Entrepreneurial Edge

Small Business
Toolkit

Girandola Press
Entrepreneurial Edge Series

Books by Tiffany McVeety
Entrepreneurial Edge Incubator Toolkit (Licensed Edition)
Entrepreneurial Edge Small Business Toolkit
Entrepreneurial Edge Inventor's Toolkit
Entrepreneurial Edge Inventor's Notebook

Entrepreneurial Edge Academy
Entrepreneurial Edge Idea to Launch
Entrepreneurial Edge Tools for Success
Entrepreneurial Edge The Strategic Start
Entrepreneurial Edge Startup Success
Entrepreneurial Edge The Quick Plan
Entrepreneurial Edge Designing a Sustainable Business
Entrepreneurial Edge The Executive Business Plan
Entrepreneurial Edge Money Rules
Entrepreneurial Edge Show Me the Money!
Entrepreneurial Edge Leading My Business
Entrepreneurial Edge Share Your World

Edge Series On Demand Video
10 Keys to Success

Entrepreneurial Edge

Small Business
Toolkit

Tiffany
McVeety, MBA

GIRANDOLA

PUBLISHED BY

Girandola Press
www.GirandolaPress.com
Seattle, Washington

ISBN-13: 978-0615451329

ISBN-10: 0615451322

Library of Congress Control Number: 2011923003

Printed and bound in the United States of America.

Girandola Press books are available through booksellers and distributors worldwide. For further information, please visit our website at www.GirandolaPress.com. For information on obtaining permission for reprints and excerpts, or to arrange a speaking or train the trainer engagement, please email Girandola Press at Speaking@GirandolaPress.com.

Articles or inserts, if applicable, have been reprinted with permission.

About the Publisher:
Girandola Press. Supporting your entrepreneurial process.
Girandola [Italian]. Pinwheel.
To move a pinwheel, one must only apply breath.
The pinwheel signifies an entrepreneur's unique ability to apply energy to create.
Turn your dreams into reality today with Girandola publications.
We support your entrepreneurial process.

In order to play the game,
you simply need to know the rules.

Forward

It was clear to me when I hired Tiffany as director of the Northwest Women's Business Center, she was was already on a mission to help small businesses grow and be successful. Tiffany McVeety has been a small business counselor and mentor, small business banker, business instructor, and advocate for entrepreneurs.

Her mission is embodied in the *Small Business Toolkit*. Her approach to business planning is distinctive and valuable. She breaks down complex business concepts into easy-to-follow steps.

In this workbook, she shares simple solutions and strategies that can help an existing business owner, or potential entrepreneur, navigate the intricacies of starting—and funding—a business.

When I first picked up her book I wondered, what else could be said about starting a business that has not already been written? The answer: *A lot!*

Use the book and grow a successful business that can thrive today, tomorrow, and into the future. I recommend this book as a must read for any person interested in starting a business.

Jim Thomas
President & CEO, Community Capital Development
Seattle, Washington

From the Author: I was honored when Jim Thomas agreed to write the forward for my book. Mr. Thomas was an appointed an advisor to the United States Small Business Administration and operates several of their business centers and loan funds. Mr. Thomas is Founder and Chief Executive Officer of one of the most successful Community Development Financial Institutions in Washington State, and serves on the boards of microenterprise development associations—advocates of entrepreneurship training best practices.

Contents

Author's Message

The passion and persistence you have as an entrepreneur drives your success perhaps greater than any other factor. Passion and persistence without a game plan and a rulebook can lead to a waste of your precious resources—time, money and talent.

Entrepreneurs— your glass is always full when you know the rules of the game.

According to the US Small Business Administration, an entrepreneur will start an average of seven businesses before they launch the one that successful for them. We want to mitigate your risk and help you get it right the first time.

The Entrepreneurial Edge Series levels the playing field and arms you with the rules of the game so you can play. A business is not built in a box. There are strategic steps to starting your business, a model for professional business planning, and a business plan your banker wants to see. Business design is an art, not a science. But there are rules.

Throughout the *Entrepreneurial Edge Small Business Toolkit* and the *Entrepreneurial Edge Academy* online classes we present complex solutions—made simple—to help you design the business of your dreams and turn your passion into profit. I have spent the past decade teaching, presenting, and fine-tuning these guides through hundreds of presentations and workshops to entrepreneurs and trainers alike.

Entrepreneurs and incubator professionals from over sixty countries have been taught these startup solutions and strategies through leading business support organizations like the:
- National Business Incubation Association
- US Small Business Administration
- US Small Business Development Centers
- US Navy Transitional Assistance Program (TAP)
- US Small Business Administration Women's Business Centers

Certified for use in Self Employment Training (SET) and Assistance (SEAP) programs in certain states, this *Toolkit* may be the only entrepreneurial planning book you ever need. Play the game. Know the rules.

Acknowledgements

I wish to acknowledge my clients, workshop participants, and students who have shared their business vision, goals, and challenges with me over the years, and who allowed me to co-create their perfect business.

Specifically, I wish to recognize and thank my entrepreneurial mentors who, over the years, helped me refine the rules of the game. Seattle Pacific University Professors and lecturers Herb Kierulff, Jim Goebelbecker, John Castle, and Dr. Larry Nyland respectively, who encouraged me to start a company, introduced me to the world of alternative business financing and equity investing, and engaged me to write business plans and leadership conference presentations. Greg Amadon, for making me a 'friend of the company', a millionaire on paper, and for lessons on the art of serial entrepreneurship. Joe Shocken, for my experience in investment banking. Small Business Development Center Legend, Ron Battles, for teaching me the art of professional business planning. Jamie Curtismith for leading the path and paving a way. Jim Thomas, for letting me lead the Women's Business Center, and for teaching me the art of the balance sheet, which served me well as small business and international trade banker. Danielle Ellingston, Washington State Department of Commerce Export Voucher pioneer, for catching the vision of global entrepreneurship training.

My tools are simple—I worried too simple. Presenting my rules of the finance game to business incubator professionals from more than sixty countries unveiled the benefits of simplicity. I wish to thank the National Business Incubation Association (NBIA) for including my curriculum in the client-funding category of their Professional Incubator Manager Certificate program.

I especially want to thank GROW Washington founder, Mayor Carolyn Eslick, who believed in my program and road tested these principles. Her knowledge and feedback was invaluable. Thanks to Ann Holt Grove for the time we spent in Tucson working on the book; and to Sheryn Hara of the Publisher's Network for her editing team. Lastly, thanks to my husband, and best friend, Mark for his love and support.

How to Use this Toolkit

Welcome to the *Entrepreneurial Edge Small Business Toolkit.* This guidebook is for all types of entrepreneurs: micro-entrepreneurs, solopreneurs, serial entrepreneurs, social entrepreneurs, and those who mentor and train them.

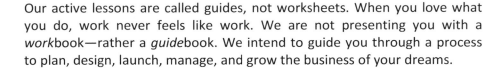

You are holding a guidebook—not a workbook.

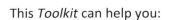

When you love what you do, work never feels like work.

Our active lessons are called guides, not worksheets. When you love what you do, work never feels like work. We are not presenting you with a *work*book—rather a *guide*book. We intend to guide you through a process to plan, design, launch, manage, and grow the business of your dreams.

This *Small Business Toolkit* includes solutions and strategies, resources and tips to guide you on your path to success. The 10 Keys to Success, Money Rules!, a single page business plan called The Quick Plan, and a more intensive business design guide to help you complete a business plan for your banker, investor or spouse, called the Executive Business Plan. The Toolkit is just that—consider visiting the List of Guides Index in the back of the book to give you a feeling for the types of tools you will find. Jump around. Use what you need, when you need it. The Toolkit is not meant to read strait through—but to use. Learn something—then get back to designing, planning, or running your business.

This *Toolkit* can help you:
- Turn your creativity into a sustainable business
- Write a business plan your banker wants to see
- Discover your entrepreneurial strengths
- Learn 3 key factors in entrepreneurial goal setting
- Build your dream team using an advisory board agreement
- Learn to talk with your banker – and stay ahead of your cash flow
- Answer the question: *Will I make money?*
- Connect with customers using Facebook, Twitter, and more!

The Keystone

Whether you are an artist, inventor, or entrepreneur, you can turn your dreams into reality using these simple and effective tools and guides. Throughout the *Entrepreneurial Edge Small Business Toolkit* and *Entrepreneurial Edge Academy* online classes, you will see pictures in the margins. Here is your key to those images.

 A light bulb represents a bright idea for your startup or business.

 An image of US currency represents a tip, tool, strategy, or resource related to saving money, making money, managing money, securing money, and may also represent a Money Rule.

 A light bulb with a sprout inside can help you grow fast, mobilize resources, or mobilize communities to support your business. These tips are especially for the social entrepreneur or philanthropic entrepreneur.

 A Key represents one of the 10 Keys to Success.

 The circle within a letter "C" is the Core Business Principle logo. It identifies one of the 20 Core Business Principles.

 The image of a hand writing on a notepad means "Take Action". It represents a guide for you to complete to support your learning and may be a requirement of the Edge Series Certificate Program.

Small Business Toolkit Key

Bright Idea   **Money Wise**   **SPROUT!**   **Key to Success**   **Core Business Principle**   **Take Action**

Chapter 1: **Tools for Success**

Guides

Guide 1: 10 Keys to Success
Guide 2: Money Rules
Guide 3: 20 Core Business Principles
Guide 4: Key to Free
Guide 5: Getting Certified
Guide 6: Small Business Grants
Guide 7: Startup Do's and Don'ts
Guide 8: Startup Checklist
Guide 9: Talking the Talk
Guide 10: Test Your Knowledge
Last: Next Steps
Certificate of Completion

Takeaways:

Describe the "10 keys to success" and examine how they relate to you.
Define the five "money rules" and understand their importance in your venture.
Understand the importance of "core business principles" and recognize them throughout the guidebook.
Access "tools for success" like free resources for your business.

Guide 1: 10 Keys to Success

Did you know that there are a set of tools that uniquely contribute to and speed up your entrepreneurial success? These key concepts, when implemented, will jumpstart your new venture and help mitigate your risk. Entrepreneurs start an average of 7 businesses. The 10 Keys to Success can help you find success the first time—instead of the seventh.

Key to Success

Entrepreneurial Edge 10 Keys to Success

Eighty percent of entrepreneurs expect to have five or fewer employees—a microenterprise. Business planning is personal planning when you have a microenterprise. Tools like those in this chapter will arm you with the rules of the business game so you can fully engage on a level playing field.

**Business Planning
is Personal Planning**

The **10 Keys of Success** are identified throughout the Entrepreneurial Edge Series of guidebooks and instructional tools with an image of a key. Keep the **10 Keys** in mind as you plan, start, and grow your business.

The 10 Keys will help you fast track and focus your entrepreneurial success.

10 Keys to Success
1. Know what you want
2. Seek advice and counsel
3. Understand your options
4. Plan with the future in mind
5. Design your perfect business
6. Know how to access OPA (Other People's Assets)
7. Protect your intellectual assets
8. Create a Strategic Marketing Plan
9. Develop and Implement a sales process and plan
10. Design and use a leadership dashboard

Key to Success

10 Keys Primer

You already know there are a set of tools—keys rather—that will uniquely contribute to your entrepreneurial success. Here are the *10 Keys* defined.

The 10 Keys to Success

1. Know what you want.

Sounds basic—but this is critical to any person's success—on both a personal level and business level. When you know what you want serendipity happens. You also position yourself to seek assistance from others.

2. Seek advice and counsel.

Even if you are a solopreneur, micro-entrepreneur, or inventor, you need not go it alone! There are strategies to identifying, engaging, and mobilizing human resources to assist you, accelerate your growth, and broaden your opportunities. You just need to know what the options and alternatives are.

3. Understand your options.

Understanding your options is one of the most important keys to success. You don't know what you don't know—until you do. Did you know there are free resources to help you sell to the largest US buyer? That there are certifications that make you a more likely candidate for winning contracts and bids? That strategic partnerships, joint ventures, and stock options are strategic tools that even the smallest business owner can employ. Know more. Get more. You have to know what your options are before you can keep your options open.

4. Plan with the future in mind.

There is an art to the start. When designing your perfect business use your forward thinking muscles. Plan for the highest and best possible outcome. Whether you want to grow fast, import, export, raise investment capital, sell, or transfer the business to a family member when it's time—these all take planning from the start. There are strategies to the start that can position you for future success. When you know what you want, and understand your options, you can then design the perfect business.

5. Design your perfect business.

You are your business. Eighty percent of all businesses in the US are Small Businesses. Small business usually means micro enterprise—if you plan to have five or fewer employees, you are a micro-entrepreneur. If you plan to live your business, then design the business of your dreams. Design the perfect business for you. It's up to you. You are in full control—from business formation strategies to choosing your perfect customer.

6. Know how to access OPA (Other People's Assets).

Investment capital. Small Business Loans. Alternative lenders. Angel Investors. Patient capital. Green Money. Government Grants. Co-signors. Guarantors. OPM (Other People's Money). The alternatives for funding your business, project, or idea are limitless. Know what your options are. Be able to identify the best sources of funds for you. Learn winning strategies. *Show Me the Money!*

7. Protect your intellectual assets.

Knowledge is power. Your intellectual property is an asset. When you know how to protect what you have and what you create, you position yourself for greater choices—and possibly a higher valuation. Two years ago Google had less than 5,000 patents. Today they have over 75,000. Learn to protect and maximize your intellectual assts.

8. Create a strategic marketing plan.

Marketing is the window to the soul. Not exactly—but it is the single most critical means of reaching your perfect customer. Learn strategic direct marketing tools, the components of a traditional marketing plan, write an Inventor's Marketing Plan, and create a social media marketing plan.

9. Develop and implement a sales process and plan.

There are very detailed, in-depth, and frankly onerous sales strategies and selling tools in the market covering everything from direct selling, indirect sales, channel sales, white label sales, value added sales—so many options. Yes, you need to sell your product or service—but let's stick to the basics: have a financial goal, identify your perfect customer, create a marketing plan, and execute the plan. Follow simple and proven sales processes to create sales relationships. Marketing and sales are all about relationship building. Learn how to do it right and make an impact. A positive impact.

10. Design and use a leadership dashboard.

You are in control. But of what? There are key leadership metrics for each business. Learn what financial controls are important to your business success and implement a leadership dashboard. Be able to identify and encourage the strengths of your team. What marketing returns are you expecting or sales goals do you need to hit? Your financial dashboard puts you in control of the key benchmarks and metrics for your business growth. Create a leadership dashboard for your business and set up for success.

Guide 2: Money Rules

Money Rules Primer
In small business—any business really—cash is king. You must master the Money Rules. It helps that there are only five.

Core Business Principle

The Money Rules
1. Project It*!*
2. Present It*!*
3. Access It*!*
4. Control It*!*
5. Manage It*!*

Money Rules

The five "Money Rules" were first introduced at GROW Washington and were expanded in the *Entrepreneurial Edge On-Demand* training program. We integrate the Money Rules throughout the Entrepreneurial Edge Series of Guidebooks.

Use the Money Rules Key to help you identify the Money Rules in the *Small Business Toolkit*. Here is our Primer:

Money Rule 1: Project It*!*
Being able to design your perfect business is one of the *10 Keys to Success.* Projecting your income, expenses, profit, and cash flow break even are a part of your perfect business design. If you can project your income, expenses, cash flow, timing of cash, break even, and the value of your business upon capital investment or exit – *you have this one down!* Money Rule #1.

Money Rule 2: Present It*!*

Accessing OPA is a *Key to Success.* In order to access OPM—Other People's Money—whether it is a capital investment from a friend or family member or securing a business line of credit from your favorite banker—is all about presentation. You will likely not be the one to present your loan request to a loan committee. Your presentation will speak for you. Lean how to present properly—to a banker, angel investor, or even your spouse.

When you can present your business on paper – the history, the current position, your future expectations, your future value—to bankers, investors, and even your spouse—you nailed Money Rule #2.

Money Rule 3: Access It*!*

Knowing how to access OPM—and your own—is a part of understanding your options and is one of the *Key to Success.* In this section of the *Toolkit*, you will learn what the difference between equity and debt financing looks like, where to get both types of capital investment, and the rule of the capital investment game. We even prepare you for the perfect 10-minute angel investment presentation. When you know what your banker wants to see in terms of financial statements, financial projections and your business plan—and you know what an angel investor needs to see, are ready to negotiate a deal with a banker, alternative lender, or private investor— then you have mastered Money Rule #3.

Money Rule 4: Control It*!*

When you control your cash—you control your future. Learn to set up financial controls for your business, understand cash management options, and learn to leverage before you need to. When you know what's coming in and going out—and you hold the reigns—and you control the Controller Money Rule #4 is in the bag.

Money Rule 5: Manage It*!*

We are not our business—we need to manage our business. Managing Money is all about knowing the rules of the financial game—putting you in the driver's seat. Learn to orchestrate your future through profit mastery. Finally, whether cash flow is flowing or not—you know what to do. You know how to manage your future, your cash, your leverage, your currency, your accountant, and your profit. You rule Money Rule #5.

Money Rules Key

Guides in the *Toolkit* integrate each of the the five money rules. Here is an overview of what is to come and where to look for specifics. Look for the Money Rules Logo to help you stay on track. For a broader introduction and an overview, jump to the chapter called "Money Rules".

Money Wise

Money Rules	Project It!	Present It!	Access It!	Control It!	Manage It!
Chapter 1			X		
Chapter 2	X		X		
Chapter 3	X	X	X		
Chapter 4	X	X	X	X	
Chapter 5	X	X	X	X	X
Chapter 6	X	X	X		
Chapter 7	X	X	X	X	X
Chapter 8	X	X	X	X	X
Chapter 9	X	X	X	X	X
Chapter 10			X	X	X

Core Business Principle

Guide 3: 20 Core Business Principles

Entrepreneurial Edge Core Business Principles

Did you know there are 20 core business principles that once mastered help heighten your chance of entrepreneurial success?

Core Business Principles are best practices taught by certified business incubators, advocated by Microentrepreneur Development Organizations (MDO's), and delivered to you throughout the Entrepreneurial Edge Series. The *Entrepreneurial Edge Small Business Toolkit* covers 18 of the 20 Core Business Principles, while some of the Edge Series of publications are more focused on a single core principle to deepen learning.

> *Knowing the rules is a part of the game.*
> *These are your ground rules.*

Entrepreneurial Edge Series of guides present the Core Business Principles uniquely from other business planning resources in that each learning tool comes from real world business practices. As you ease through the guides in the Series, you will gain mastery of each of the 20 Core Business Principles. Take note when you see the Core Business Principle logo. This image represents a pivotal tool for *your* small business toolkit.

The Core Business Principles are separated into categories to further define the optimal timing or use during the lifecycle of your business, fundraising activity, or product or service deployment.

5 Core Categories
1. Startup Success
2. Designing Your Perfect Business
3. Idea to Market
4. Show Me the Money
5. Managing Your Venture

Core Business Principles

No single Core Business Principle is more or less important than the other. Each of these business principles is proven to have impact on your venture activities.

Core Business Principle

Core Categories	The Core Business Principles
Startup Success	1. Values 2. Vision 3. Business Formation Strategies 4. Business Model 5. Advisory Board
Designing Your Perfect Business	6. Revenue Model 7. Pricing Model 8. Customer Identification 9. Competitive Advantage 10. Market Opportunity 11. Target Market
Idea to Market	12. Features vs. Benefits 13. Strategic Direct Marketing 14. Components of a Marketing Plan 15. Intellectual Property Protection 16. Sales Process Design
Show Me the Money	17. Debt vs. Equity 18. Pro forma Financial Statements
Managing Your Venture	19. Chart of Accounts 20. Business Benchmarks (RMA Ratios)

Core Business Principles Categories

Core Business Principles are taught in different ways by different business centers. However, the concepts remain unchanged. We take lessons learned from successful entrepreneurs and turn their plan, start, and grow strategies into simple solutions you can immediately implement. Each of the guides in this *Toolkit* employs real world best practices and many incorporate Core Business Principles.

The Entrepreneurial Edge Series introduces you eighteen of the twenty core business principles in five categories:

1. Startup Success
2. Designing Your Perfect Business
3. Idea to Market
4. Show Me the Money
5. Managing Your Venture

Core Business Principle

5 Principals at the core of your startup success

In the very earliest stage of your business planning process, before you employ the strategies of the start and design the perfect business model to turn your vision into reality—even before you decide what success in this venture means to you—you have an empty canvas.

You have certain characteristics, strengths, and values that will define what your business becomes, where it will fit in the world, and what you intend to do with it. In fact, your personal values and entrepreneurial quotient—your EQ—will define and shape what success means to you as an entrepreneur. You are unique—as your business will be. The first set of Core Business Principles relate to your startup success. Each principle may be revisited at any time during your business lifecycle. Change happens. The five Startup Success Core Business Principles are:

1. **Values**—Your venture will reflect your personal values. Discover your values so you can thoughtfully design the business of your dreams.

2. **Vision**—A business' vision is different than its mission. It frames each strategic move, decision, option you choose, and goal you set. Leadership requires vision. Be the leader of your business. You not only set the stage—you create it.

3. **Business Formation Strategies**—Skip the strategic start and you will miss the mark. Master the art of business formation. There is a perfect structure to your business. It may be based on your values, your exit strategy, income and growth goals, intended key personnel, strategic positioning for capital investment strategies, or a global plan. Learn to launch right the first time around not the second or third.

4. **Business Model**—There is a perfect business model for your venture. You simply need to know what your options are, and design the business of your dreams.

5. **Advisory Board**—Some refer to it as a mastermind group, team of advisors, or dream team. We all know that people make the world go 'round. Using strategic advisory boards for the various stages of your business lifecycle will not only help you achieve your goals, but in record time.

6 Principles to help you design your perfect business

Strategies and solutions to designing your perfect business begin with the basics. When you master the following fundamentals, you will be on your way to making your dream of entrepreneurial success a reality—whatever *success* means to you.

Core Business Principle

6. **Revenue Model**—Learn to determine your primary sources of revenue, and secondary sources—incremental revenue. Determine how much time you will spend on probono—or donated time or products. Your partners may have a completely different idea of perfect revenue model for your perfect business. Get on the same page early with tips, tools, and guides surrounding your revenue model.

7. **Pricing Model**—A key part of your marketing strategy, one of the "4 P's of Marketing", is pricing. Learn how it balances quality, creates prestige, and can make or break a business.

8. **Customer Identification**—Whom do you want to play with? Being able to identify your perfect customer is part of designing your perfect business.

9. **Competitive Advantage**—What pain do you solve in the market place? What gap have you identified to fill? What is your value proposition? How are your products or services better or different than what is available already? Being able to address each of these questions is critical to your success and will help you position your business for

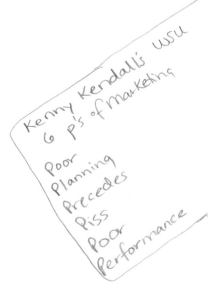

Kenny Kendall's WSU
6 P's of marketing

Poor
Planning
Precedes
Piss
Poor
Performance

strategic partnerships, OPM (Other People's Money), even a solid business valuation.

10. **Market Opportunity**—Knowing your place in the big picture – the macro-economic perspective—may sound lofty. It's important to investors—so it should be important to you!

11. **Target Market**—Take a step toward the micro market opportunity—your target market. You should not only be able to identify the market opportunity, but your target market and the growth rate, trends, and even more granular, the value of your target customer on an annual and monthly basis. Sound impossible to project? It's not. You will master this process and more as you design your perfect business and write your Executive Business Plan.

Core Business Principle

5 Principles to guide your idea to market

Idea to market—that's what it's all about. Starting, and then growing your business. The Core Business Principles in this section pertain to reaching that perfect customer you identified for your business.

12. **Features vs. Benefits**—There is a method to the madness of the features and benefits exercise. Understand what drives your perfect customer to make buying decisions and you can package, position, price, and achieve sales success. People buy benefits. What are the benefits of your next big idea?

13. **Strategic Direct Marketing**—Not the direct marketing of old. Strategic direct marketing is a marketing strategy taught to business incubator professionals—the trainers of entrepreneurs—at conferences worldwide. Ever heard of it? Now you have.

14. **Components of a Marketing Plan**—Marketing is key. A marketing plan holds the strategy. Knowing the components of a marketing plan is considered a Core Business Principle. But—please—do yourself a favor and actually write one.

15. **Intellectual Property Protection**—Knowledge is power. Intellectual property is an asset. Learn to use an Inventor's Notebook and the 'Prove it or Lose it' rules to protecting your intellectual assets.

16. **Sales Process Design**—Learn the strategies of sales and design your perfect sales process. Then manage it and monitor it. Control the outcomes and reap the financial rewards. From Coopetition, relationship selling—there is a perfect sales strategy for your perfect

business. Once you know the options, design a sales plan and process that works for you.

2 Principles that will show you the money

Some people say that the pinnacle of success in the lifecycle of a new venture is when you can successfully access OPM (Other People's Money). When you have successfully been able to seek and raise investment capital—whether debt or equity—then, and only then have you made it.

Core Business Principle

We might not agree—however, we will arm you with the knowledge, tools, skills, and resources to raise investment capital when and if you need it. Until you know the rules of the financial game, you can't play. It's your turn. Play to win. Here are the bare necessities.

17. **Debt vs. Equity**—There are two types of capital. Debt and Equity. You need to know what they are and how to get it—before you need it.

18. **Pro forma Financial Statements**—Understanding financial statements is important. Not for your accountant to understand—for *you* to understand. If you don't know what they are, how to manage them, and how to monitor them, other people control your potential for growth, expansion, and financial success. Know your options. Control your options. Get to know the numbers.

2 Principles to help you manage your venture

In this *Toolkit* we focus on the art of the start. We arm you with solutions and strategies focused on the startup and seed stage venture. There are two Core Principles which relate to designing your business so that you can manage it better later. One is the creation of your chart of accounts. Another is knowing how to benchmark for success using key ratios.

Core Business Principle

19. **Chart of Accounts**—If there is one way that you can position your company for a future sale, it is setting up a chart of accounts in the very beginning and keeping the same chart of accounts through the life of your business. Learn how and why this is a strategy not to miss.

20. **RMA Ratios**—Call it profit mastery. How do you really know what success looks like? Achievement. Success. Accomplishment. Record breaking. Benchmarks. Best practices. What do these concepts have in common? When you know the RMA ratios or other Key Performance Indicators (KPIs), you have the tools the bankers use to determine your level of achievement, success, accomplishment based on accepted benchmarks gathered from financial statements of other like companies nationwide.

**Understand
your options**

Guide 4: Your Key to Free

All entrepreneurs wish they had a magic wand when it comes to launching a new venture. While you may not have startup magic, this *Toolkit* will arm you with proven strategies, solutions, insider secrets, and tips to guide you through the adventure of the art of the startup.

Armed with the *Entrepreneurial Edge Series Small Business Toolkit*, it will feel like magic when you are introduced to the largest purchasing agent in the world and your products or services are included in their pre-approved buying catalog; and when the same group acts like your new sales person, feeding you sales leads daily, weekly, or when you want them.

> *Did you know...*
> - *There are free resources to help you sell to the largest US buyer.*
> - *There are certifications that make you a better candidate for winning government contracts.*
> *...Know more. Get more.*

A publically traded company in Seattle offered these services for up to $5,000 a month. Is it worth that? Many would say, yes. But wouldn't you rather have the same access for free? Read on for these and other free business resources that can make a positive impact on your business.

It will feel like magic when you can create a business plan in a day, when you have never written one before, even if you got your MBA and never went through the process.

It will seem like magic when, for the first time, you are armed with all the documents you need to land the capital investment you want—when you need it.

It will look like magic when the blinders are taken from your eyes and you see for the first time how possible it is to make the dreams of owning a business a reality. These resources and others just as powerful will make your business planning process feel like startup magic.

We almost called this book Startup Magic because clients have shared with us that the tips and tools you have before you made such a positive difference in their strategic business planning that the fast results felt like magic. A focus group chose another name—but the magic is still here.

**Seek advice
and counsel**

Top Free Business Resources

We want to do more than simply hand you a list of our favorite resources. In this guide, we highlight our favorite free business resources and tell you why they are important to you and your business.

Mobilize resources to support your business vision.

Our goal is to increase your comfort level so you actually make the call, set the meeting, and reap the rewards. In no order of importance, here are our favorite free business resources.

US Small Business Administration

The US Small Business Administration (SBA) is a division of the Administrative arm of your government (the Office of the President). We all pay federal taxes. So, you are already paying for the services and programs the SBA offers. The SBA programs tend to be overlooked and underutilized by entrepreneurs of all stages of business. Perhaps because their programs are misunderstood. Perhaps, it is that most of the programs are free and that some may feel 'you get what you pay for', so free means sub-standard.

*The US Small Business Administration provides entrepreneurs business and financial assistance throughout the country.
www.sba.gov*

We have found the SBA and their programs to be pure gold for the entrepreneur, veteran, import and export company, company seeking financing, and for rural, disadvantaged, and women entrepreneurs. The SBA has created specialized programs to help you plan, start, grow, expand, and fund your companies. You paid for the programs, so use them.

The following are our favorite SBA programs.

Don't go it alone!

First, the SBA has two functional categories (access to capital and access to markets) and five main programs:

- Access to Markets
    1. SCORE (Service Corps of Retires Executives)
    2. WBC (Women's Business Centers)
    3. SBDC (Small Business Development Centers)
    4. Import (Trade) Assistance
- Access to Capital
    5. Government Guaranteed Loans
        - SBA 7a
        - SBA 504
        - SBA Micro Loans (up to $50,000)

Expand your opportunities.
Discover your options and alternatives.

SCORE®
Counselors to America's Small Business

SCORE Program

SCORE is a free business assistance program of the US Small Business Administration. About a $5 million nationwide program operated by the federal government, SCORE, Service Corps of Retired Executives, utilizes trained volunteers to provide business consulting for free to business owners with fewer than 500 employees. According to the SBA, a business with fewer than 500 employees is a Small Business. A Business, which needs less than $35,000 in capital investment, is a Micro-Business. It's good to know their definitions.

SCORE business counselors can help you with any issue you may face in the lifecycle of your business. You may use a SCORE counselor daily, weekly, monthly, or when you need them—it's up to you and their availability. There is no limit to the time you may use a SCORE Counselor, nor a limit on the business questions that can be asked. They will not do the work for you. For example, if you need a business plan written, they will guide you through the steps to complete a business plan, but they will not write it for you.

Bright Idea

TIP: If a SCORE counselor tries to get you to hire them directly, consider reporting the counselor to the SBA office. SCORE counselors are volunteers.

If you don't fit with the SCORE counselor you are first introduced to, that's okay—ask for another one. There are several, dozens really, of SCORE volunteers in each state. You may have a specific need. Be sure you and your free business consultant are a good fit and that they have the knowledge you are seeking. www.score.org

SMALL BUSINESS TOOLKIT 19

WBC Programs

The Women's Business Centers (WBC) were created as another usually free business technical assistance program. Business Technical Assistance (TA) is the term used by the industry that means on-on-one or very small group business consulting, coaching, or mentoring. This is another definition that can help you as you navigate through all the free business resources available to you.

Women start over 50% of all businesses

In serving millions of entrepreneurs all over the US, the SBA realized that although women were starting businesses as fast as men, they were not using the free business technical assistance or access to capital programs that were available to them. To reach this special population, they created a separate program called the Women's Business Centers. The interesting thing about the Centers—as a former WBC Director, I can attest to this—is they provide services to both men and women. Men are more comfortable seeking free business help wherever they are offered. While women tend to want a special invitation to participate.

You will find WBC's in each state—sometimes several in each state. Not all WBC's use their program name. For example, there is a WBC in Washington that changed its name to the Washington Business Center – keeping the acronym of the WBC and changing nothing other than its name.

TIP: Visit the SBA.gov website for a list of all the Women's Business Center programs in your state. Greater than 50% of all businesses started in the United States are launched by women. These are amazing resources. Use them!

Bright Idea

SBDC Program

The Small Business Development Center (SBDC) programs are tailored to the existing business owner, although they might not turn away a startup. Each state is awarded a single contract for the SBDCs, and usually are operated by an institution of higher education.

For example, in the State of Washington, Washington State University in Spokane has the statewide SBDC contract. They will hire various SBDC Business Counselors, train them, and fund their offices and operations from a central budget, using the central administrative staff. This reduces costs that might otherwise be associated with such a program.

Small Business Development Center (SBDC) programs are tailored to the existing business owner.

You will likely find an SBDC officer, sometimes called a business consultant or director, at a college.

However they might be located within a non-profit, or in a business incubator or other business center. Some SBDCs provide business technical assistance only (on-on-one counseling), while others might provide training and counseling (TA). The SBDC training budget or funding is separate than that of TA—not all offices will provide the same services.

Interestingly, a WBC director is required to have a Master's degree, and a Master of Business Administration (MBA) is preferred. The SBDC counselors go through specialized training to become a certified SBDC business counselor. SCORE counselors are volunteers who are trained on how to maintain confidentiality and similar concepts though are not vetted to the extent of WBC and SBDC program personnel.

**Understand
your options**

SBA Trade Offices

The US Small Business Administration (SBA) recognizes the importance of trade, and export in particular, to our continued growth and success as a country. In March of 2011, the SBA launched a new program called State Trade and Export Promotion (STEP). By this time, there should be a US Export Assistance Centers operated by the SBA in each state.

If you feel your company might be ready to go global, this is a terrific place to start! The office hours tend to be limited, so call in advance.

Global can be big business for a small business.

If you think your small business can't go global, think again! Here are some examples of small businesses—micro-enterprises in fact—doing international business.

- Example 1: A husband and wife team that imports fireworks and wholesales them to stores like Wallmart, Bartelle's, and Walgreens earns over $250,000 a year in their business.

- Example 2: A women owned business imports wine from Argentina and distributes to specialty shops all over the country, earning more than she did in the corporate world.

- Example 3: A one-person, home based business generates over $2 Million a year exporting lumber to Korea.

- Example 4: A two-person, home-based business, generates nearly $20 million a year buying, than selling fish to big box stores like Costco.

- Example 5: A one-person business generates nearly $6 million exporting recycled paper to paper packaging companies worldwide.

- Example 6: A husband and wife team imports silk from Thailand, and sells to the high-end interior designers of boats and aircrafts generating nearly $250,000 a year.

International sales—import and export—can mean big business to small business.

You don't know what you don't know—until you do.

SBA Access to Capital Programs

An entire section of this *Toolkit* dedicated to OPM (Other People's Money), types of funding, sources of funding, the structure of debt financing, and angel investing. In fact, you are entitled to a bonus with the purchase of this *Toolkit—a* comprehensive list of all the angel investment groups in the US, and all the alternative lenders in the US we could identify. Visit the website for this Free download: www.EntrepreneurialEdgeSeries.com.

Access OPA

This section on access to capital programs, however, focuses on the Small Business Administration loan programs in particular. Specifically, we hope to ease the confusion over what the program is and how to access these unique sources of debt financing.

If your banker:
   1. Is not a business banker
   2. Has never done an SBA loan or
   3. Does not know what the SBA is...
find yourself a real business banker.

TIP: It is the responsibility of your business banker to listen to your financing needs, your business growth plans, and to you. Then, based on their exceptional listening skills, and knowledge of their industry, they will be able to recommend the best sources of funds and options for your business. You are not to be expected to know what the SBA is, what their loan programs are, and whether you qualify for one or another.

Bright Idea

In the guides in the OPM section of this *Toolkit* there are descriptions of all the types of banks. Use that section of the *Toolkit* to help you identify the perfect financial institution for you and your business.

**Understand
your options**

Choosing a bank is a strategic decision—not just an administrative one. It can be difficult to change banks once you are well established, so choose wisely.

SBA Lending 101

The SBA does not lend to the business owner. They guarantee a specific level of repayment to the bank in case you fail to repay your loan (aka: go out of business). There are several, and specific, purposed for which can SBA loan may be used. Your business banker will know all the options, or you can visit the SBA.gov website for a list of current programs. The details are many.

*You have to know what your options are
before you can keep your options open.*

Government Guarantee Small Business Loan Process

You apply for a business loan from your financial institution. Be sure your lender is a preferred SBA lender. Your banker determines if you are qualified for a traditional business loan. If not, they determine your eligibility for a SBA (government guaranteed) loan. SBA loans may have a higher interest rate and more paperwork than a traditional business loan, but the requirements may be slightly more relaxed than a traditional loan.

**Call the SBA – Get
referred to a local
bank with a
proven record of
accomplishment.**

With an SBA Loan, the SBA acts like a personal guarantor on your loan. If you default on your business loan, the SBA guarantees a certain level of repayment to the bank. That level of repayment depends on the type of loan program you participated in. An SBA 7a loan, for example, can guarantee repayment of up to 80% of the defaulted loan amount. An SBA Express loan on the other hand can repay up to 50% of the loan default amount. Different banks have approval to offer different SBA loan products. Check with your banker or local SBA office for the latest and greatest. The programs, requirements, and availability change based on the federal budget.

Money Wise

TIP: Call the SBA office nearest to you and ask them to refer you to the bank in your state with the most SBA loan approvals. Then ask for a referral to a business banker at that bank. The referred banker will be one of the most experienced SBA lenders around. This translates to a faster loan process for you. The banker will also be able to tell you more quickly whether you will qualify for a business loan or not, and what you need to change to be able to qualify.

PTAC

The Procurement and Technical Assistance Center (PTAC) is a unique, and frankly amazing, program that can help you get set up to sell to the government, get on the General Services Administration (GSA) Schedule.

Seek advice and counsel

The GSA Schedule is the purchasing catalog for the entire US Government. PTAC is a free program that can also help you get certified with any number of government certifications, and even put you on a system that sends you sales leads based on the parameters you set up in their system.

PTAC is funded by the Department of Defense, and there is usually a single contract issued per state that manages all the state's PTAC counselors—similar to the SBDC program noted above. There are also Native American PTAC offices that serve the Indian Nations.

A PTAC (pronounced "pee tack") contract tends to be awarded to an active and large Economic Development Council (EDC), but may be awarded to a college, or other well managed program. In fact, there may be several PTAC officers or employees across the state so visit the PTAC website to find your nearest office. This is a free business technical assistance resource that is helpful for any small business owner. www.dla.mil/db/procurem.htm

Locate the nearest PTAC office in your state and list the contact information here:

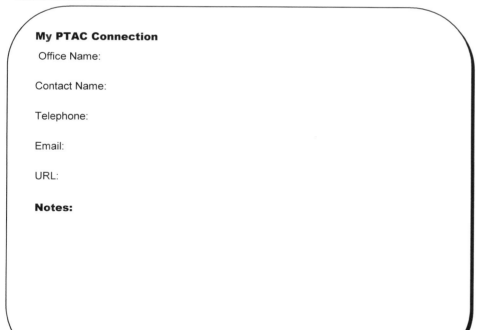

My PTAC Connection

Office Name:

Contact Name:

Telephone:

Email:

URL:

Notes:

**Understand
your options**

Guide 5: Getting Certified

Our government is the largest buyer of goods and services in the entire US. Are you certified to do business with the government? Did you know there are free resources that help walk you through the process?

The government wants the greatest number of options when it comes to making a buying decision. If you are not positioned to sell to the government, you are possibly holding yourself back from business development opportunities.

Government Certifications

Before you can begin business with the government, your business must obtain the proper certifications. Small business certifications are like professional certifications; they document a special capability or status that will help you compete in the marketplace.

Small Business Certifications for Minority, Woman, and Service Disabled Veteran Owned Businesses

The US Small Business Administration can be contacted regarding participation in the following programs:
- HUBZone Certification
- 8(a) Business Development
- Small Business Certification
- Women-Owned Small Business Federal Contract Program
- Veteran & Service-Disabled Veteran Owned
- Native Americans
- Alaskan Owned Corporations
- Native Hawaiian Owned

Depending on the Administration, there may be programs that encourage government procurement officers to utilize women-owned firms, minority owned forms, or disadvantaged businesses at a higher level in both the number of firms awarded contracts and the dollar amounts awarded to them. The following three certifications could help you in this instance.

MBE Certification

Minority Business Enterprises (MBEs) are entities that are at least 51% owned and/or controlled by socially and economically disadvantaged individuals. An MBE certification is issued through National Minority Supplier Development Council (formerly known as the Minority Supplier Council, or MSC.) Their website is www.nmsdc.org.

DBE Certifications

Disadvantaged Business Enterprises (DBEs) include those which are:
- Owned and/or controlled by a socially and economically disadvantaged individuals as described by Title X of the Clean Air Act Amendments of 1990;
- A Small Business Enterprise (SBE);
- A Small Business in a Rural Area (SBRA);
- A Labor Surplus Area Firm (LSAF); or
- A Historically Underutilized Business (HUB) Zone Small Business Concern or a concern under a successor program.

WBE Certification

Any Minority Business Enterprise that is women-owned can be certified as a Woman Owned Business Enterprise (WBE). This certification is an important business development strategy for women business owners for two primary reasons: First, most local and national government purchasing agencies track and/or have programs for doing business with women business owners. Having WBE Certification is the only way the purchasing agents have confidence that a business representing itself as woman-owned is, in fact, woman-owned and controlled.

Second, many publicly-held corporations, as well as larger private corporations, also track and have programs for doing business with women-owned vendor companies. They, too, rely on WBE Certification.

Access OPA

Guide 6: Small Business Grants

Some say there are no such things as a business grant. Look no further! There is a program that I have personally participated in and seen great success for my business clients and associates: the SBIR and STTR programs (The letters are pronounced individually).

These grants tend to be unknown to and underutilized by entrepreneurs and inventors—especially those in rural and small cities. More information on these grants and other resources for inventors can be found in the inventor's Workshop section of the *Toolkit*. I list them here to both introduce you to the resource, and to encourage you to find out how you can qualify for these, sometimes recurring, large grants.

SBIR/STTR 101

All Federal Agencies recognize that innovation and invention comes from the non public sector—namely you, the entrepreneur. So, each of the Agencies participate in two grant programs, the Small Business Innovation Research Program (SBIR) and Small Business Technology Transfer (STTR) program.

In a nutshell, funds may be invested into a small business or research institution that is creating, improving, developing, or commercializing something the Agency may be interested in buying in the future.

If you are awarded one of these grants, you are agreeing that at some time in the future, you will sell, license, or otherwise make available your new invention to the agency which funded you. Basically, the government is paying you to do R&D for them.

If they decide not to use your invention, no problem, it was a grant. Free money that enabled you to create something new for your business or to bring to market yourself. If they like it, they might want to buy it, at the market rate after they pay you to commercialize it. Win Win!

Money Wise

These programs provide grants to eligible small businesses and or research institutions that accomplish two things in two phases.

First, the grants fund the research and development of an innovation, invention, concept, product or process. This is called Phase I of the grant process. Second, the grant can provide funding for the commercialization, or bringing to market, of that new invention. This is called Phase II. Check with your PTAC office for current grant values, as they tend to change.

The grants amounts for each grant and each phase are:
    SBIR
    Phase I: $150,000 total costs for 6 month
    Phase II: $1,000,000 total costs for 2 years
    STTR
    Phase I: $100,000 total costs for 12 months
    Phase II: $750,000 total costs for 2 years

**SBIR
Gateway**

The grants may be applied for again and again. In fact, some companies that are in the business of inventing and developing new products, technology, or innovations, generate millions each year on these grants.

Each Agency has their own SBIR/STTR programs. To overcome this massive hurdle in research and trying to identify an opportunity to fit your business, use the resources in the back of the *Toolkit*. There are websites that aggregate all the SBIR and STTR opportunities in one location, workshops to help you learn more about the grants and the process to apply, and more. Here is the link for the SBIR/STTR Gateway—the single best secret out there related to these grants. This one website aggregates all agency SBIR Solicitations in one website. And it's free. www.zyn.com/sbir/

Bright Idea

Another issue is that the approval process is both very difficult and very competitive. Use your local University technology transfer programs to learn about any training offered surrounding these grants. In Washington State, for example, Innovate Washington (formerly Washington Technology Center) provides access to training, workshops, and one-on-one consultations with actual Agency grant reviewers to help local businesses gain access to these important grant programs.

**Seek advice
and counsel**

Having written and secured a Phase I SBIR grant for a client, I know the daunting process, and the importance of accessing the resources around you to make the process palatable. The following is a bold statement, we know. Here it goes. No small business can be successful winning a Phase I SBIR grant on their own. It is a relationship process. Like any other competitive grant process.

Bright Idea

TIP: If an actual grant reviewer is in your state teaching a class or speaking: pay the fee, take the class, and meet the reviewer. Grant writing is a relationship based sport. You need to be a known, vetted, and perceived as a secure investment for the Agency to accept the risk. There is no preferential treatment. However, if you are applying for a NIH SBIR Grant and have an NIH Grant Reviewer on your advisory board, you may float to the top of the pile of applicants.

Check your local SBIR/STTR service providers for the latest in amounts, eligibility, etc., as these programs are government funded and can change frequently.

SBIR / STTR Notes:

Resource Name:

Contact Person:

URL:

Notes:

GROWWashington
Guide 7: Startup Do's and Don'ts

GROW Washington is an entrepreneurial development Center in a small destination city called Snohomish, Washington. Carolyn Eslick, Mayor of a neighboring small rural city, and former restaurant and bar owner, runs the business incubator. Over her years of running successful businesses, and helping business owners get their start, she and her staff have come up with some basic business planning do's and don'ts.

Use the following as a guide or simply as sage advice—either way, these business tips are gold. Follow the GROW Washington business Do's and Don'ts to save you time and money.

Business Startup Do's

Do what you love!

It should be wildly accepted that to start a business, it should be in an area that you love. Somehow that concept escapes many. Don't let it escape you!

Do consult an accountant, attorney, and banker.

We really like this one for several reasons. First, your local service providers know a ton about the local businesses. They have experience and are willing to share it with you. All you need to do is ask!

Seek advice and counsel

Do get your state licenses before setting up your bank account.

This is another really good piece of advice. In order to open a bank account, or to be able to accept money in your business name, you need a legal business. Determining your corporate structure—the type of business entity you plan to launch—is an important business planning step. Later in this *Toolkit*, there is a guide to help you through this important and strategic process.

Plan with the future in mind

Do your research on the industry and your competition.
You need to know how large of an industry it is. Whether it is growing or shrinking, and at what rate. Most importantly, you need to know where you fit in the micro scheme of things. You need to be able to answer the questions: Who are my direct and indirect competition? Who are my ideal customers? What geographic location will I be serving?

Business Startup Don'ts

Don't sign a lease before securing financing.
This is a biggie! As former bankers, we have seen what can happen to a business owner when their excitement for a location gets the better of them. It is advised that you have so many customers or clients that you absolutely have the cash flow to cover your lease before you sign on the bottom line.

Money Wise

TIP: Worst case, one 'out' is to only execute a lease that is contingent on financing at the level you determine is appropriate for your business. That way if you don't get the business loan you were hoping for, you are not hooked. Further, lease agreements tend to have a personal guarantee. Meaning, even if your business fails, you are personally responsible to pay for the full term of the lease. Last, there may be a clause that prevents you from subleasing the space which could again limit your options.

We are not attorneys, and throughout this *Toolkit*, we present best practices, strategies, and solutions to common business startup hurdles. We are not presenting legal advice. We recommend that you seek council when executing any legal agreement. Company formation is a legal process, and so is executing a lease.

Don't spend money before checking regulations with the city or county.
This is important. Know what licenses, permits, and regulations may affect your business venture before you start. If you are operating a home-based business, check for license or other special requirements.

The City and County administer things like:
- Zoning permits and fees
- Building permits and inspections
- Utilities and taxes
- Specialty licenses

GROWWashington
Guide 8: Startup Checklist

☐   Define your business vision and goals

☐   Design your perfect business

☐   Develop a business plan and financial model

☐   Decide on a business structure (Sole Prop, LLC, Corp, Coop, other)

TIP: If an LLC, file with the Secretary of State first to ensure your chosen business name is available. This may save you time and money in the business entity formation process.

Money Wise

☐   Obtain licenses, permits, and bank accounts

☐   Determine regulatory, record keeping and insurance needs

☐   Build your dream team—create an advisory board

☐   Secure capital as needed and know your credit

☐   Develop your sales process, goals, and marketing strategy

☐   Launch marketing initiatives, pre sales activities, and grand opening events

Visit GROW Washington online at ww.GrowWashignton.biz to learn more about this product-focused business incubator serving rural and small cities and how to join or or bring one to your community.

Guide 9: Talking the Talk

Summary of Definitions

There are so many acronyms in the world of Microenterprise and small business development. Here are some definitions to help you navigate.

7a	US Small Business Administration loan
8a	US Small Business Administration certification as a small business, to help secure government contracts
504	US Small Business Administration loan
DBE	Disadvantaged Business Enterprise. US Small Business Administration designation and certification, to help secure government contracts
EDC	Economic Development Centers. Usually operated in counties, e.g.: Hennepin County EDC. A Resource for small business owners for demographic research, properties for sale, sometimes technical assistance programs, and potential advisory board members
HUBZone	US Small Business Administration designation and certification, to help secure government contracts
MBE	Minority Business Enterprise. US Small Business Administration designation and certification, to help secure government contracts
Microloan	A small business loan or very small business loan. According to the SBA, a loan under $50,000. According to various microenterprise associations, a loan under $35,000
OPA	Other People's Assets
OPM	Other People's Money

PTAC	Procurement and Technical Assistance Center, a business technical assistance program funded by the Department of Defense to support the small business owners access to government markets and to facilitate technology transfer from the private sector (business) to the government or public sector through the SBIR and STTR programs.
SBA	US Small Business Administration, a division within the Office of The president, which supports small business through access to capital, access to markets, and access to information programs for entrepreneurs.
SBDC	Small Business Development Center, a business training and technical assistance program funded by the US Small Business Administration
SBIR	Small Business Innovation Research Program. Research, Development and Commercialization government grants to promote technology transfer from the private sector to the public sector.
SCORE	Service Corps of Retires Executives. A volunteer program administered by the US Small Business Administration to provide business counseling and mentoring to small business owners and pre-startup entrepreneurs.
STEP	State Trade and Export Promotion. A free international trade technical assistance program for small business owners interested in exporting their products or services.
STTR	Small Business Technology Transfer. Research, Development and Commercialization government grants to promote technology transfer from the private sector to the public sector.
TA	Technical Assistance, One-on-one business consulting, business counseling, business mentoring, or small group coaching
WBC	Women's Business Center, a business technical assistance program administered by the SBA to serve women entrepreneurs
WBE	Woman-owned Business Enterprise. US Small Business Administration designation and certification, to help secure government contracts

On the next page, you have the opportunity to test your knowledge. Hint: from the list above there is one acronym missing in the quiz.
Can you identify which one?

Guide 10: Test Your Knowledge

You already walk the walk…let's examine your 'talk the talk'. In this section on Tools for Success so many acronyms were presented that we thought the following exercise might be fun. Test your knowledge by matching the definitions with the acronym.

Acronyms
SCORE
SBA
WBC
TA
SBDC
7a
8a
Microloan
504
OPM
PTAC
EDC
HUBZone
MBE
DBE
WBE
SBIR
STTR
STEP

#	Definition
1	A business loan under $50,000.
2	Disadvantaged Business Enterprise
3	Economic Development Centers
4	Minority Business Enterprise
5	Other People's Money
6	Procurement and Technical Assistance Center
7	Service Corps of Retires Executives
8	Small Business Development Center
9	Small Business Innovation Research Program
10	Small Business Technology Transfer.
11	State Trade and Export Promotion.
12	Technical Assistance
13	US Small Business Administration certification
14	US Small Business Administration certification
15	US Small Business Administration loan
16	US Small Business Administration loan
17	US Small Business Administration
18	Woman-owned Business Enterprise
19	Women's Business Center

Last: Next Steps

There are a set of core business principles that—once mastered—heighten your chance of entrepreneurial success. Knowing the rules is a part of the game. The 20 Core Business Principles are your ground rules.

In this chapter, you learned the rules and were armed with the Keys to your entrepreneurial success. Now—reach out! Seek the advice and counsel of those organizations presented here that stand out to you. The next chapter will introduce you to several tools that will set the stage and lay the groundwork for the design of your perfect business.

Tools for Success To Do's

- Visit EntrepreneuialEdgeSeries.com and print the 10 Keys to Success Image to place on my desk.
- Contact the SBA to locate the nearest program:
  - ＿＿ WBC
  - ＿＿ SCORE
  - ＿＿ SBDC
  - ＿＿ STEP
- Contact the PTAC office in my state to learn more about government contracting

Still Ahead

- Learn about corporate structure and the types of business entities
- Craft my ideal company structure
- Fill any leadership gaps with an advisory board or team
- Write a single-page business plan

Tools for Success
Certificate of Completion

You have successfully taken a step toward turning your dream of business ownership into reality.

In this section of the *Small Business Toolkit* we introduced you to the microenterprise industry best practice in business planning—the Entrepreneurial Edge *Core Business Principles* and you were armed with the *10 Keys to Success.* Key free resources to help you plan, launch, or build your business, secure government contracts, or government grants were shared, and you had a chance to test your knowledge.

You completed guides 1 through 10 and now it's time to reward the commitment.

Completed Guides:

> The Keystone
> Guide 1: 10 Keys to Success
> Guide 2: Money Rules
> Guide 3: 20 Core Business Principles
> Guide 4: Your Key to Free
> Guide 5: Getting Certified
> Guide 6: Small Business Grants
> Guide 7: Startup Do's and Don'ts
> Guide 8: Startup Checklist
> Guide 9: Talking the Talk
> Guide 10: Test Your Knowledge

Complete your certificate of completion on the following page to memorialize your accomplishments before we move ahead.

Congratulations!

Entrepreneurial Edge

Small Business
Toolkit

Certificate of Completion

I certify that I, _____, have successfully completed

Tools for Success

Including: *10 Keys to Success™, Money Rules, Core Business Principles™, Keys to Free, Getting Certified*

Signature: _____   Date: _____

SPROUT!

Chapter 2: **The Strategic Start**

Guides

Guide 11: Determining Your EQ

Guide 12: Realizing Your Values

Guide 13: Aligning Your Entrepreneurial Intention

Guide 14: Discovering Your Strengths

Guide 15: Entrepreneurial Goal Setting

Guide 16: Defining Your Vision

Guide 17: The Art of Business Formation

Guide 18: Steps to the Start

Guide 19: Identifying Advisors

Guide 20: Engaging Advisors

Last: Next Steps

Certificate of Completion

Takeaways:

Understand your unique entrepreneurial personality.

Describe how your entrepreneurial intention is supported by your core values.

Asses your entrepreneurial strengths and weaknesses, identify gaps to
overcome, and evaluate your potential as an entrepreneur.

Define "SMART" goals and the four factors in entrepreneurial goal setting.

Write a vision statement for your new venture.

Understand the types of business entities and evaluate which corporate
structure is right for you.

Describe the value of a business advisor.

Guide 11: Determining Your EQ*

So, you want to be your own boss. Do you have what it takes to be an entrepreneur? Only you can answer that question, but this Toolkit should help you.

The Strategic Start is all about pre-planning your entrepreneurial initiative and learning the steps to the start—before you pull the trigger. Even if you already have a business, the guides in this section of the *Small Business Toolkit* will put you on the fast track toward your entrepreneurial goals and share time-tested strategies to fast track your venture.

Know what you want

Whether you are already a business owner, or just thinking about it, the guides in this part of the book will remind you why you got into business in the first place, let you revisit your values—some may have changed, and learn the three factors in entrepreneurial goal setting.

You will discover the key characteristics of a successful entrepreneur, uncover your strengths, and learn to share your vision with a room full of influencers. There's even a quiz that will allow you to assess your entrepreneurial potential.

Are you interested in starting a business but aren't sure if you have what it takes? Do you have a hobby business that you are considering taking to the next level?

So what are you waiting for? Let's determine your EQ now.

*Entrepreneurial Quotient

**Know what
you want**

Be your own Boss

Every year, hundreds of thousands of people like you make the transition from employee to entrepreneur. How do you know if the entrepreneurial life is for you?

Through surveys and research, experts have found that entrepreneurs share some common personality traits, the most important of which is confidence. They possess confidence in themselves to sell their ideas, set up a business, and trust their intuition.

Measure your potential for entrepreneurship success with the self assessment guide. If a test indicates you have the appropriate personality for entrepreneurial success, that doesn't necessarily mean you're ready right now.

Many questions remain, for example:
- Do I have enough money?
- Is my family ready for this?
- Do people need a product or service like mine?
- Do I have clear business and personal goals?
- Have I identified possible customers?
- Have I identified people to support me in this venture?

If you answered "yes" to most of these questions, Congratulations! You may be on your way to becoming a business owner.

**EQ:
Entrepreneurial
Quotient**

The Entrepreneurial Personality

Each business owner, artist, and entrepreneur are unique. Even if you run the same type of company, in the same industry, and perhaps the same city or town as another business owner, you are still different.

Each entrepreneur brings unique strengths, values, experience, and goals to their ventures. For example, if you assessment two businesses that do pet portraiture, could you assume they have the same earning or income potential? Could you assume they have the same 'perfect customer' or even the same financial goals? Of course not! One business owner may create custom portraits for the very wealthy, and another's market might be doggy day-care centers, or even hotels that offer pet care.

What's Your EQ?

The Entrepreneurial Quotient Quiz self-assessment can help you decide if starting a business is right for you. Take this quiz to determine your Entrepreneurial Quotient.

Determine Your EQ: Questions

	Yes	Unsure	No
I am passionate about my business idea			
I am persistent			
I am willing to tap all my resources			
I have the savings to invest on my own			
If something can't be done, I still find a way			
I have adequate experience			
I am competitive			
I am prepared to work long hours every day for an indefinite period			
I have a unique service or product			
My family is supportive of me			
I am willing to make short-term sacrifices for long-term success			
I am an excellent communicator			
I have access to more money if I need it			
I know this business inside and out			
TOTAL			

TIP: Analyze your totals. Are you where you want to be? If not, how can you get there?

Determine Your EQ: Answers

	Yes	Unsure	No
I am passionate about my business idea	?	?	?
I am persistent	?	?	?
I am willing to tap all my resources	?	?	?
I have the savings to invest on my own	?	?	?
If something can't be done, I still find a way	?	?	?
I have adequate experience	?	?	?
I am competitive	?	?	?
I am prepared to work long hours every day for an indefinite period	?	?	?
I have a unique service or product	?	?	?
My family is supportive of me	?	?	?
I am willing to make short-term sacrifices for long-term success	?	?	?
I am an excellent communicator	?	?	?
I have access to more money if I need it	?	?	?
I know this business inside and out	?	?	?
TOTAL	?	?	?

On the other hand...
Entrepreneurs are a unique! It's okay not to fit this or any other mold!

Guide 12: Realizing Your Values

Personal values and entrepreneurial intention are directly related. Awareness and understanding of your personal values is essential to successful business planning. What a person values is a good predictor of where you choose to invest your energy.

When your values and goals are aligned, you jump on a fast track to success. A mismatch between your personal and business goals can have a substantive impact on your life, business and personal. This mismatch can produce self-sabotage, burnout, and can even lead to business failure.

Core Business Principle

A value is not the same as a motive.

Values play an important role in your job, especially when your job is CEO of your business. If your business or job requirements align with what you value, there will be less conflict. For example if you have a high value for power and the job requires influencing behaviors, there is no conflict. Alternatively, if you have a low value for power but a high value for tranquility and your business is as a lobbyist in Washington DC, there may be conflict.

Conflict and tension may arise in business relationships, partnerships, between co-workers, even between family and friends, when one of your 'high values' buts against a 'low value' requirements. For example, if you feel the need to influence others in a job that has a low job requirement for helping others succeed, you will find your efforts counterproductive.

When your business is in a growth stage, it is common to find yourself with a gap between your values and your expanding business opportunities. If you know where those gaps exist, you can close them.

Motives are natural drivers whereas values are chosen areas of importance. Values are conscious whereas motives are unconscious.

Values are adaptive. They are developed from your life experiences. While motives are basic, influenced by early emotional experiences and might be genetic. Motives are difficult to change whereas values can be changed.

Values Change. Assess Frequently.

Over time, your values may change. Common catalysts for changing values are a change in or expansion of personal or business goals, exposure to new influences, immersion in a new environment, and even the recognition of your current values.

Uncover Your Values

Uncovering your personal values will help you solidify your entrepreneurial goals. Once you have set entrepreneurial goals, you will be able to design the business of your dreams. Complete this guide in three steps:

Step 1: Explore your values
Step 2: Identify your core values
Step 3: Determine what you value most

Once you have identified what matters to you most, you can align your entrepreneurial intentions and goals with your personal values.

1
Step

Step 1: Explore Your Values
Answer the question: What do I value most?

From the following list of values, circle the **10** that are most important to you as guides for how to behave, or as components of a valued way of life. Feel free to add any values of your own to this list.

Circle your top 10 (most important) values from the following two pages.

Abundance	Driving others to achieve
Accountability	Ecological awareness
Achievement	Economic security
Adaptability	Education
Advancement and promotion	Effectiveness
Adventure	Efficiency
Affection—love and caring	Empathy
Arts	Ethical practice
Autonomy	Excellence
Challenging problems	Excitement
Change and variety	Fairness
Close relationships	Fast living
Collective action	Financial gain
Communication	Focus
Competence	Freedom
Competition	Friendships
Concern for Community	Good health
Connectedness	Growth
Connections	Happiness
Control	Harmony
Cooperation	Having a family
Country	Helping other people
Creativity	Helping society
Cultural Diversity	Honesty
Decisiveness	Idea Generation
Democracy	Impact (significance)
Diplomacy	Inclusiveness
Discipline	Independence
Discussion	Influencing others
Diversity	Inner harmony

Did we miss any?
Use this space to add your own here:

Spirituality

Innovation

× Integrity

Intellectual status

× Joy

Knowledge

Leadership

Logic

Loyalty

Making things happen

× Meaningful work

Merit

Mobilizing others

Mobilizing resources

Money

Mutual benefit

× Nature

× Opportunity to teach

Order (conformity)

Organization

Owning (home, business)

Partnership

× Personal development

Physical challenge

Physical fitness

× Pleasure

Power and authority

Privacy

× Public service

Purity

× Quality (in what you do)

× Quality relationships

Recognition (status)

Religion

× Reputation

× Respect

× Responsibility

Restoration

Security

Self-respect

Serenity

Sophistication

Stability

Status

Strategy

× Strong moral values

Strong religious values

Supervising others

Sustainable regeneration

Time

× To be a leader

× To be remembered

× To help others

Training

Tranquility

× Truth

Wealth

× Wellbeing

Wellness

× Wisdom

Working alone

Working under pressure

Working with others

World leadership

Step 2: Identify Your Core Values

Now that you have identified ten values, imagine that you are only permitted to have five values. Which five would they be? List them now.

2
Step

My Top 5 Values   Today's Date: _____

1.

2.

3.

4.

5.

Now imagine that you are only permitted four.
Which would you give up, which would you keep?

My Top 4 Values   Today's Date: _____

1.

2.

3.

4.

Now eliminate another, to bring your list down to three.

My Top 3 Values   Today's Date: _____

1.

2.

3.

Another round of elimination to bring your list down to two.

My Top 2 Values   Today's Date: _____

1.

2.

3
Step

Step 3: Determine What You Value Most
Finally cross off one of your top two most important values.
Which one item on the list do you care about most?

What I Value Most: Today's Date: _____

1.

Guide 13: Aligning Your Entrepreneurial Intention

Ask yourself the following questions to help align your personal values with your entrepreneurial intention.

Does your entrepreneurial intention right now reflect your values? Is the way you spend your time consistent with your priorities?

Your venture reflects your values

If the way you spend your time is not consistent with your priorities, how can you make it so?

Are there some parts of your entrepreneurial life that you would like to change but cannot right now? If so, what is your timetable for bringing your lifestyle more into harmony with your values?

How do you think your most important personal values will affect your business?

The Vision and Entrepreneurial Intention guides were adapted from the Hay Group Values Assessment and from *Training for Life: A Practical Guide to Career and Life Planning,* Fifth Edition (1994).

Guide 14: Discovering Your Strengths

Most successful entrepreneurs have launched their entrepreneurial initiative from an opportunity that presented itself, and not from necessity. If you fall into this category, you might be an opportunity-driven entrepreneur.

Opportunity-Driven Entrepreneurship

For example, you may be an opportunity-driven entrepreneur if you were working for Microsoft, came up with a way to solve a software problem outside your scope of work, and started your own company to sell that product or service back into your former employer. In this example, you identified an opportunity, and started a business. An Opportunity-driven venture has a greater chance of success than one that is started out of necessity.

Know your strengths— make it count!

If you're primary motivation to start a company is independence or to increase your income, you may be a necessity-driven entrepreneur. You may fall into this category of entrepreneur if you need to start a business because you are fired, downsized, outsourced, or you believe it's time to 'be your own boss'.

The great news is that we can turn necessity into opportunity!

Opportunity-driven entrepreneurs know their strengths.

In a period of economic growth, eighty percent of new companies launched are opportunity-driven.

In a recessionary time, the tables are turned. Business ventures launched out of necessity, rather than from opportunity, tend to have a higher failure rate according to the Global Entrepreneurship Monitor (GEM). If you feel you may be a necessity-driven entrepreneur, there's hope!

Bright Idea

TIP: Following a business design process helps you identify opportunities in the marketplace and can turn you into an opportunity-driven entrepreneur. How do you turn your necessity-driven business into one of opportunity? Most successful entrepreneurs recall starting their own business with a sense of urgency, not just a desire. Not all entrepreneurs have the knowledge, support, or financial backing to make their business a success.

Opportunity-driven entrepreneurs know their strengths and launch their ventures with economic goals in mind. The following Entrepreneurial Assessment guide will set you on the track of an opportunity-driven entrepreneur.

A Microenterprise has 5 or less employees.

And what about success? Success to one person can look very different from success to another. If you need buy-in or financial support, how you share your strengths and the opportunity presented by your business becomes vital. The guide on the following pages will help you discover and articulate your strengths and weaknesses, evaluate your entrepreneurial advantages, and set some goals.

As micro entrepreneurs, we wear many hats in our business. It is rare that one person has all the knowledge of each functional area of business or all the qualities needed to be successful in business.

Functional Areas of Business

Entrepreneur Assessment

What is important is to understand individual strengths and weaknesses, and to be able to mitigate, or overcome, any weaknesses that we might have. Every entrepreneur needs some expertise in the main functional business areas—management, marketing, operations, sales, and financial management—but you don't need to be an expert.

You may have experience from past business ownership or management, work as an employee or an entrepreneur, or through a past jobs or training, experience may also come from others like relatives, employees, board members, friends, or advisors.

As a microentreprenreur, you manage everything from leadership to customer service.

Spend a few moments to document your personal experience in each of the business functional areas to help you determine where there may be gaps, and to help you ultimately create your strategy for success.

From this assessment you will be able to mitigate any lack of expertise with Advisory Board members, key employees, or other outsourced (software or cloud based) resources.

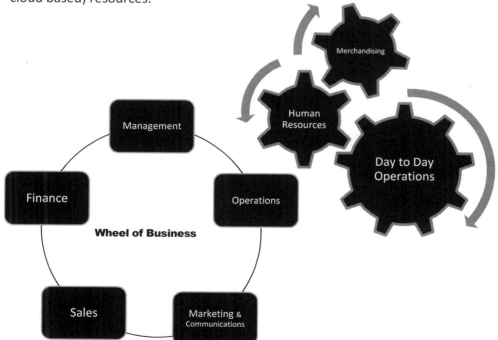

Each spoke of the wheel can have many sub-functions.

My Management Assessment

Business Functions	My Strengths and Experience	My Weaknesses / Gaps to Fill	How I Plan to Overcome any Weaknesses
Business Formation			
Business Planning			
Business Launch			
Strategic Planning			
Leadership and Team Building			

My Marketing Assessment

Business Functions	My Strengths and Experience	My Weaknesses Gaps to Fill	How I Plan to Overcome any Weaknesses
Identifying Markets			
Target Marketing			
Strategic Direct Marketing			
Social Media Marketing			
Pricing			
Advertising			
Public Relations			

My Operations Assessment

Business Functions	My Strengths and Experience	My Weaknesses Gaps to Fill	How I Plan to Overcome any Weaknesses
Quality Assurance			
People Management			
Supply Chain Management			
Product Management			
Services Management			
Equipment Management			
Managing the day to day of your business			

My Sales Assessment

Business Functions	My Strengths and Experience	My Weaknesses Gaps to Fill	How I Plan to Overcome any Weaknesses
Sales Process Design			
Sales Projections			
Sales Tracking and Benchmarking			
Business Sales			
Consumer Sales			
Retail / Wholesale			
Relationship Sales			
Channel Sales			

My Financial Management Assessment

Business Functions	My Strengths and Experience	My Weaknesses Gaps to Fill	How I Plan to Overcome any Weaknesses
Accounting / Book-keeping			
Creating and Managing Financial Controls			
Tax Strategies			
Cash Management			
Creating and Monitoring Budgets			
Fundraising / Capital Investment Strategies / Leverage			

Guide 15: Entrepreneurial Goal Setting

Goal setting is powerful. In this *Toolkit*, we differentiate between personal goals and entrepreneurial goals. However, all goals have similar attributes. This section covers the basics and is a baseline to help you craft both personal and entrepreneurial goals.

In personal planning, setting goals on a routine basis helps you decide what you want to achieve, and then move step-by-step towards achieving the desired outcome.

Plan with the future in mind

Setting goals allows you to choose where you want to go in life. If you know what you want to achieve, you'll know what you have to concentrate on in order to make things happen. You can set your path, and factor out things that are merely distractions.

Goals give you long-term vision and short-term motivation

Top-level athletes, successful business-people, and achievers in all fields use goal-setting techniques. They focus your acquisition of knowledge and help you to organize your time and your resources so that you can make the very most of your life.

By setting sharp, clearly defined goals, you can measure and take pride in the achievement of those goals. You can see forward progress in what might previously have seemed a long pointless grind. By setting goals, you will also raise your self-confidence, as you recognize your ability and competence in achieving the goals that you have set.

Goals are set on a number of different levels: First, you decide what you want to do with your life and what large-scale goals you want to achieve. Second, you break these down into the smaller and smaller targets that you must hit so that you reach your lifetime goals. Finally, once you have your plan, you start working towards achieving it.

The importance of setting goals cannot be stressed enough. Goals give us something to work toward, and help us feel like we are moving along a specific path. Establishing goals invites us to look at the big picture, break it down into smaller pieces, and get started toward accomplishing our important hopes and dreams.

A problem that arises most often is that many people aren't quite sure how to set goals. Where to start, what kind of goals to set, how big or how small, how long a time frame to allow. One of the most common problems is that their goals tend to be too big. It is much easier to achieve smaller goals that fit with a larger objective, than to try to accomplish everything all at once. It's time to start getting smart about goal setting.

Bright Idea

TIP: Refer back to the values guide when setting your goals.

Know your personal goals.
Set SMART business goals.

Goal setting is an integral part of successful business planning. In addition to evaluating your strengths, weaknesses, and values it's important to be able to define your entrepreneurial goals.

As an entrepreneur, you may be your business. So, listing your personal goals is very important. For some people, the goal is the freedom to do what they want when they want, without anyone telling them otherwise. For others, the personal goal may be financial security.

Setting SMART Goals
SMART goals are Specific, Measurable, Achievable, Relevant, and Time-related. This is a tried and true method used by business centers, entrepreneur mentors, and college programs nation-wide, for effective entrepreneurial and personal goal setting.

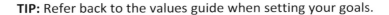

When defining goals for your personal or business life, try the SMART technique.

Know what you want

SMART Goals	
Specific	Set clear, concrete goals. Some examples might be writing a business plan, implementing a marketing plan, writing in your inventor's journal when you have a new idea, or creating a business advisory board.
Measurable	Identify markers that will indicate success for you. If your goal is to implement a social media marketing plan, a reasonable measurement of success might be to secure your Facebook and Twitter account names within one week, to have twenty followers within three weeks, and to have schedule one quarter's worth of postings using Hootsuite. Learn how to accomplish all this in the chapter on social media.
Achievable	Ensure that your goals are realistic. For example, setting the goal of writing your Executive Business Plan in one week may be difficult. However writing a QuickPlan, the single page business plan, in one week would be doable. However, if you want to complete an Executive Business Plan, break your project into small enough tasks so that each task is part of the overall accomplishment.
Relevant	Choose goals that are applicable to your entrepreneurial initiative and which align with your values. Make sure your goals are something you are truly invested in, because you will be focusing a great deal of time and energy on them. Ask yourself what success would look like when you do achieve your goal, and if this goal makes sense.
Time-Related	Set a timeline that will guide your progress. Specifying a goal for two years down the road is not as powerful a motivator as one that you set for the next six months, three months, or three weeks.

**Plan with the
future in mind**

4 Factors in Entrepreneurial Goal Setting

When setting entrepreneurial goals, think about the following four factors:

1. Income
2. Lifestyle
3. Type of Work
4. Social Responsibility

*Entrepreneurial goal setting
is holistic goal setting.*

1.

The Income Goal

Every entrepreneur is different. We each have very different goals and expectations for ourselves as we plan our business. In terms of an income goal – be real! How much do you need to earn from your business activities in order for you to quit your current job? Consider how many hours you can actually commit to the business and what type of income goal for the business is realistic. What business income goal is worth your energy and time in this new venture?

2.

The Lifestyle Goal

A lifestyle goal is an important consideration for business owners and those planning to launch a business venture. Why? The majority of business owners actually operate a micro enterprise, a business with five or fewer employees.

Some Lifestyle questions to consider:

- How many weeks a year do I want to work?
- How many hours a week do I plan to dedicate to my business?
- Will I need an office other than my home?
- How many times a year do I want to travel for business? How long do I want to be gone? International or domestic?
- Will my business be family focused?
- How can I structure the business to align with my values and personal goals?

3.

The Type of Work Goal

Type of Work goals may be the most simple, but are still important. When you are the main driver of your business, why not design the perfect work environment for yourself? For example, if you dislike talking on the phone, don't plan a business that demands long-distance client relationships. Instead, design a business where you can meet with clients and customers face to face.

Consider your ideal working environment. Do you want to work in an office? Would you prefer to work outdoors? Do you want a computer focused job? How often do you want to interface with others? You know the work environment that will contribute best to your success. Write it down.

4.

Social Responsibility

Have you considered the broader responsibility or contribution your company can make in the world? Most large companies have a social responsibility component to their business. HSBC, the largest international bank in the world, makes it a point to support environmental causes and education around the globe. They not only fund organizations and causes that align with their socially responsible commitment, but they pay their employees, through providing paid time off to volunteer, to support their social mission.

SPROUT!

A social enterprise is any for-profit or non-profit business that has found financially viable ways to integrate social and/or environmental value into their business processes or design. Some organizations support global health, renewable energy, sustainable agriculture, base-of-the-pyramid economies the list goes on.

**Know what
you want**

My Entrepreneurial Goal Setting

Some ways to consider if you intend to add a socially responsible component to your business might be to answer the following questions:

- What can my business do that will create meaning and impact?
- Am I creating a social innovation—a new solution to a social problem that is more effective, efficient, sustainable than existing solutions?
- What social indictors might my business track to gage how successful we are at achieving our business mission?

Use these questions to help you assess your income, lifestyle, and type of work goals here.

Income:

Many entrepreneurs go into business to achieve financial security. Consider how much money you want to make during your first year of operation and each year thereafter, up to five years.

My Income Goals:

My Lifestyle Goals:

Plan with the future in mind

Lifestyle:

Consider travel, family commitment, hours worked, geographic location, and personal investment when you assess your lifestyle goals.

Know what you want

Type of work:
Determine whether you like working outdoors, in an office, with computers, on the phone, with lots of people, with children and so on. You might even visualize what you would be wearing on your best day!

My Work Style Goals:

My Social Enterprise Goals:

SPROUT!

Social Aspect:

Many entrepreneurs today start their businesses in order to leave the world a better place. You may have a passion for children, renewable or green energy, indigenous populations, or maybe animal welfare.

Think about how your company or new business venture might contribute to the greater good.

**Core Business
Principle**

Guide 16: Defining Your Vision

You may have a business idea and are not sure where to start. Maybe you're not sure what step is next in your business planning process, or even that there are steps to planning for a successful business.

Business planning can be a never-ending process. Depending on your goal at any given time, the process of planning allows you to adjust and readjust your business dreams and goals. The Business Process Diagram is a starting point to help you plan.

It really is quite simple. Business planning starts with your vision and you work from there to create a model that will support your vision and purpose. Your business vision defines its future direction and business makeup. It is a guiding concept for what the organization is trying to do and to become.

A strategic vision is a roadmap of a company's future – the direction it is headed, the customer focus it should have, the market position it should try to occupy, the business activities to be pursued, and the capabilities it plans to develop

Start with an overall vision or purpose for getting into business. This will simplify designing the business to support your vision and goals. Answer the questions in this Guide to help prepare you to write your vision statement.

**Business planning
is personal planning.**

What drove me on this path toward entrepreneurship?

Plan with the future in mind

What will our business look like in 5 to 10 years from now?

I started on the path of business ownership because...

If I had my way, my business would...

Business planning is an art – not a science.

The reason my business ~~exits~~ exists and its purpose are...

My business is committed to...

My business will be recognized by its clients and employees as...

When it succeeds, its accomplishments will include...

My Business Vision Statement

You have spent time on the vision statement preparation questions in this guide. Use the space below to create your own business vision statement.

Core Business Principle

Sample Business Vision Statements:

Anheuser-Busch
Be the world's beer company. Through all of our products, services and relationships, we will add to life's enjoyment.

Avon
To be the company that best understands and satisfies the product, service, and self-fulfillment needs of women - globally.

IKEA
The IKEA vision is to create a better everyday life for the many people. We make this possible by offering a wide range of well-designed, functional home furnishing products at process so low that as many people as possible will be able to afford them.

Volkswagen
At Volkswagen, they don't use the word "Vision" – rather, they word it like this: Our strategy pursues a clear objective: By 2018 the Volkswagen Group is to be the world's most successful and fascinating automobile manufacturer – and the leading light when it comes to sustainability

Guide 17: The Art of Business Formation

Core Business Principle

We love business planning. More than any other part of planning, a good discussion about business formation strategy and corporate structure is most exciting. Corporate structure? Business formation strategy? What could be so important about that?

Corporate structure is more than just having an understanding of the difference between the types of business entities and what benefits they might offer you (like an LLC, S Corp, C-Corp, Coop, Non Profit, Association, Joint Venture, Sole Proprietorship, etc.)

Business formation strategy is also more than the knowledge of the perfect process of choosing a company name and securing it with company formation procedures in order to save the most time and money. Yes, there is a perfect process. We share that with you in this section of the *Toolkit*. Business formation strategy is more than setting up a company for today just because you can—it's about forming the business that will let you accomplish your dreams.

My Company

Corporate structure can be looked at like an umbrella. You, as the business owner, have a unique opportunity to create something, an entity, your business, that will last into the future. A business, that if set up correctly from the beginning, will never need to go through a stock split (turning your existing units or stock into more because you didn't plan ahead and diluting the shares of all your investors in the process), because you planned for the future growth of your company.

In short, think of corporate structure and more broadly, your business formation strategy, as that all important planning time to think three, five, and twenty five years down the road.

Plan with the future in mind

What do you think your company will look like? Will it have separate divisions based on the types of services you provide or products you sell (like a Coca-Cola or Ford Motor Company). Will you want to raise money from friends and family, or through an investment banker or angel investor? Might you want to buy another company? What if you want to purchase that other company with your equity and not all cash?

So much to think about and so many options.

You are the owner, you are in control. It's not too late to start...even if you've been in business for years and never thought about the future or the number of units you allocated for your limited liability company. Even better if you are a sole proprietor now, and are planning to change into an LLC. Today is always the perfect time to consider the steps of a start!

A Sole Proprietorship is "*you, you and you*".

Sole Proprietorship

DBA

DBA

DBA

First, let's start with some questions to help you start thinking in more broad terms about your corporate structure. Use the Umbrella on the following page to begin to consider the ideal corporate structure of your business.

Question 1: Do I want to bring in outside funding?
From Friends and family? From angel investment groups? From venture capitalists? If the answer is yes, you and your investors might want a business structure that is a separate entity from yourself.

Remember a Sole Proprietorship is 'you, yourself, and you'. You retain the liability for the business; you retain the assets of the business. It is not a separate entity from you. Investor's, whether you are raising debt or equity financing, are going to want to invest in a business entity other than a Sole Proprietorship.

Consider the LLC as a simple and inexpensive way to avoid possible double taxation, but to have an entity that is separate from you.

Question 2: Do you have other people, employees, clients, or customers crossing your threshold–or coming into your physical business location? Do you conduct your business on another person's property?

If so, then definitely consider moving from a sole proprietor structure to a LLC or another business entity that is separate from you. If for nothing but for liability protection reasons, as if that wasn't enough.

Questions 3: Lastly, consider the future of partnerships, joint ventures, buying another business for which you may want to maintain separate books, taxes, and accounting practices. Do you plan in the future to buy a business? Would you want the option of offering stock options or ownership to a partner or key employees? Might you consider having a nonprofit or charitable arm of your business at some point?

If any of the above applies to your business as you take a forward look, then consider a more sophisticated corporate structure than a sole proprietorship, and create your own business formation strategy.

Business Structure Decision Example
Plant Jive – A landscaping business

Plant Jive is a landscaping business that generates revenue for the owner through yard maintenance, landscape design, and wholesale plant sales. In addition, the business owner owns a network marketing business on the side for incremental income—additional income. In interviewing the entrepreneur, here is what they had to say about their corporate structure and plans for the future.

Today:

"I filed my master business license several years ago as a sole proprietorship. I hire some contract employees. I bring them in based on my workload. I hope to build business credit and grow this into a viable future for me and my family. However, I know I can't do this type of work forever, at least not in the same way. Now, I do most of the labor intensive work myself. Also, I bought into a network marketing company and do some consulting on the side. I use trade names (doing business as) when I wear my different business hats."

Future:

"I want a larger landscaping business that will have a commercial [business to business or B2B] division, a business to consumer division (B2C), and wholesale plant material sales. I want to have employees, so I can move away from the day to day labor intensive part of the business. I want to be able to offer my employees some sort of ownership in the company to keep them interested and so that they have a vested interest in the company's success. Also, I may need to bring in a partner/investor to help me grow the business. I may want the option of selling the business to my partner down the road. "

**Know what
you want**

Question: "What are my corporate structure options?"

*Business planning is an art,
not a science.*

Takeaways:

Business formation planning—also called corporate structure or design—is an art, not a science. There is no single correct way to structure your business. Further, all businesses are different. One landscape design company might look very different from another in terms of structure depending on the owners' goals and plans for growth, expansion, succession, income, and taxes.

**Seek advice
and counsel**

It is always recommended that you seek the counsel of a tax advisor or attorney when considering corporate structure. There are free resources available as well.

In this example, the company owner has placed themselves and their family's assets at risk by doing business as a Sole Proprietorship. If a customer becomes lawsuit happy, the company offers no liability protection under this type of corporate structure. Another issue is that the owner is interested in bringing in a partner or investor in the near term. As a Sole Proprietorship, the investor would be investing in the business owner as a person and not a business. A new business structure would be needed to bring n outside investors. There are several ways to do this, and considering the tax implications of each business type should be considered for both the owner and the new equity owner. Lastly, the owner is interested in granting some ownership rights to current or future employees. As a Sole Proprietorship, this is not a viable option.

However, there are several ways that the "right" corporate structure can enable the owner to accomplish all of his goals.

I love free resources. You might consider visiting a Small Business Administration SCORE counselor or Small Business Development Center for further advice on the types of business entities and which one might be the right fit based on your future business goals. A business attorney will have the inside scoop on corporate structure options too. For tax considerations, talk to a tax attorney or a business accountant. There are tax implications for every business formation strategy.

Knowledge is power - learn what the options are before diving in. That way you can keep your options open and plan for success.

Strategic Business Formation

Consider forming a Limited Liability Company to replace your Sole Proprietorship.

When creating the LLC, be sure to create enough member units that will allow you to 'give' some away – to investors and or employees—but that the amount you give away won't dilute your ownership too much.

Limited Liability Company

An LLC is a separate entity from yourself, so as long as you don't 'pierce the corporate veil', your business liability will remain just that–a business liability and not a personal liability. "Piercing the corporate veil" is the term that is used to describe when a business has mixed or blended some of their personal assets or liabilities with business ones. The business is no longer legally a separate entity from the owner any longer, and becomes a mess for legal and tax reasons.

Some simple ways a business owner can work toward maintaining a clean separation of their business assets and liabilities from personal ones are to:
1. Set up a business checking account separate from your personal accounts.
2. Maintain business record keeping and bills separate from those for your household.
3. Avoid using your own funds to purchase items for the business or to 'float' the business with a personal cash infusion during tough times. Instead, consider making a loan to the business. That way you have avoided mingling your personal and business funds.

There are other ways to ensure you retain your clean bill of health as a business entity. There are some of the most common though. I recommend talking with a business accountant or CPA to be sure, you don't pierce the corporate veil.

Alternative Company Structure

Alternatively consider creating a Holding Company or a Parent Company to 'hold' your various business ventures. The Parent can own other business entities, assets like real estate, and even joint ventures. You can structure the business units so that business income rolls up into the Parent company. Cash Management strategies are an art and the options are many. A good business banker and their treasury representative will have all the options.

Companies with separate divisions, those who do business in several states, or even in multiple countries, might want to consider this structure.

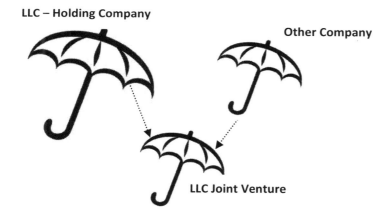

LLC – Holding Company

Other Company

LLC Joint Venture

This new company, on the lower middle, represents a Joint Venture: a new company formed by two different companies, and owned by both. Each company owner may have invested time or capital, or both, to form the new company. Ownership of the new company does not need to reflect equal parts...this is an art after all! Not a science. This might occur when you want to buy a building or piece of equipment and need a financial partner and want to keep the new business, venture, or assets separate from your existing companies.

Design your perfect business

If you consider creating a holding or parent company, think *big picture* when you consider a name for this entity. You may have this business forever! Consider using your family name with the word "International" tacked onto the end. Be bold. Be creative!

Core Business Principle

My Strategic Business Structure

Consider the resources and information in the previous guides to help you design your idea business entity. Use the space below to craft your ideal future business formation. This model is something you can take to a business attorney, one of your advisors or business coaches to make it so. It the structure isn't too complex, you can do it on your own online. Use the space below to draw your ideal company structure.

My New Venture Looks Like...

Guide 18: Steps to the Start

There is a right way to start a business. We feel the right way is the option that lets you meet your goals (whether they be speed, cost effectiveness, fundraising options, maintaining long term ownership and control, etc.) in the most simple and cost effective way.

This guide will introduce the types of business entities and strategies surrounding each.

**Core Business
Principle**

Sole Proprietorship

The simplest type of business formation is the Sole Proprietorship. Buyer beware! This option really means you. You may have a trade name (later in this guide) but the business becomes you, yourself and you. Your assets are the business' assets. Your liabilities are the business' liabilities. If you are sued, your personal assets, including your house, may be at risk. This is only an option for the very small micro-entrepreneur or solopreneur who is not at risk of losing it all. More specific, it is a good option for the small business owner who does not 'cross another person's threshold' meaning – your product or service does not step into another person's space. Food companies, pet day cars, and all similar companies are not a good fit for a sole proprietorship. A jewelry company, on the other hand, might be.

How to Register:
You need only file a Master Business License with the Department of Revenue in your State. Some cities may have their own license as well. Before you file, read on. You will want to consider Trade names for your business.

Fees: Typically Under $100.

Trade Names

If you choose to license your business as a Sole Proprietor, I recommend selecting up to five "Doing Business As" trade names before you file. You need a legal Business Name, Trade Name, or DBA in order to open a bank account and cash a check (i.e.: get paid by customers).

Bright Idea

Think big. Think about your future business operations. It is wise to think into the future and plan for several trade names before you file to become a Sole Proprietorship. If you come up with a brilliant Trade Name later, you will have to pay the Master Business Application fee a second time just to add a new Trade name. There does not seem to be a limit on Trade names today. You do not have to use the Trade Names you select. You are simply buying the option to use them into the future as long as your business license is valid, or open.

Trade Name Ideas:
- Your Name
- Your Name Consulting
- Your Family Name International
- Your Last Name Real Estate
- Your Last Name Productions
- Some Cool Name Software

How to Resister:
To register a Sole Proprietorship, simply visit your State's Department of Revenue or Department of Corporations website, and complete their Master Business Application as a Sole Proprietorship.

Fees:
This process can be done online, and will cost less than $100 in most states. In Washington State, for example, a Master Business Application costs USD $35.00 plus an additional USD $5.00 per Trade Name (DBA name). Sometimes you need to start small and simple due to cost restrictions.

Limited Liability Company

The next most common business formation is the Limited Liability Company or LLC. We love the LLC as a business formation strategy for a few key reasons:

- Simple to form
- Simple reporting requirements (in most states, you simply file an annual report online each year, and renew your business license)
- Relatively inexpensive (Usually less than USD $300)
- Provides liability protection (when you follow the rules)
- Is a separate legal entity from the owner
- Allows sole members (a single person can own a LLC with no other partners, members, board of directors, etc.)

How to Register?

There is a cost effective strategy for filing as a LLC.

1. First, file with the Secretary of State in your state.

2. Second, file the Master Business Application with your State's Department of Revenue.

Money Wise

Why in this order? The Secretary of State will approve or disallow the business name you choose. The Secretary of State will perform a name search and will only approve your selected business name if another business is not already using that business name. If you file as a LLC, and happen to select a business name that is too closely related to another business, your name will be declined and you will, for no additional fee, have the opportunity to choose another name.

If you chose to file your Master Business Application first, and then went to the Secretary of State to file as an LLC, and your business name was not approved, you would have spent more money ad time that necessary. As you would then have to start the process again, this time in the correct order.

To save money and re-filing fees, start with the Secretary of State office in your state. Select your business entity name. Be strategic with this name, as you may own it for a *really* long time. You may use your various Trade Names (see above) as your business name and for doing business. Think of the LLC Name as your holding company or parent company name and your Trade names as your various business names under which you operate.

Some day you may want to own a film production company, or a start a micro loan fund. Consider a more generic and long lasting name for your LLC, and more specific or fun trade names under which you may want to operate your various hobby businesses.

There are tax implications to choosing to file as a LLC. In fact, you have a choice. You must choose or select how you want to be taxed within a certain period of time otherwise your tax structure will be selected for you. Look at the options and seek tax advice before making the selection. Maintain your right to choose by following the deadlines.

Other Business Entity Types

There are C Corps, S Corps, Non Profit Corps, and other creative entities as well. However, as the LLC and Sole Proprietorship are the most common today among small business owners and micro-entrepreneurs.

There is great debate about the best entities in order to encourage the solicitation of angel and venture capital investors (namely C Corp vs. S Corp). It is relatively painless to convert a clean (limited number of members/owners) LLC into another entity type (about USD $2,500 if using an attorney) if you decide to raise outside funds and a conversion is required by the investor.

We have participated in successful fundraising efforts using the LLC corporate structure with no pain or complaint from the investors. You can even issue member units to employees as golden handcuffs using an LLC – similar to stock options in the S and C Corporation corporate structures.

Bright Idea

Don't let the simplicity of an LLC stop you from setting up the entity the way you need to in order to meet your needs, whether it be a future fundraising round or golden handcuffs for key employees.

TIP: Visit your local US Small Business Administration office for detailed information about business entity types and for free business planning advice and counsel.

Types of Business Entities – Comparison Table

	Sole Prop	LLC	S Corp	C Corp
Limited liability protection	No	Yes	Yes	Yes
Perpetual duration of the business	No	Maybe	Yes	Yes
Business taxed at entity level	No	Maybe	No	Yes
Double taxation	No	No	No	Yes
Pass-through income/loss	Yes	Yes	Yes	No
Ease of raising capital	No	Maybe	Yes	Yes

Which Type of Corporate Structure best fits my business goals?

My Top 5 Holding or Parent Company Names:

My Top 5 Trade Names:

Guide 19: Identifying Advisors

A Board of Advisors is a small group, from five to fifteen, experts who you engage for a specific period, like a year, to help you accomplish a goal. They may advise you in exchange for equity in your project, joint venture, or company. Many companies have more than one advisory board. One to help with business operations, another for seeking investment capital, and another if your business is high tech or international.

Team of Advisor's Exercise

Your Dream Team can be a team of advisors, an actual Advisory board, or a pool of people you may even want to hire down the road. Consider the question: What type of team do you need to support your goals?

Who do you know, or who do you want to know, who could be of help to you as you plan and launch your business? Think broadly.

In what areas might you need help? Accounting, hiring, taxes, real estate, supply chain, legal advice, the permitting process, supplies, taxes, zoning, customer service, social media assessment, sales marketing, sales management, logo development, letterhead, look and image development, sales leads, pricing—this list of the functional needs is long.

If we expect to do all of these on our own, we will struggle. By getting help, we will decrease our time-to-market and increase the chance of success.

Uncovering Potential Advisors

One member of your Dream Team might include a COI (Center of Influence). A Center of Influence is someone who champions you or supports your introduction to contacts, markets, or business development opportunities. Another member of your Dream Team might be a successful entrepreneur who would advise you as you plan and grow your business.

Take this opportunity to brainstorm potential best in class leaders in their field—worldwide—who you want on your advisory board.

For each person you identify, take the opportunity—before you contact them—to learn all you can about them, their interests, the board seats they hold, and other companies they have helped to grow.

Research the following for each potential advisor. **TIP:** Use a student or intern to help you with this potentially time-intensive project and have them report to you on their findings. Have them create a spreadsheet to track their results. Use the one on the following page as a model.

Bright Idea

Contact Information
Name

Email

Phone

Experience and Interests
Personal URL / Twitter / Linked In Profile

Current Employer / Company Name

Company Address

Company URL

Recent Press Releases

Board of Directors

Investors

Special Projects

Books Written

Blog(s)

Company Growth Plan – where might you fit?

Why Them?

Why would they want to or be able to help you?

What have they done in the past that caught your attention?

What would you like them to do for you?

Personal Advisor. Financial Advisor. Technical Advisor? Other?

My Potential Dream Team

Management / Leadership:

Operations:

Financial Management:

Sales / Merchandising / Export:

Marketing / Communications:

Technical / R&D:

Identifying Potential Advisors

Use the following space, or create your own spreadsheet, to track your contacts with potential advisory board members for your business.

Advisory Board Candidate	Referred by	Expertise Desired	Telephone	Email	Value Proposition	Contact Date	Notes

**Core Business
Principle**

Guide 20: Engaging Advisors

Mobilizing Resources

Building a supporting environment for entrepreneurship, innovation, and micro-enterprise to flourish requires the engagement of all stakeholders. The same goes for the development of a successful emerging growth Company. Broad stakeholder involvement and support is required to build a fast growth or capital-intensive company.

Engaging Strategic Partners

An Advisory board is an extremely useful tool that can help you build a management team, and a team of experts in each functional area of your business, without the formality of a Board of Directors, and without giving up control of your company. It is also a useful tool for mobilizing strategic human resources, people power, for non-profits and community projects, in addition to your entrepreneurial venture.

For each broad-based community or economic development initiative, we recommend the formation of an advisory board—for the startup business, it is critical to success.

Advisory Board vs. Board of Directors

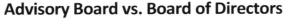

Access OPA

An advisory board is not a board of directors. A traditional board of directors maintains some control, in terms of voting power, over your business operations and company. An advisory board or team of advisors is just that – advisors to you and your business. They maintain no control over your business, and you can choose how, when and if you want to compensate them.

Some Advisors will want something in return for their participation and counsel to you – like ownership in your company. Many will not even ask!

We recommend providing an advisor with a certificate that celebrates their service to the initiative, or an actual agreement that summarizes their compensation—equity or otherwise. You will find a sample Advisory Board Agreement in this Guide.

Seek advice and counsel

Do you expect rapid growth and rapid returns?

An emerging growth company is one that expects rapid growth and rapid returns. An emerging growth company may want to have up to three (3) advisory boards: a financial advisory board to assist with fundraising, a technical advisory board (if your business is technical in nature), and a business advisory board (the more general team of advisors who are awesome at day to day business functions like people management, merchandising, customer relations, marketing, public relations, and sales.)

Depending on your company goals, the advisor may seek some level of commitment from your company so that there is an *upside* to them for helping you grow your business, build your non-profit, or launch your latest program or event.

TIP: For a social enterprise or economic development initiative—like a business incubator program—we recommend having separate business advisory boards for the various initiatives of your program.

SPROUT!

Advisor Compensation

If you are an emerging growth company that expects to raise millions in venture capital or angel money, and you are looking to build an advisory board, then you would expect to have a formal agreement and offer some ownership that would vest over the period of the contract(like 1-2% max). The amount of expected ownership changes depending on the fundraising climate and the experience and prestige the advisor brings.

TIP: Seek the advice of local angel investment groups, entrepreneurial support organizations, and networking groups to be sure you are not giving up too much or offering too little to your prospective advisors. You want a team member who will support you after all, so you don't want to undervalue them at the start of the relationship. You may get one chance to engage any one individual, so plan for success.

Bright Idea

Access OPA

Small Business Seeking Patient Capital

Do you consider your business to be more traditional—one that may or may not be seeking outside capital—but still seeks the advice and counsel of a seasoned small business owner or professional? Ad advisory board is right for you too! The compensation for these advisors may be very different from that of an emerging growth venture.

Some professionals will allow you to use their name on their business plan as an advisor, and offer you counsel, on a limited basis for no compensation at all. An appropriate offer might be equity in the company at some level that feels appropriate. Alternatively, you may barter for services. If you have a massage practice, and are seeking loan advice from a former banker, and don't have the corporate structure to allow for equity give up, perhaps you offer a package of massages for their time.

Be creative. People tend to want to help others. Especially service professionals. Bankers, accountants, lawyers, bookkeepers, insurance, and real estate professional typically will have ample experience and time to offer the emerging entrepreneur or economic development initiative.

Seeking counsel of another business owner is a good idea, but don't feel put off or rejected if they are too busy managing their own business to offer their support to you.

Bright Idea

TIP: If you are filling your advisory board with local business owners, choose a business leader with 50 plus employees. This way they will have enough of an internal infrastructure where they might be good candidates to serve on your advisory board, have financial resources to contribute, or better yet, in kind support such as administrative help when you need it. Seek out the business owners with 50 plus employees who are leaders in their industry.

Money Wise

TIP: If you are a small business owner who is seeking advice, on a monthly or quarterly basis, as you start or grow your business, likely the business professional will allow you to call them and seek their counsel for free. Most people really are helpful and kind. Be thoughtful not to take more of their time than you promised.

Engaging an Advisor

It is a simple process to engage an advisor. First, know what you need, and who you want to support your initiative or business. Identify all the potential stakeholders—those who may have an interest in seeing your success. Identify any person or company that can fill any gaps from your Entrepreneur Assessment earlier in the *Toolkit*. Last—make the call. Invite others to help and support you in your endeavor. It's as simple as 1. 2. 3.

Access OPA
Access OPA

If you are an entrepreneur, first, know what you need and identify who you want to fill your management gaps. Contact your potential Dream Team member and let them know you are building a company and have identified them as an expert in their field, and that their expertise and knowledge would help your business venture. Tell them you would like them as a part of your advisory board and what that would mean to them.

One idea is to compose an email introduction—the ask—that you could also use on the phone. Identify someone, like a board member or colleague, who can provide you a warm introduction. Today, there are ample ways to find a warm connection to your possible stakeholder so that you are not calling the "cold".

Describe to the potential advisor what the time commitment may be. For example, it may mean that they could expect a telephone call or email from you once a quarter, they would not be required to have any group advisory board meetings, and that you would like to use their name in your business plan as an advisory a board member.

Typically, that would be enough of a pitch.

Most people will say "yes". Others will let you know they are too busy or over committed with other Board responsibilities. If you do happen to get a "no", ask them for a referral. You will likely be introduced to another industry-leader who may be able to assist you. Learn how to structure a relationship that is win-win. Learn how on the following pages.

So, what's in it for them?

Find out on the following pages.

Access OPA

Advisor Compensation

Advisor compensation comes in all shapes and sizes. However, the most common three types include: 1.) vesting equity, 2.) equity-only, and 3.)a blend of gifted products or services and equity.

A. Vesting Equity. Member units (if LLC) or an Option to Purchase Shares (if Corporation) that vest (accrue) quarterly during the period of the agreement – typically one year. You will need an actual stock option plan agreement to make this possible ($$).

B. Equity. Member units (if LLC) or Shares (if Corporation) that are fully vested (owned) upon execution of the agreement. This would be typical for a trusted advisor; someone who's name or credibility or influence will help you accomplish a goal (like fundraising) more quickly.

C. Mix of Product or Service and Equity. Member units (if LLC) or Shares (if Corporation) that are fully vested (owned) upon execution of the agreement PLUS discounted services or products. For example, a massage practitioner might gift a package of massages at a value of $2,000 in addition to equity. A retailer might entice an advisor with products at cost plus equity.

Money Wise

TIP: Be sure to set a value limit to both the value of equity and gifts. Depending on the arrangement, the equity and or products and services may be taxable.

Things to consider
What am I—or is my company—willing to give up?
- Time
- Products or services
- Equity (ownership)
- Vesting equity over time? or a "Thanks" for signing the agreement?
- Cash – If so, in what increments?

Consider these questions:
How many investors can you bring in before you run into Securities Exchange Commission jurisdiction and are you planning on working within the system – and do you know the rules? Is venture capital or angel capital in your future? Have you made promises of equity that could slow the fundraising process—or make it more expensive than it needs to be?

There are many ways to keep your options open while bringing in other peoples assets (time, knowledge, experience, capital). A sample advisory board agreement is on the following page. However, have a plan and know what you have to offer—and are authorized to offer—before you execute your first agreement.

Be sure the value is palatable to you as the business owner. You would not want to give up so much of the company that you limit your options for a clean corporate structure for future investors or bigger money down the road.

Revisit the concept of corporate structure and recognize that you as the business owner need to plan, control, and manage the equity in your company. Consider questions like "How much control do you need after raising outside capital one, two, or more times?"

TIP: Most LLC's are formed and filed online. This means you may not have an operating agreement or authorized or issued member units. Member units are to an LLC as "stock or shares" are to a corporation. Review your filed corporate formation documents if you have already filed. Check with your secretary of state to ask how to authorize and issue member units.

Bright Idea

It is very likely that you need to a) perform a member unit split to issue more units or b) you need to set an authorized and issues unit amount by filing your operating plan. Again—this is a strategic step—think big! You don't want to have to go back to investors to ask for permission to issue more units later—and dilute their and your ownership—when you want to raise money or bring in an outside advisor. Happy hunting!

Advisory Board Agreement

In this section, we decided to provide you with a sample Advisory Board Agreement. We are not attorneys and are not offering legal advice. We recommend that you use a service like Go Small Biz (a pre-paid business legal service) or find a legal advisor to assist you with the agreement for your company. To learn how Go Small Biz can help you with the legal affairs of your business (agreements, contracts employee manuals, etc.) for a low monthly fee, visit the Entrepreneurial Edge Series website for more information.

It is important for you to see what an advisory agreement might look like. Each is tailored specifically to the needs of your business. I have personally served on dozens of advisory boards. I find helping other business owners rewarding, as will your new advisors!

Sample Advisory Board Agreement

SPROUT!

[Name and Address of Advisor]

DATE

Dear NAME OF ADVISOR:

Thank you for your interest and support of **Your Company Name Here** (the "Company"). We are very pleased that you have agreed to join the Company's Advisory Board to assist in its ongoing success.

As we value your active participation as an Advisory Board member, the Company would like to offer you (**Your Number Here e.g.: Five Thousand (5,000) units**) of the LLC's membership units (the "Units") to formalize your commitment to our future growth.

The issuance of these Units is conditioned upon your agreement and execution of the terms and conditions within this agreement.

As a condition of joining the Company's Advisory Board, we need your agreement to the following terms and conditions: **(Insert your company's terms and conditions, e.g. Non Disclosure Agreement, Non Solicitation of Employees, Non Agency)**.

Please recognize that this offer is not an offer of employment and your position as an Advisory Board member is terminable at will by you and the Company. Any modification of this voluntary relationship must be expressed in a formal written contract. We consider you an important addition to the Company's Advisory Board and we look forward to working with you in furthering the growth and success of the Company.

Sincerely,
Your Name, Your Company Name

Acknowledgement and Agreement of Receipt of Advisor
(Signed and Dated)

Last: Next Steps

In this chapter we armed you with some tools to help you reach out to others who can help you plan, start, and grow your business into the success that you want it to be. Many of these tools will set the stage for designing your perfect business. Here is a list of to-do's to help keep you on task and a list of some of what's to come.

The Strategic Start To Do's	Still Ahead
• Complete my business vision statement • Set SMART business goals • Determine my four types of entrepreneurial goals. • Complete my management assessment, operations assesment, financial management assessment, and sales and marketing assessments • Identify potential advisors to fill any leadership gaps	• Be introduced to the Business Design Roadmap • Discover the most important question • Write a Grounding Statement • Identify my ideal customers • Describe my competitive advantage • Get introduced to strategic coopetition

The Strategic Start Certificate of Completion

You have successfully taken a step toward turning your dream of business ownership into reality.

Business planning is personal planning. It's all about you. The Strategic Start guides in the *Entrepreneurial Edge Small Business Toolkit* focus on your entrepreneurial intention and strategies to set the foundation for perfect business design.

Throughout this entrepreneur development chapter, we introduced you to four of the five Startup Success Core Business Principles. They were:
- Values
- Vision
- Business Formation Strategies
- Advisory Board

You completed guides 11 through 20 and now it's time to reward the commitment.

Completed Guides:

Guide 11: Determining Your EQ

Guide 12: Realizing Your Values

Guide 13: Aligning Your Entrepreneurial Intention

Guide 14: Discovering Your Strengths

Guide 15: Entrepreneurial Goal Setting

Guide 16: Defining Your Vision

Guide 17: The Art of Business Formation

Guide 18: Steps to the Start

Guide 19: Identifying Advisors

Guide 20: Engaging Advisors

Complete your certificate of completion on the following page to memorialize your accomplishments before we move ahead.

Congratulations!

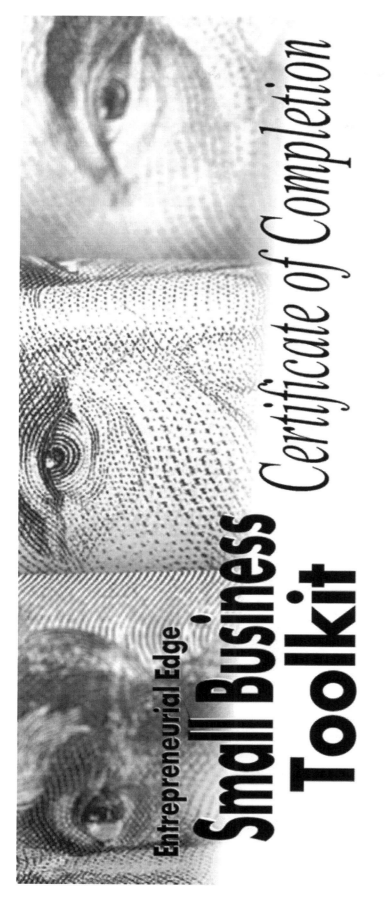

Entrepreneurial Edge

Small Business Toolkit

Certificate of Completion

I certify that I, _____, have successfully completed

The Strategic Start

Core Business Principles™: Values, Vision, Strategic Business Formation, Advisory Board Formation

SPROUT!

Signature: _____   Date: _____

Chapter 3: **Startup Success**

Guides

Takeaways:

Describe your business goals and identify resources to support your success.

Complete a grounding statement for your business.

Explain how small businesses can pinpoint their ideal customers.

Explain the differences between direct and indirect competition.

Describe your company's unique selling factors as a competitive advantage.

Define strategic direct marketing.

Guide 21: Business Design Roadmap

For whatever reason, entrepreneurs tend to launch businesses and begin development of a new product, or design a new service before deciding specifically short term, long term and exit goals or dreams. The activity draws us in. The new venture draws us in. There's so much to do that there's no time to think.

Core Business Principle

> *How can you decide what to do*
> *if you don't know where you want to be*
> *after you've done it?*

Business planning can be a never-ending process. Depending on your goal at any given time, the process of planning allows you to adjust and readjust your business dreams and goals. The Business Process Diagram is your business planning roadmap.

Here are the basic steps:
1. Set a $ Goal
2. Design Your Business
3. Determine its Financial Viability (Will it work?)
4. Decide to fix it, keep it, or start over.

So you know where you're going.

Business planning starts with your vision and you work from there to create a model that will support your vision and purpose. Refer back to the Guide *Defining Your Vision* to help you identify your vision. You may have a business idea and are not sure where to start. Maybe you're not sure what step is next in your business planning process, or even that there are steps to planning for a successful business.

**Know what
you want**

How much after tax income do you want your business to generate this year? You will come back to this number later when we design your business around your goals. You can, and likely will, change this number as opportunities arise, so don't feel like this number is set in stone—it's not.

Write that number down here. Yes, *now.* **$**_____

Step 1: Define My Financial Goal:

_____

Step 2: Design My Business.

Thoroughly research your market, trade or industry. Identify your ideal customers. Create a pricing strategy to uncover your income potential. Design the business of your dreams.

Step 3: Create a Plan.

A business plan is your dream on paper. Write your business plan.

Step 4: Develop My Financial Model.

Whoa! Numbers! This should be simple. You did the hard work! In the design step you defined your customer, determined how often they will buy, at what quantities, over what period of time, and for what price. Turn these numbers into a financial model that will validate your business idea.

If the number don't support your financial goal, go back to Step 2. If they do, SUCCESS!

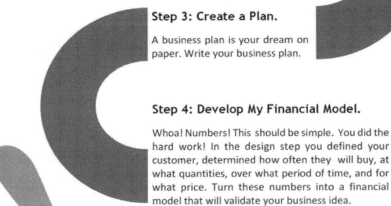

Guide 22: The Most Important Question

The Most Important Question

To thrive in business and not just survive, coach yourself to ask the most important question. "who can help me achieve my goals?" Instead of asking what needs to be done or how in the world can I accomplish what has been asked of me.

The first question an entrepreneur might ask when considering a problem to be solved, a market to enter, or a business to launch is what.

'What do I need to do in order to make [insert goal here] happen?'

The second question a person might ask is how.

'How can I make this happen?'

The most important question a person should ask always begins with who.

Who can help me achieve my goals?

Some questions might be: Who can help me? Who do I need support from? Who is already successful at what I need to accomplish? And who I can partner with to accelerate my success.

TIP: Accomplish goals faster by asking who can help.

SPROUT!

Who can help you achieve your goals is the most strategic question you can ask. If you want to thrive in business and not merely survive, start by asking the right question.

Guide 23: Achieving Greatness

Strategic Goal Setting

In a Small Business Leadership Summit at Microsoft a facilitator led us through a challenging exercise to teach us how to thrive in business.

**Seek advice
and counsel**

The facilitator asked for a volunteer in the goal setting exercise, and before I knew it he was asking me to state my most pressing business goal. At that time I worked for WaMu (now JP Morgan Chase Bank) and I was sponsoring business events to generate market interest and new business clients for the bank. The marketing dollar return on investment generated for the bank through my marketing plan far surpassed my colleagues' business development activities.

My goal, I stated, was to sponsor ten events each with a minimum of 100 attendees during the next year. My banking colleagues looked at me like I was crazy. They knew how much work this meant—the event at Microsoft was one of mine after all.

Step 1: Set a goal

Ten events was not a bold enough goal for the facilitator. He asked me if managing ten events was doable for me. I responded *"Yes"*. It would be a lot of work, but I said it was definitely doable. He forced me to come up with a more outrageous goal, a stretch goal. So, I raised the number to twenty-five. *Ugg.*

I was asked to select a goal that would scare me—yes scare—but that would really be amazing once achieved. Twenty five events. I committed to this bold, audacious, stretch goal in front of colleagues and partners.

My banking colleagues were astonished, and frankly, they wanted nothing to do with events or marketing on a broad scale. They wanted to get back to what they perceived as their job. They wanted to get back to the safety of their desks. But we know the business is not inside our offices—*it's out there*.

Step 2: Your goal isn't bold enough! Set a stretch goal.

I knew better. I was practicing what I teach—strategic direct marketing. I knew the best way to reach my business goals was to determine "who" was available to help me see my project through. I jointly hosted the leadership event with Microsoft, so I had to stay until the day's strategic planning and goal setting activities were over anyway. I was stuck. And I was on stage!

The facilitator then asked me how I felt about this new goal I had set. My answer included the words overwhelmed and scared. I could pull of ten events, but 25 was a major stretch. Then something wonderful happened.

The facilitator told me I could ask the room any question I wanted that would help me accomplish my new goal.

Step 3: Ask the most important question.

Wow. He gave me the opportunity to ask a roomful of CEOs and the leadership team of Microsoft's Local Engagement Group anything. So I asked: "Who in this room can help me sponsor, speak at, and participate in 25 business events in the next 12 months?"

The facilitator yelled "Yes! You asked the right question!" The single most important question you can ever ask is *who*. With my question to the room, I had tapped into what the core message of his presentation. He went on for the afternoon training that to thrive in business and not merely survive; we must always start with the questions beginning with "who".

To my astonishment, arms raised. The Microsoft team had already planned ten events and said I could be a sponsor and speaker at the events across the United State. Ten down. *Easy!*

The arms kept rising. Within moments, I had enough partners in the room, so that I was no longer worried about the stretch goal. I was more worried about my schedule! This would be a great year.

It can be difficult write down your entrepreneurial stretch goal without first stating what reality looks like now. Once you write down where you are today and state your starting point, your desired new reality becomes clearer.

1
Step

3 Bold Steps

First, consider what your business looks like today. Use the space below to write down your current business reality. Consider questions like:

- In what stage is your business?
- What income are you generating?
- From what main sources are you generating that income?

My Current Reality:

Next, think about your biggest and best possible outcome. Picture your future success like a snapshot in your mind.

- What does business—or life—look like when the best of all possible business scenarios have happened?
- From where are you working?
- Who are your top clients?
- How much money are you generating?
- How many events do you need to be a part of to exceed your income goal?

Consider your big picture, best possible outcome scenario. Once you have the best possible goal in mind, take it a step further—ten steps even.

What is your totally outrageous,
best possible scenario for your business?

This desired new reality must be a stretch from what you believe you can accomplish. Once you have identified the desired new reality for your business, write it down.

For me, it was to have sponsored twenty-five business events within twelve months. I knew from experience each event would give me a higher than required return on marketing investment and make my employer ecstatic. Which it did. I became the number 1 ranked banker in the 2nd largest bank in the nation within the year.

Plan with the future in mind

2
Step

My Desired Reality:

3
Step

Almost done. Consider and list the top three bold steps you can take to move you in the direction to achieve your new desired reality.

Bold Step 1

- Action
- Action
- Action

Bold Step 2

- Action
- Action
- Action

Bold Step 3

- Action
- Action
- Action

Keep your eye on the prize

Sometimes even the bold steps seem too great a challenge. If that is the case, if you run into a block, then consider what simple, doable steps that will help you accomplish each of your bold steps. Identify the small steps you can take in the near term to put you on the path toward achieving your three bold steps and ultimately your new desired reality.

What can I do to reach my new desired reality?

This can also be the beginning of your sales plan. Consider using this tool to help get your sales goals on paper.

Last, answer the most important question: Who can help you accomplish your stretch business goal?

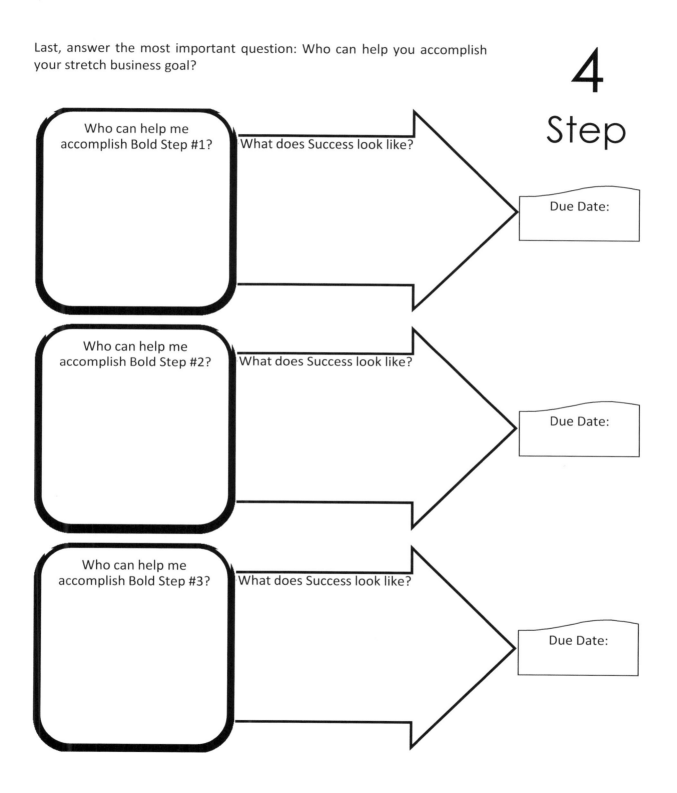

4
Step

Who can help me accomplish Bold Step #1?

What does Success look like?

Due Date:

Who can help me accomplish Bold Step #2?

What does Success look like?

Due Date:

Who can help me accomplish Bold Step #3?

What does Success look like?

Due Date:

The Most Important Question Answered

Last, think about who the people are in your center of influence, or even several degrees of separation from you, who can help you reach your stretch goal? (people, organizations, new network)?

List 10 resources you have available to you to help make this new desired reality happen:

1. _____

2. _____

3. _____

4. _____

5. _____

6. _____

7. _____

8. _____

9. _____

10. _____

Access OPA

If you are in a workshop or in a group setting, as participants ask who in this room wants to participate in my stretch goal today?

1. _____

2. _____

3. _____

This is a great tool to help you mobilize the resources around you to support your vision and goals.

Entrepreneurial Edge Academy

3 Bold Steps

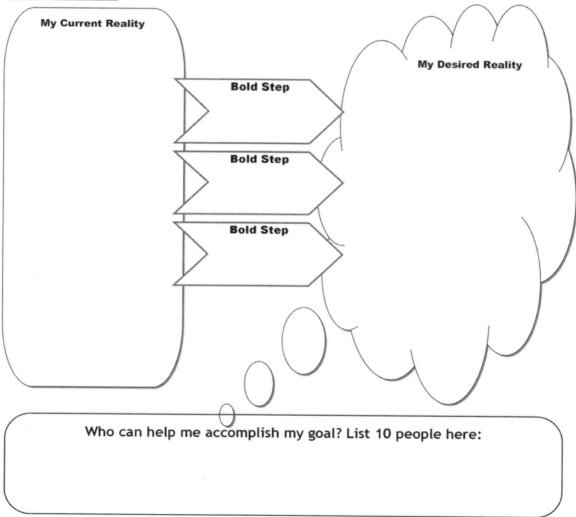

My Current Reality

Bold Step

Bold Step

Bold Step

My Desired Reality

Who can help me accomplish my goal? List 10 people here:

Visit Entrepreneurial Edge Academy online free downloads and online classes.

Source: This exercise was adapted from "3 Bold Steps" as delivered to the Women's Business Exchange by Alchemy, 2006 and from the Microsoft Local Engagement Team Small Business Leadership Summit at Lincoln Square, 2007.

Core Business Principle

Guide 24: Your Grounding Statement

Every entrepreneur can benefit from a written Grounding Statement. The Grounding Statement is a way to help you define and clarify your business model. It will not only help you stay focused and on track, but will keep marketing spending in line with your business core competency, and will help ground the business through its stages of growth.

The Grounding Statement is both different and less difficult than a mission or vision statement. It is for you, the entrepreneur. You need not share a Grounding Statement with your customers, however it may help you focus your elevator pitch in a group networking environment.

It is a *tool* to help you stay focused on your core business and the business model you designed.

Focus with your Grounding Statement

Just answer the three questions. It's ***that*** simple!

1. What do you do?

2. Who is your customer?

3. Where are your customers located?

> **RULES:**
> Okay, there are some rules, but not many!
> - You may not do "Everything"
> - You may not sell to "Everyone"
> - You cannot be "Everywhere" (even if you are selling on the Internet).
>
> **GOAL:**
> Describe your core business in as few words as possible.

My Grounding Statement

What

_____

To Whom

_____

Where

_____

**Design your
perfect business**

Example 1:
I <u>design, manufacture, and sell</u>

<u>hand-made metal yard art shaped like fish</u>

for the <u>10,000 people who own Koi Ponds</u>

in the <u>greater Puget Sound Area</u>.

Example 2: Merchant Artisan – Social Entrepreneurship Example
Pristine Tea is Washington State Limited Liability Company founded in 2011 in order to import and distribute organic green tea from Chinese farms to meet the growing demand for organic Asian teas left by the gap from the Japanese nuclear disaster. Teas will imported through free trade zones, packaged by a company that provides work opportunities for the disabled, and 50% of profits will be reinvested in displaced Japanese tea farms.

Example 3: Technology Company
Versaly is a Seattle-based mobile media and entertainment company for the "always-connected" generation. Versaly developed and is marketing a cloud-based multi-channel B2B bulk video delivery platform that reduces the cost and improves efficiency of global video syndication. Our customers include media companies, video distributors, global mobile carriers, independent mobile video portals and online video destinations.

Keep focused on your _core_ business!

Core Business Principle

Guide 25: Whom Do You Want to Play With?

Identifying Your Ideal Customer

In this target market exercise, you will answer the questions: "What are the characteristics of my ideal customer?"

Whom do you want to play with?

Whom do you want to play with? This is a simple, but great question to help you think about the type of customer you want to spend your time with. Have you ever spent any time on this question?

Here's your chance! This is an opportunity for you to plan who you want to play with and preselect your customers. In that you may spend a significant number of hours a day on your business, consider which whom you want to spend that time.

Design your perfect business

If you already have customers, think hard about your favorites. Think about why they are your favorite customers. Perhaps they buy consistently, spend the dollar amount you require, are easy to work with, their business is growing at the same rate as yours, they buy at a good price point, etc. This is not a time to restate all of your current customers, but rather to identify desirable characteristics of your ideal customers.

You might also want to identify those characteristics you want to avoid. This will give you a picture to analyze or visualize your perfect customer and plan for the future. Maybe your current clients or customers are not the ones you want to work with into the future. That's okay.

Visioning, or visualization, is a great tool to help you determine who you want to spend all those hours with before you spend precious marketing money trying to reach a customer you never wanted in the first place.

Design your perfect business

Research in the field of positive psychology shows that simply thinking about an event makes it seem more likely that it will actually happen. As you think about an event, you begin to construct mental scenarios of how it might occur, and even more importantly, how you might make it happen.

Visualization goes by many names, including mental practice and covert rehearsal. It's been a favorite tool of sports psychology experts for many years. Now you will use the tool to help design your perfect business.

Ideal Customer Exercise

Close your eyes, picture yourself working with, and selling to your ideal customers, are you on the phone? Are they in your office? Are they in your retail shop? Or are they in the audience? What do they look like? Could you characterize their attire: business formal, business casual, software developer, surfer, granola, elegant, fashionista?

And, what about you? What are you wearing? Are you in front of a crowd? Did you travel far in order to meet with this customer or group? How did you get there? Car, ferry, private plane, walking, riding a bike, in your company car?

Here's a question career coaches love: pretend you are having the best business day ever. Something great just happened – maybe you landed a new client. What do your shoes look like? This will give you a strong sense of who your perfect customer might look like.

Think about the ideal characteristics of your ideal customer—not necessarily the customer you are serving today.

Characteristics of your ideal customer will include the following four categories:
- Geographic Location
- Demographic Characteristics
- Psychographic Characteristics
- Buying Behavior

When you know what you want serendipity happens.

The following guides will help you identify your perfect future customer. Your ideal customer will be a part of your target market. Your ability to identify these characteristics is important. Note: You will not be considered biased, judgmental, or politically incorrect by defining the characteristics of your ideal customer. Business planning is personal planning. You have the opportunity to identify whom you want to work with.

This important information will be used as you design your perfect business and plan to reach your ideal customer in the most effective, inexpensive and successful way.

Business planning is personal planning.

The primary customer will be the group of potential customers or clients you most want to reach and around whom your product, service, or company brand will be developed. The secondary customer will be the target of promotional efforts but not of brand development.

Use the following guides to help identify some characteristics of your ideal primary customer. Consider the demographic and "psychographic" characteristics of these target audiences.

Characteristics of your perfect customer
Demographic Characteristics
Types of demographic and diversity characteristics may include:

- Age
- Income
- Socioeconomic status
- Ethnicity
- Gender Sexual Orientation (affinity)
- Religion
- Geographical differences (rural versus urban; inner city versus suburban)
- Occupation
- Differences in skills and abilities
- Personality traits

Psychographic Characteristics

Psychographic characteristics of our primary target customer can be used like demographic (age, income, occupation) and geographic (place of business or residence) criteria to describe and identify customers and prospective customers and to aid in developing marketing and promotion strategies that will appeal to specific psychographic segments of the market.

For example, the market for your restaurant may include several psychographic segments described by their primary purchase motives (eating, entertainment, drinking), usage styles (daily, weekly, special occasion only), or lifestyle (busy professional, parents with young children, empty nesters, hipsters).

Psychographic characteristics of your customer can include attitudes, beliefs, emotions, values, personality, and buying motives are the factors that influence their purchasing decision. Understand these criteria to create targeted promotional materials, choose appropriate distribution channels, and create strategic marketing partnerships.

Psychographic data includes lifestyle characteristics, usage patterns, motivators, etc. (Examples of psychographic characteristics are "Web savvy," "Busy lives," "Value convenience".)

Describe your perfect customer now:

Are they an individual (person or group?) or a business? If you are selling to businesses as customers, what size is there business? How many employees might they have?

My perfect customer or client is:

Identify what percentage of your revenue you expect to generate from both individual customers and business customers. You might have a mix of the two types of customer:

Business Customers: _____ % Business

Individual (Consumer): _____ % Individual

**Core Business
Principle**

Guide 26: B2B or B2C

Business to Business (B2B) or Business to Consumer (B2C)

Uncover the demographic, geographic, psychographic, and behavioral characteristics of the customer you want into the future. Take some time to identify the main characteristics of your ideal customer.

This is business planning, so think ahead to your perfect or ideal future customer. Don't get stuck on who your customer is today.

Business planning is future planning. Will you be targeting a business customer or a consumer, or the end user? The guide on the following pages can help direct your research as you discover your perfect customer.

Consider the following characteristics of a consumer market and a business market as you define your perfect customers.

Consumer Market Considerations

Age

Income

Gender

Profession

Education

Family Size

Homeowner

Marital Status

Business Market Considerations

Geographic Location

Size of Company

Annual revenue

Number of Branches

Number of Employees

Industry

Age of Company

**Business planning
is future planning**

Describe the demographic, geographic, and buying behavior traits of your future perfect customer in the space below.

My Ideal Customer Demographic Characteristics:

My Ideal Customer Psychographic (lifestyle trends):

Activities, Interests, Values, Opinions, and Attitudes

Examples: Baby Boomer, Gen X, Y, Millennium, Cultural-Creative, Green

My Ideal Customer and Product Questions:

Describe your perfect customer's geographic location:

How far are you willing to drive? Travel?

How many customers do you want?

How many units of product (especially important if hand crafted) can you create a year?

Do you want to limit yourself to create a certain quantity each year?

Guide 27: Customer Buying Behavior

Your customer's ideal buying behavior will determine your income potential. This too can be designed by you! You don't have to sell to anyone that walks through your door. You can plan, design your perfect business, and identify who your perfect or ideal customer for the future is. When you know whom you want to play with, you can begin to develop a marketing strategy—that includes strategic direct marketing—that will help you reach your financial goals.

Be Specific. Customer buying behavior determines income.

Describe your perfect customer's buying behavior:

What is the average dollar amount your perfect customer will spend with you a month?

How often will they buy from you? Monthly _____ Yearly _____

Will your business be seasonal? What months will you realize the most income? Separate by percentage, month to month.

What % of Max Income or other trends expected

Q1	Q2	Q3	Q4

Jan _____	Apr_____	Jul_____	Oct_____
Feb_____	May_____	Aug_____	Nov_____
Mar_____	June_____	Sept_____	Dec_____

Guide 28: Uniqueness Advantage

Uncovering Your Competitive Advantage

Determining your Competitive Advantage is key to the successful marketing of any product or service. You must be able to identify who your competition is—both direct and indirect—and describe how you are better or different—making your business unique. Ask yourself: What pain or problem will your new company, product, or service solve for the ideal customer?

Core Business Principle

Factors that influence the competitive position of your business in an industry or market include: supplier or buyer power, barriers to entry, and alternatives in the marketplace. Consider the following to help you design your competitive advantage: cost advantage, product differentiation advantage, price-performance trade offs, price sensitivity, brand identity, and your distinctive competencies.

List and expound on your direct competition and indirect competition in the following space. This lends credibility to your plan and will help you create a sustainable revenue model later.

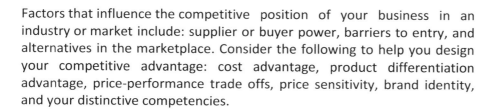

Direct Competition: *Who does exactly what I do?* Competitive Advantage: *How I am better or different?* List up to five direct competitors.

In-direct Competition:
What can my customers spend their $$ on other than my product or service?
List up to five indirect competitors.

Stop playing checkers and start playing chess.

My Competitive Advantage
Describe how new product or service differentiates itself from competitors.

Guide 29: Competitive Matrix

Determine your competitive advantage and market comparables
The Competitive Matrix is a tool to help you communicate your businesses direct competition, indirect competition and competitive advantage in a format that is visually compelling.

This exercise can be very strategic. Use your Competitive matrix to uncover possible acquisition targets if your exit strategy is to be bought someday. This model can be the start of your market comparables (just called "comps" or "comparables" in the finance industry).

Also use the Competitive Matrix to share with potential investors your understanding of the market, which in turn lends to your capacity as a successful CEO or business owner.

Use data from the Competitive Advantage exercise to complete the table - or create your own visually compelling way to present your company's direct competition, indirect competition, and competitive advantage. Use a table format to display direct competition, and simply silt indirect competition categories.

Unique Selling Factors to consider:

**Understand
your options**

- Advertising
- Appearance
- Credit Policies
- Hours of Operation
- Image
- Price
- Products
- Quality
- Sales Method

- Company Reputation
- Reliability
- Expertise
- Service
- Location
- Ease of Use
- Selection
- Exclusivity
- Stability

List your other unique selling factors here:

Direct Competition

Research and list all major direct competitors and place them in this Competitive Matrix format. A Competitive Matrix is a part of the Executive Business Plan.

Company Name	Company Location	Product or Service	How am I Better or Different

Market Comparables in 3 Simple Steps

How do you value your new company, product or idea? How do you determine what a larger, liquid company, might consider paying for a portion of your idea, invention, marketing rights, or a joint venture?

Market comparables, also called comps in the investment world, are pulled from usually public, though sometimes private, information that when pulled together can help you determine the value of your business or a product. As a former investment banker, this is the process we used to determine the value of private companies or inventions for the potential investors.

Step 1: Aggregate data about investment activity, acquisition activity, and joint venture activity though public information.

Step 2: Determine value of transaction (if public company look at published financial statements). If you aren't great at financial analysis, bring on board a student intern from a local MBA program or finance person to help.

Step 3: Determine value of company (smaller one) at time of transaction. Deduct from financial statements, press releases, or announcements.

Insider Tip: If a public company—look at published financial statements found on websites like Hoovers.com or MSN money. For both private and public companies, look for press releases, research the board of directors— research their names—uncover companies for which they participate on boards. Likely they serve because their company made an investment of some kind and are watching their investment by securing a place of decision making power. Sign up for a board-watch service to be automatically notified of board activity in a particular company or sign up for Google or Facebook alerts on the company target.

Bright Idea

Use the example on the following page as a model for your company market comparables. This sample market comparables table was derived from public information. Your model should look similar. Here's how:

Gather between six and twenty comparables to complete your market comparables background research. To do that, first identify 20 companies who could benefit from your product, company, customers, or concept (US and International).

Identity what investments, acquisitions have they made in the past two years. Determine the value of any relevant transaction and identify the transaction date. Explain how your company is different such as: earlier stage, more or less revenue, greater market potential, complementary product or company, etc.

Use this information gathering to demonstrate the following information:

- *Company.* The Company that made the investment or acquisition of a company in the same industry as your business.
- *Target.* Identifies the smaller company that was purchased or invested in.
- *Date.* The date of the investment or acquisition.
- *Transaction Value.* Actual value of the transaction (be sure you have the source data.)
- *Revenue Multiple.* When you know the revenue of the acquired company, you can determine if a premium was paid by the investor and at what value. For example, if a business is generating one million a year, but were bought for ten million dollars, the revenue multiple would be ten.
- *Discount.* If the same business were bought for less than it was earning a discount would be considered instead of a revenue multiple. Determine what the discount value is, and the reason.

Once you have gathered this type of data for your company comparables representing transaction such as investments, joint ventures, strategic partnerships, or acquisitions—whole company or part—you can average the data and place a value on your own company or product. The company for which this data was aggregated both secured SBIR funding, then was acquired by a public company.

Selected Company Transactions

ACQUISITIONS

Company	Target	DATE	Transaction Value	Revenue Multiple
GE Industrial Systems, a division of the General Electric Company (NYSE: GE),	Sensing Solutions group of Spirent plc(NYSE: SPM)	SEP-10-01	$220 million cash	Revenues in 2000 were $137 million.
Danaher Corporation's (NYSE: DHR)	Cooper Industries, Inc. (NYSE: CBE	AUG-08-01	$5.5 billion cash transaction ($54 to $58 a share)	30 percent to 39 percent premium
Fisher Scientific International, Inc. (NYSE: FSH)	Cole-Parmer Instrument Company	SEP-05-01	$205 million cash transaction	
Fluke Networks, Inc., Danaher family of companies (NYSE: DHR) and Microtest, Inc. (Nasdaq: MTST)	Microtest, Inc.	JUN-13-01	$74 million cash transaction	

Guide 30: Strategic Coopetition

Developing Strategic Marketing Relationships

Unless you are McDonald's, it's too expensive to market directly to your ideal customer. Strategic direct marketing is taught as a best practice to business incubator professionals (small business coaches) at the National Business Incubation Association. It's a strategic selling model that every small business owner needs to master.

Core Business Principle

Strategic direct marketing answers the question: "Who is *already selling* to my ideal customer?" You will not likely market directly to your ideal customer—it's too expensive. Instead, identify who is already selling to them and develop a joint marketing relationship (collaborate with) that group, company or organization.

To help guide you, ask yourself:
- To which organizations does my ideal customer belong?
- Might they be affiliated with a religious institution? Which one?
- To which professional organizations do they belong?
- From where did they graduate? To which alumni groups might they be a part?
- Are they a member of a health club?
- Where do they shop?
- What magazines do they buy?

Your list may be different. When your list complete, consider the most complementary business relationships you might develop with these affinity groups to help you market to your joint customer base.

SPROUT!

This is where you will spend your valuable time, energy, and marketing dollars. Be Strategic! When you have spent some time thinking about who is selling or marketing to your perfect customer, the next steps is to think of ways you can work with them, join up in some way, to use them as a marketing channel for you and your business.

The old way of business was 'mine is mine, and yours is yours'. The world of social media was not yet born, and organizations like BizNik, Groupon, Tippr, and Facebook were not around yet to facilitate unique joint marketing relationships and connections. It used to be more difficult to find the perfect partners. Today, entrepreneurs need to seek new and outside-the-box ways to get in front of new prospective customers.

Old: Hypercompetition
New: Coopetition

**Coopetition applies.
Relationships rule.**

The new marketing reality in the age of social media.

- **Old:** It takes seven (7) contacts with a prospective client before they choose to buy from you.

- **New:** In the world of social media, it takes 44 impressions, or touches before someone has built enough trust to consider buying from you.

Collaborating with, partnering with, or reaching out to your competition for a joint marketing effort, co-branded solution, or co-sponsorship of an event for your clients is a key part of creating a loyal customer base and reaching new prospective clients.

Today coopetition is key. Partnering, and playing together, with your *perceived* competition, creates greater opportunity for all.

Think of unique ways you can partner with those organizations that are already selling to your perfect customers. Coopetition is not giving up the farm. Work to create a win-win in ways that protect your current client base, your brand, and your intellectual property. Some call it strategic direct marketing. We call it strategic coopetition- and it's smart.

Last: Next Steps

The guides in Startup Success set the stage for the designing your perfect business. Now you have a grasp of the business planning process, and are armed with some tools to help focus your business vision and purpose.

You have begun to master the 10 Keys of Success—and gained a more solid understanding of why knowing what you want, understanding your options, and seeking advice and counsel are so critical in the business startup success. Your Grounding Statement is the perfect tool to keep you focused on the core of your business and is a starting point for your elevator pitch.

Business planning is personal planning and future planning. A business is not created in a box. We need other people's assets, financial and otherwise–time, talent, experience, and lessons learned—so we don't have to make the same mistakes.

Startup Success To Do's

- Complete my Grounding Statement
- Identify the top 10 people who can contribute resources toward my success
- Determine my ideal customer and their buying behavior
- Complete my competitive matrix
- Identify businesses affilliaated with my ideal customers

Still Ahead

- Learn to write the single page business plan for artists and microentrepreneurs--a QuickPlan

Startup Success
Certificate of Completion

You have successfully taken a step toward designing the business of your dreams.

In this section of the *Entrepreneurial Edge Small Business Toolkit* you were introduced to the Grounding Statement--the modern mission statement that helps you stay focused on your business vision and purpose. You learned the most important question to ask to thrive in business—'Who' — not 'what' or 'how'. You completed a competitive matrix and are on your entrepreneurial path with a competitive edge.

You completed guides 21-30 and were introduced to several Core Business Principles: Business Model, Revenue Model, Customer Identification, Competitive Advantage, Market Opportunity, Target Market, and Strategic Direct Marketing through the following guides:

> Guide 21: Business Design Roadmap
> Guide 22: The Most important Question
> Guide 23: Achieving Greatness
> Guide 24: Your Grounding Statement
> Guide 25: Whom Do You Want to Play With?
> Guide 26: B2B or B2C
> Guide 27: Customer Buying Behavior
> Guide 28: Uniqueness Advantage
> Guide 29: Competitive Matrix
> Guide 30: Strategic Coopetition

Complete your certificate of completion on the following page to memorialize your accomplishments before we move ahead.

Congratulations!

Entrepreneurial Edge

Small Business Toolkit

Certificate of Completion

Startup Success

I certify that I, _____, have successfully completed

Including: Core Business Principles™ Customer Identification, Competitive Advantage, Strategic Coopetition

Signature: _____   Date: _____

SPROUT!

Chapter 4: **The Quick Plan**

Guide 31: The Quick Plan
>**5 Steps to a Quick Plan**
>>**Step 1. Create Your Grounding Statement**
>>**Step 2: Identify Your Dream Team**
>>***Step 3: Determine Your Ideal Customer***
>>**Step 4: Get Coopetive!**
>>**Step 5: Set Success-Based Goals**
>**Quick Plan Template**
>**Completed Quick Plan Example**
>**Last: Next Steps**
>**Certificate of Completion**

The Micro-Entrepreneur's Business Plan

Takeaways:
>Put together the following concepts to create a single-page business plan: grounding statement, management team, customer identification, strategic direct marketing, and entrepreneurial goals setting.

Guide 31: The Quick Plan

In this chapter, you will find a tool to help you write a simple single-page business plan we call a Quick Plan. It can be difficult to put your dreams on paper when someone tells you that you need a business plan, and you don't know where to start.

Merchant artisans, musicians, home-based business owners, and Internet-based businesses use these business design guide to get their dreams on paper—now you can too!

Design your perfect business

The Quick Plan is a simple way to create a single-page business plan. It is a tool that every business owner—or potential business owner—should use in business planning, new product development, or business feasibility testing as a part of the business planning process. Use the Quick Plan to help you put your personal dreams and aspirations on paper.

5 Steps to a Quick Plan

To complete your Quick Plan or vision plan in just five simple steps, simply complete the following worksheets. You already completed most of the actual work in the previous guides–the questions here should be a review. Summarize your thoughts using the Quick Plan template for a clean look and a simple presentation format. There is an example of a completed Quick Plan in the back of this section.

**Core Business
Principle**

1
Step

**Know what
you want**

Step 1. Create Your Grounding Statement

This is where you describe your business. First, state what you do—or what you want to do. Second, identify your ideal customers. And finally describe your geographic focus—recognizing that that 80% of your business will come from within a twenty mile radius of your headquarters or home base. See the *Grounding Statement* guide for more details.

What do I do, to whom, and where?

Step 2: Identify Your Dream Team

Do you want to be your business or manage your business? I bet you aren't planning to do everything yourself! What areas might we need help with? Accounting, hiring, taxes, real estate, supply chain, legal advice, permitting, supplies, taxes, zoning, customer service, social media, marketing, sales management, logo-letterhead/look-and-feel development, merchandising, pricing—or something else altogether? This list of the functional needs of your business might go on and on as described in the *Entrepreneur Assessment* guide.

If we expect to do all of these on our own we will struggle, and by getting help, we will decrease our time-to-market and general chance of success. Your Dream Team can be a team of advisors, an actual Advisory board, or a pool of people you may even want to hire down the road.

What type of team do I need who can support my goals?

Whom do you know, or who do you want to know, that could be of help to you as you plan and launch your business? Think big! You could use this section to identify your management team or to list anyone you have identified that can fill management gaps identified earlier in the *Toolkit*. We can't all be experts at managing, operations, marketing, and financial management for our venture.

Seek advice and counsel

One part of your Dream Team might be a COI (Center of Influence). A center of influence is someone who champions you into multiple contacts, markets, or business development opportunities. Another part of your Dream Team might be a successful entrepreneur you can count on as an advisor to you as you plan and grow your business.

Don't be afraid to think big ...list your ultimate dream team.

Refer to the *Identifying Advisors* and *Engaging Advisors* guides for tools and templates to help you with this step.

2
Step

List your Dream Team here.

This is where you list your management team.

Answer the question: *Who can support me to achieve my business goals?*

My Dream Team

Step 3: Determine Your Ideal Customer

In this target market exercise, you will answer the question: "What does my ideal customer look like?"

You may spend up to fourteen—or more—hours a day on your business. With whom do you want to spend that time?

Whom do you want to play with?

Have you ever spent any time on this question? Well, now you have the chance! This is a unique opportunity for you to plan, who you want to play with. If you completed *Who Do You Want to Play With*, *B2B or B2C*, and *Customer Buying Behavior* guides, you should have this information readily available. If not, revisit that those guides for direction.

Include the four main target customer categories: Demographic Characteristics (age, education, income...), Psychographic Profile (interests, activities, opinions, values and attitude), Geographic Location, and Buying Behavior (frequency and amount of average sale per customer) when identifying your perfect future client or customer.

Core Business Principle

3
Step

Describe your perfect customer now:

> **Demographic Characteristics:**
>
>
> **Psychographic Characteristics:**
>
>
> **Geographic Location:**
>
>
> **Buying Behavior:**

**Core Business
Principle**

Step 4: Get Coopetitive!

Strategic direct marketing is all about answering the question: "Who is *already selling* to my ideal customer?" This is important! You will likely not market directly to your ideal customer...it's just too expensive. You need to identify who is already selling to them, then market to—collaborate with— that group, company, or organization.

Based on your determination of 'who is already selling or marketing to your ideal customer', write down the most logical partnerships, joint marketing efforts, or existing marketing campaign, event or promotion that could help you reach your ideal customer faster and cheaper than on your own.

Consider these examples: If you are a personal trainer, consider partnering your marketing efforts with a well-known personal chef that creates health good for the busy professional? If you paint animal portraits, consider advertising at your local animal day care or veterinarian's office.

Micro-entrepreneurs should not market directly to your ideal customer. Take a moment to identify five potential strategic partners. Review the *Strategic Coopetition* guide for more details.

4
Step

**Who already sells
to your perfect
customer?**

My Potential Strategic Partners

Step 5: Set Success-Based Goals

Last but not least—goal setting. Visit the goal setting guides *Entrepreneurial Goal Setting* and *Achieving Greatness* if you want to learn more about SMART Goals before completing this step of your Quick Plan. If you're ready, create a one month, three month, and one year plan to get you on your way!

Plan with the future in mind

1 Month Goal *(What do I want to accomplish in one month?):*

Action items *(What do I need to do to make that happen?):*

Success looks like:

**Ignite Results:
Clearly define
goals, objectives,
and time lines.**

3 Month Goal *(What do I want to accomplish in one quarter?):*

Action items *(What do I need to do to make that happen?):*

Success looks like:

1 Year Goal *(What do I want to accomplish in one year?):*

Action items *(What do I need to do to make that happen?):*

Success looks like:

Quick Plan Template

Use this simple single page business plan template to summarize the information from your planning and goal-setting on the previous pages. Notice the steps and section titles are the same as those on the previous pages. Find an example of a completed Quick Plan on the next page.

Company Name:

Owner Name:

Purpose of Business Plan:

Capital Needed:

1

Grounding Statement

2

Dream Team

3

Ideal Customer

4

Marketing Strategy

5

Goals

Completed Quick Plan Example

Fish Sticks, LLC

> Company Name: *Fish Sticks, LLC*
> Owner Name: *Jill Owner*
> Purpose of Business Plan:
> *To create an initial plan for my startup.*
> Capital Needed: *None*

1
Grounding Statement

I design, manufacture and sell hand-made metal yard art shaped like fish for the 10,000 people who own Koi Ponds in the in the greater Puget Sound Area.

2
Dream Team

Jill Brottman, Owner, Experienced artist and former gallery owner. Dan Green, Accountant, responsible for bookkeeping and taxes. Kathy Jones, Koi farm owner, Advisor to the company. Needed: sales and marketing expertise. Currently hiring for that position.

3
Ideal Customer

Customer Profile: Koi Fish owners and enthusiasts, Professional Men and Women, Upper Income, Home Owners.
Strategic Coopetition: Those selling to my ideal customer are:
- Garden Stores (with water plants), Pond Stores, Fish Stores, Koi Fish Stores
- Koi Farmers (that sell to individuals)
- Japanese Garden Stores

4
Marketing Strategy

Develop co-marketing relationships with my newly identified marketing channels and distributors. Pricing Strategy: Upper end pricing (not competing with fairs). Place: Wholesale to stores; Retail online through website, Facebook, and Google. Product Line: Hand crafted, one-of a kind, garden art. Promotion: In-store promotions, garden show, garden tours, magazines and e-zines for Koi aficionados. Annual Marketing Budget: $2,000

5

Goals

Goal: Have top three garden stores selling my "Fish Sticks" by summer.
Tasks 1. Identify and create a contact list for all individuals and stores that sell Koi ponds, fish and products. 1 Month.
Task 2. Create marketing collateral, pricing, and sales pitch for stores to sell my garden art. Review materials with advisors. 2 Months.
Task 3: Begin selling products through new distributors by end of Q1.
Financial Goal: $24,000 – 300 Fishsticks annually.

Last: Next Steps

In this section of the *Entrepreneurial Edge Small Business Toolkit* you were introduced to business design tools for artists and micro enterprises. It can be difficult to put your dreams on paper when someone tells you you need a business plan, and you don't know where to start!

The Quick Plan—with its five steps—you completed a simple single page business plan designed to help you focus on your core business idea, vision, and goals.

Merchant artisans, musicians, home-based business owners, and Internet-based business owners have used this business design tool to help get their business goals on paper. Here is a list of To-Do's to help keep you on task and a list of some of what's to come.

The Quick Plan To Do's

- Complete the single page business plan for micro-entrepreneurs, artists and musicians: The Quick Plan™

Still Ahead

- Take my business to the next level with the art of professional business design.
- Learn to write the single page business plan my banker wants to see – The Executive Business Plan™

The Quick Plan
Certificate of Completion

You have successfully taken a step toward
planning your perfect business.

The Quick Plan
The Quick Business Plan—*Complete!*

In this chapter of the *Entrepreneurial Edge Small Business Toolkit* we
introduced you to the simple solution to a single-page business plan—the
Quick Plan. You were able to draw from your completed guides to
complete a single-page business plan. You identified potential business
advisors, determined your target market, gained an edge with strategic
direct marketing, and set business goals.

You mastered the following Core Business Principles: Business Model,
Customer Identification, and Strategic Direct Marketing. You also gained
the following Keys to Success: Design Your perfect Business, Seek Advice
and Counsel, and Plan with the Future in Mind.

Completed Guide: Guide 31: The Quick Plan

Your certificate of completion is on the next page.

Sometimes we fail to celebrate our successes! Not this time! Simply fill out
your certificate of completion with your name and date you completed this
section of the *Toolkit*.

Congratulations!

Entrepreneurial Edge

Small Business Toolkit

Certificate of Completion

I certify that I, _____, have successfully completed

The Quick Plan™

The Quick Business Plan for Micro-Entrepreneurs

Including: Core Business Principles™ Business Model, Customer Identification, Strategic Direct Marketing

SPROUT!

Signature: _____   Date: _____

Chapter 5: **Designing Your** *Perfect* **Business**

Guides

Takeaways:

Define the five components of a business model.

Explain the importance of designing your revenue model.

Describe the benefits of your product or service to your ideal customer.

Compare market opportunity with the concept of a target market.

Understand pricing techniques and determine a pricing strategy for introducing your new product or service to market.

Project your income potential using the professional business design process.

Guide 32: The Art of Business Design

In this section of the *Entrepreneurial Edge Small Business Toolkit*, you will find business planning tools used by investment bankers and Fortune 500 company executives made simple and a single page business plan your banker wants to see—the Executive Business Plan.

Professional Business Design

The business design tools found in these guides will lead you through the process of designing a perfect business.

Fortune 500 business product managers developed these business design models to help them identify whether or not one product would likely do better, or generate more revenue, than another product.

A Fortune 500 executive who joined the ranks of Small Business Development managers handed down the model to me. The former executive turned public servant (director of an SBDC program) had modified the executive planning tool he formerly used to use as a product management executive so that he could mentor and coach his small business clients, arming them with the same business planning process the big guys used.

Thousands of small business owners have used it to discover their business earning potential and define their perfect customers. They simply answered the question:

"Will this company, product, or service make money?"

We teach this professional business design tool to incubator professionals, business coaches, and in college entrepreneurship programs. Now you have it too!

You can use the business model guide to:
- Plan and refine income projections
- Identify market opportunities
- Define target customers
- Refine a product marketing mix

Use these models on a macro level or on a micro level for business planning. You can use the guides on the following pages to design a service-based or product-based business.

Macro: Use it to plan for the entire business at once! Include all revenue lines in one model.

Micro: Use a separate Business Model Worksheet for each type of income you generate, or for each separate product line or line of service.

5 Steps to Professional Business Design

Use the following worksheets as guides to help you design your business. There are separate worksheets, templates, and samples for a product-based business and for service companies.

Professional Business Design Outline

There are five main components of a business model. Understanding each of these components will help you complete your own business model and design the business you have always wanted. Complete the following guides to design your perfect business!

1. Business Revenue Description
   a. Primary
   b. Incremental Revenue
2. Ideal Customer Identification
   a. Business to Business
   b. Business to Consumer
   c. Characteristics of the Ideal Customer
3. Market Opportunity
   a. Overall Industry
   b. Market Potential and Trends
4. Target Market
   a. Actual Market
   b. Reality Check
5. Income Potential

Guide 33: Show Me the Money!

Professional Business Design Step 1: Business Revenue Description

Core Business Principle

The business revenue description and guide is the first step in professional business design. This business design tool will help you identify each of the possible income opportunities for your business, project them out based on your interest in working that business line, and based on the overall potential income.

Once you are armed with the numbers, you, your business partners, and your investors can make an educated decision about which direction to take the venture.

The goal is to list each of the primary sources of income, the main revenue drivers, for your business. You may be able to generate revenue from multiple activities. For this exercise, try to limit the total number of sources of income to your top five revenue-generating activities—even if there are more. Try to focus on your top two or three top revenue drivers.

For example, a restaurant may want to differentiate between food sales, non-alcoholic beverages, alcoholic beverages, catering, and events. If an event is a very small revenue generating activity, like renting your facility as a commercial kitchen, you may want to leave that out of the mix for planning purposes.

If you have an existing business, include the top (highest 20 percent) income-generating activities for your business.

Money Wise

TIP: Don't group together all of your possible revenue into one category and call it *income*. Use this model to help you differentiate between the various sources of revenue you have or want and determine upon which areas of your business to focus your time, energy, and marketing dollars.

This can be a useful tool for service providers and partnerships to help focus their marketing and service offerings. We have used the model to lead newly formed law firm partnerships through a roadmap to designing their perfect practice.

In one real world example, two attorneys had existing practices in a rural city, and were joining forces. They created a limited liability limited partnership (LLLP)—a unique corporate structure used by professionals like accountants, attorneys, and venture capitalists. These two business partners bought an older home zoned as commercial, and set up shop. Their conflicts began when the income they had generated while independent was not translating into the newly formed partnership.

First, we used the following guide to help the partners, working separate from one another, identify all their sources of income (Step 1 in Professional Business Design).

One attorney was heavily focused on business law, with a subset of K-12 education law (his primary interest) and was spending about 10 percent of their time on volunteer work for which he actually had no passion or intrinsic interest.

The other attorney was heavily weighted in litigation, and was interested in doing education legal work.

Next, each partner was to estimate what percentage of his or her total income would come from each revenue-generating activity. For example, the pro bono (free) work was taking up about 25 percent of one attorney's time, but generating no income or referrals to new business. This was one of the many eye-openers an exercise like this one can bring to light.

Each attorney was asked to give weight to the amount of time—on a percentage basis—that he or she wanted to focus on for each possible revenue generating activity.

Finally, they were able to compare notes.

Primary Source of Revenue	Income from Source as %	Income from Source in $	% of Time Allocated CURRENT	% of Time Allocated GOAL
Example:				
Business Law	95%	$95,000	50%	50%
Education Law	5%	$5,000	10%	40%
Education Pro Bono	0	0	30%	10%
Various Pro Bono	0	0	10%	0

What do you notice about this example?

By using a revenue sourcing guide like the one above, you can design a business model that meets your business goals—financial and otherwise. For this professional service business, this model allowed the partners to meet their goals which were to:

- allocate time to bro-bono activities based on their interest,
- create a marketing strategy to increase the business they both enjoyed—namely education, and to
- be more strategic with the business lines that, however laborious, generated the majority of the income—litigation and business law—using the 80-20 *Rule* and *Strategic Direct Marketing*.

Now that you see how the revenue model design worked for another company—it's your turn. Identify all the sources of revenue your new business might have. Primary revenue is your main sources of income, and incremental revenue is the secondary sources of revenue. Second, break out the income you are generating from each activity. List the amount of time you currently spend on the activity. Finally, note the amount of time you want to be spending on the activity. We are designing our perfect business after all—we are not necessarily describing what we are currently doing. Business planning is future planning.

Have each partner complete the same activity. Then compare notes. You may uncover hidden business interests. We are all more happy and content when we are focusing our time on work we enjoy!

Core Business Principle

My Ideal Revenue Model

Primary Source of Revenue	Income from Source as %	Income from Source in $	% of Time Allocated CURRENT	% of Time Allocated GOAL

Assumptions:

Secondary Source of Revenue	Income from Source as %	Income from Source in $	% of Time Allocated CURRENT	% of Time Allocated GOAL

Guide 34: Selecting Your Ideal Customer

Core Business Principle

Professional Business Design Step 2: Ideal Customer

Armed with information about your ideal customer, you can prioritize your market position strategy and pricing strategy. You will want to know the characteristics of your perfect customer–that target niche of people, businesses, or industries that will most likely be interested in your new business, product or service. Your ideal customer uncovers the demographic, geographic, psychographic, and behavioral characteristics of the customer you want in the future. The purpose of being specific with your ideal potential customer is to narrow the field for your marketing activities and to design the business of your dreams. It's that simple.

Design your perfect business

As microentrepreneurs, we will not be able to deploy a mass marketing approach—like McDonalds®. Instead, we need a targeted strategic direct approach to reaching our perfect customer. Knowing which—and how many—potential perfect customers we can potentially reach will help refine our overall market opportunity. Strategic direct marketing, as a customer identification strategy, was presented at one of the international business conferences as an industry best practice. Refer to the *Strategic Coopetition* guide for the how-to's and tips.

Take some time now to identify the main characteristics of your ideal customer. This is business planning, so think ahead to your perfect or ideal future customer. Don't get stuck on who your customer is today. Traditional categories include demographic, geographic, psychographic, and buying behavior.

Will you be targeting a business customer or a consumer, or the end user? Use the guide *Whom Do I Want to Play With* as a refresher or to complete the guides or create your ideal customer profile using the following guide.

Ideal Customer Profile

B2B or B2C

Is the ideal customer a business or an individual?

Strategic direct marketing considerations

If it is an individual, what organizations, companies, or groups are already marketing and selling to this ideal customer?

If a business, what industry are they in?

What size company?

Plan with the end in mind

What would success look like in a relationship with this company? Is my business licensing a product to them? Are they a distribution partner? Are we co-developing a new product?

What would the main benefit be to them in working with me? Agility, time to market, innovation, experience, cost, barrier to market, other?

Guide 35: Where in the World?

Professional Business Design Step 3: Market Opportunity

Understanding the overall market for your product or service is an important step to the business planning process and to launching a viable business. Market opportunity describes the big picture—or overall market—for your product or service.

Core Business Principle

Researching the Potential

Understanding your target market, the segments and customers you expect to gain, and your competitive environment are a key part of researching the potential for your business, product, or service.

Follow your instincts on which section of the business model to start, and then fill in market research gaps with secondary research. Primary market research is the information you can gather on your own using focus groups, surveys, and observation. Gather secondary market research using marketing intelligence, or data gathered from other sources already published.

The market opportunity considers the macro environment for your potential product, innovation or service. For example, you would want to be able to define your opportunities in the following areas:

- Barriers to entry
- Few or weak competitors
- Gaps in existing product positions
- Growth rate of market
- High margins
- Low entry barriers
- Low entry costs
- Low investment risk
- Market not segmented
- Size of market
- Sustainable price structure
- Unfulfilled customer needs

Bright Idea

TIP: If you don't know what industry your business is in, start with determining your Standard Industrial Classification (SIC) and North American Industrial Classification System (NAICS) codes. They identify a company's primary business activity. www.census.gov/naics

My Market Opportunity

What are my primary NAICS codes?

The NAICS industry codes define establishments based on the activities in which they are primarily engaged. Understanding yours will help secure government contracts, determine tax rates, and defines your market.

What industry am I in?

Example: I develop mobile software applications (games). My market opportunity is the US$5 billion mobile industry. More specifically, I am in the US$1 billion software gaming subset of that market, a subset that is growing at a rate of 22% a year.

What other markets, perhaps smaller, am I in?

What is the global size of that Industry (in dollars)?

What is the US size of that industry (in dollars)?

Is the market growing? Shrinking?
At what increment or percent annually?

PEST (Political, Environmental, Social and Technological) Impact Analysis

What political, environmental, technological and social impacts (PEST analysis) might play a role in the increase, decrease, or future value of my industry? Consider a Strength, Weakness, Opportunity, Threat (SWOT) analysis for each major factor uncovered below (internal company strengths and weaknesses, external opportunities and possible threats to the growth of my business.)

A PEST Analysis helps you further discover and uncover the highest and best path for a new product or service launch and paves the way for market and customer identification.

Consider the political impacts and factors as they relate to the new initiative, social impacts, technological impacts, and finally the environmental impacts.

Political Impact and Strategy

Consider the political impact (positive or negative) on your new idea.
What's happening in my local government that would affect my idea?

State government?

Federal government?

Am I able to capitalize on the change?

Can these factors help me or hurt me? In what ways?

Today, it is important for all business owners to consider the environmental impacts of their business design. Investors consider the following environmental impact questions—*so why shouldn't you?*. The following questions were modified from the pre-investment sustainability questionnaire used by Angels with Attitude, an angel investment group in Seattle, Washington.

Environmental Impact and Strategy
Consider the Environmental impact, performance, and management factors.

Environmental Strategy
To what extent does the company track local and global environmental conditions and trends?

Can the company's product or service be directly applied to improving environmental conditions or solving environmental problems? How?

Resource Consumption Questions
What is company policy or commitment with regard to renewable energy sources?

What sources of energy are used in the production of your product or service? Include primary source if possible or known (e.g. hydroelectric, wind, solar, coal-fired, natural gas, etc).

Does the company use energy conservation and recovery methods? Are quantitative measures of energy savings tracked?

What is the energy impact of the company's product/service on its customer's energy consumption?

What are the company's sources of raw materials? What quantities of each are used annually?

Approximately what percentage of overall material use is recycled or reused materials?

How much water does the company consume annually?

Social Impact and Strategy

Consider the social or societal impact (positive or negative) on your new idea. Social factors include the cultural aspects and include health consciousness, population growth rate, age distribution, career attitudes and emphasis on safety. Trends in social factors affect the demand for a company's products and how that company operates.

Social Impact and Strategy

What social changes are occurring that could impact my business?

Technological Impact and Strategy

Consider the technological impact (positive or negative) on your new idea. Technological factors include technological aspects such as innovation and automation, R&D activity, technology incentives and the rate of technological change. They can determine barriers to entry, minimum efficient production level and influence outsourcing decisions.

Technological Impact and Strategy

How is technology changing in relation to my business?

A SWOT Analysis (strengths, weaknesses, opportunities, threats) uncovers:

- Strengths which are internal to the operations of your business or the execution of the idea or invention.
- Weaknesses are another internal assessment of where you need to fill any gaps in order to be the success you intend.
- Opportunities are external to your business or the execution of your idea. They might come from political environment, social environment, technology forces, or environmental factors. These four factors are also called a PEST or STEP analysis and can be completed for any new invention or business idea as a quick success test.
- Threats are external forces that could play a part in hindering or slowing down your bringing the idea to market.

Present your SWOT Analysis in a table format using the following template:

Strengths (Internal Factors)	**Weakness** (Internal Factors)
List key attributes of the organization that help achieve the project objective. *What are our strengths?*	**List key attributes of the organization that stop achievement of the project objective.** *What is stopping us from reaching our new goals?*
How can we use our strengths?	*How can we overcome each weakness?*
What human resources do we have access to that can help us get to goal?	*Who are the human resources are we missing that we need to reach success?*
Opportunity (External Factors)	**Threat** (External Factors)
List key external conditions that help achieve the project objective. **Use a PEST Analysis to Uncover Opportunities** *What is the market opportunity based on the ideal customer?*	**List key external conditions that could damage the project.** **Use a PEST Analysis to Uncover Threats** *How can we guard against each threat?*
How can we maximize each opportunity?	*What steps can we take to overcome each threat?*
Who are the human resources to get us there?	*Who are the human resources to get us there?*

Guide 36: Spotting the Target

Professional Business Design Step 4: Target Market

Once you have determined the characteristics of the customer you want in the future, now is your opportunity to further refine that data (demographic and psychographic characteristics, geographic information, and buying behavior) and determine your target market. Some emerging or fast growth companies like the percentage approach to determining their target market. For example, a target market might be a percent of a specific industry—or overall market opportunity.

Core Business Principle

That said, for most micro and small business owners, designing your business and determining your ideal customers using the "Whom do I want to play with?" approach is a better fit. You are then able to truly design your business and determine the market—target market—that we choose to serve.

If you decide to uncover your target market opportunity, rather than to take a percentage approach, refine your target market by asking the following questions to help you break down the market for your product or service into a reachable market. Consider the following questions:

- How many customers can I serve in a year? A month?
- How many units of products can I create today?
- How many will I need to create to meet the need of my customers?
- How many units of product or hours of service can I create or sell?
- Will this number allow me to earn the income goal I wrote down in the Business Design Roadmap guide? At the price point my customer will pay? Do I need to raise my prices?

Determine your target market now. Based on the total number of customers you plan to reach—sell to—and based on your business and pricing model, consider the following questions:

My Target Market

How many potential customers do I have?

Can I create (or find the resources to develop) products or offer services to meet this market demand?

If yes, this is your target market.

If no. How many customers can I reasonably serve (sell to) in year 1, 2, 3?

Based on this data, what is my target market?

This year?

Next year? (It may increase based on the growth of your overall market or your capacity.)

Guide 37: Buying Benefits

Core Business Principle

Professional Business Design Step 5: Income Potential

Once you identify your target market, you can identify your ideal customer buying from within that space. Armed with information about your ideal customer, you can prioritize your market position strategy and pricing strategy. You will want to know the characteristics of your perfect customer—that target niche of people, businesses, or industries that will most likely be interested in your new product or service. This will ensure you are both identifying the best possible market opportunity and income potential, and are spending time and marketing dollars wisely.

WIIFM—What's in it for me?—that's the question you need to be able to answer for your ideal customers.

Features tell—benefits sell.

Features vs. Benefits
A feature is what you do. Benefits are why features matter. It's easy to translate features into benefits. Simply ask yourself: "If I were the target audience, why would I care about this feature?"

Here's a feature statement:
"My business development center offers three levels of business training to entrepreneurs and inventors creating products."

Why do you care? Assume for a moment you are about to launch a membership drive for your entrepreneurial development center.

The same feature translated into a *benefit* might be:
"Our entrepreneurial and inventor training workshops help emerging growth and early stage entrepreneurs gain access to capital and access to markets. We offer three levels of workshops so you can accelerate your success—no matter what the stage of your product's lifecycle."

In this re-working, you have taken into account the audience, and you've made reasonable assumptions that training can help an entrepreneur be better prepared to secure both financing and generate sales.

Feature vs. Benefits Example
Consider three of this controller's features and benefits.

Features	Benefits
Dimensions of unit	Ease of use for travel
Wide Screen Keypad	Larger typing space makes it easier to work—even while playing
Full color video	Kids able to keep busy with movies

Now consider the benefits of your product, service, or company to your prospective ideal customers. Use the space below to list both features and benefits, as demonstrated in the example. Here's the twist—for each feature, list three to five benefits. It's all right to repeat benefits for multiple features. Actually, that is good. It means you are narrowing your *best* customer benefits.

Features and Benefits Template

Features	Benefits

**Core Business
Principle**

Guide 38: Priced to Sell

Pricing Models

Customers and pricing go hand in hand. Once you determine your ideal customer, answering the price versus quality question comes next.

Some pricing strategies are more relevant to emerging growth companies and new small owners than others. The better you have a clear definition of your perfect customer, the more on target your pricing strategy will be.

Price refers to how much you charge for your product or service. There is a number of alternative pricing strategies. Some common alternative pricing strategies include:

- Captive product
- Competitive
- Cost plus
- Discount
- Economy pricing
- Loss leader

- Penetration
- Premium
- Psychological
- Skimming
- Value based

Captive Product Pricing

Where products have complements, companies will charge a premium price where the consumer is captured. For example, a razor manufacturer will charge a low price and recoup its margin (and more) from the sale of the only design of blades which fit the razor.

Competitive Pricing

Competitive pricing and going rate pricing are when you base prices on what is being charged by other companies for competing products or services. This pricing structure is simple to follow because you maintain your price relative to your competitors' prices. This is a great model to consider when you "feel" that you should be charging less than the competition because you are a new business owner, which is entirely not relevant!

Cost-plus Pricing

Cost-plus pricing adds a standard percentage of profit above the cost of producing a product or of offering the service. This is a good place to start for many entrepreneurs and especially those producing a product. However, don't stop there. Just because there might be a standard, that doesn't mean it is the right model for you.

Discount Pricing

We love the idea of using the discount pricing method. A discount is based on a reduction in the advertised price. A coupon is an example of a discounted price. A partial barter for products or services is another way to provide a discount while maintaining your original price. Providing a discount can be a useful tool to get a first time buyer interested and buying, while leaving you the ability to maintain your original price for future sales.

Economy Pricing

This is a no frills low price. The cost of marketing and manufacture are kept at a minimum. Supermarkets often have economy brands for certain products like milk, cereal, and pasta.

Loss-leader Pricing

The Loss leader pricing model generally is a bad idea for small business owners. It is based on selling at a price lower than the cost of production to attract customers to the store to buy other products. An example of a loss leader is when a gas station and mini-mart sell milk at a lower price than the local grocery stores. They are drawing you into their retail outlet. It is a dangerous model for small business owners.

Penetration Pricing

The price charged for products and services is set artificially low in order to gain market share. Once this is achieved, the price is increased. This approach was used by France Telecom and Sky TV.

Premium Pricing

Use a high price where there is a uniqueness about the product or service. This approach is used where a substantial competitive advantage exists. Such high prices are charge for luxuries such as Hainan Airlines, Gucci, and Four Seasons Hotels.

Psychological Pricing

The psychological pricing model is based on the notion that a certain number in the price simply look better to the buyer than others, for example, $24.99 instead of $25.00, or $3.99 a pound rather than $4.00 per proud. This model can be used along with other models.

Skimming

Skimming involves the introduction of a product at a high price for affluent consumers. Later, as the market becomes saturated the price decreases. This is model new technology products usually employ. Consider the latest and greatest phone. The early adopters will spend extra money to have the hottest or latest technology. Then, sometimes only weeks or months later, the pricing model shifts to the competitive model.

Value-based Pricing

Value-based pricing is based on the buyer's perception of value (rather than on your costs). This is a good model when quantifying non-price factors such as hand-crafting, one-of-a-kind, quality, unique, limited editions, green, organic, and prestige.

Going rate is a price charged that is the common or going-rate in the marketplace. Going-rate pricing is common in markets where most firms have little or no control over the market price.

TIP: Watch out new inventors! Don't get caught trying to compete in price with large companies or even the market rate. It is likely that you have created or are providing something unique and different and deserves a higher price tag.

Bright Idea

Positioning: Pricing Strategy Matrix

Consider the pricing strategy matrix in the positioning of your new invention in the marketplace. Consider where your products or services should be placed on this pricing matrix today. Mark that spot on the pricing strategy matrix below. Then consider where you want to be in the future (12 months from now) and place a mark on the matrix. Is there a considerable difference between the two?

Core Business Principle

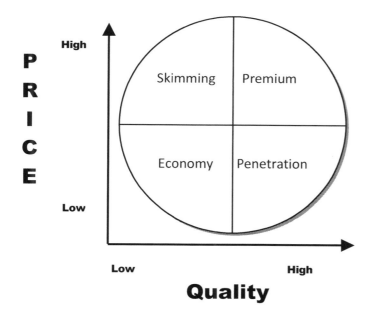

Business planning is future planning – consider 12 months from now. What pricing model have you selected for your new product or service? Why?

My Pricing Model

Guide 39: My Bottom Dollar

Income Potential

Income potential is the final section of the professional business design model. This is where you determine how much you can earn from your business activities, based on the number of potential customers, their expected purchasing behavior, and the price of your product or service.

Do the math, and then do a gut check.

Are your numbers in the ballpark of what you expected or hoped? If not, revisit the model, your perfect customers, and your pricing. There is usually a way to make a business model work the way you intended.

You will have an opportunity to complete the business design guides in the following pages to help you design your perfect business and to create your income projections. These guides will help you answer the question: "Will this business do for me financially what I had expected and hoped?"

Consider the following:
- What is my financial goal (annual for year one)?
- Will I be able to reach that goal with this business plan?
- If not, what can I change? Can I increase income? Change my target customer? Raise prices? Lower expenses?

Ideally, you should complete a projected income statement for three years. The first year should be broken down monthly. That way, you will be able to show an investor the first year's income and expenses month by month with total at the end of year one.

For years two and three, you can simply adjust your income and expenses (using a certain percent is an easy way to start) based on your planned growth. You can use the data from your business model guides to complete the following model. For more detail on how to create your own profit and loss (P&L) starting with a business budget and one-time expense guide, visit the chapter *Show Me the Money.*

Basic P&L Model

	Monthly Budget	Annual
Revenue		
Revenue 1		
Revenue 2		
Revenue 3		
Revenue 4		
Revenue 5		
Total Revenue		
Cost of Producing Goods		
Purchases 1		
Purchases 2		
Purchases 3		
Purchases 4		
Total Cost of Goods Sold		
Total Revenue - Total Cost Production		
Operating Expenses		
Salaries & Wages		
Office Expenses		
Rent Expense		
Travel Expenses		
Maintenance Expenses		
Other		
Other		
Other		
Other		
Other		
Other		
Total Operating Expenses		
Net profit or Loss		

**Core Business
Principle**

Guide 40: Designing My Perfect Business

Welcome to professional business design! These are the tools used by Fortune 500 companies to pre-plan their new products for launch. Now you have the same models.

On the following pages, you will find templates and completed examples of what your business design model might look like. The first three templates are for the product-based business. The last three templates are for the service-focused business.

Use these guides to help you plan and design your business. This process becomes your business model, will guide your marketing strategy, and will become the basis of your Executive Business Plan.

Included in this important section are the following templates:

For the Product-based Business
- Product- based Business Model Template
- Product- based Business Model Guide
- Product- based Business Model Guide: Example

For the Service-focused Business
- Product-focused Business Model Template
- Product-focused Business Model Guide
- Product-focused Business Model Guide: Example

Guide 41: Designing a Product-based Business

Use this Business Model Worksheet to help you plan for your product-based business. Notice that the first model is relatively blank. This is your template. There is a completed business model in this section so you can see what a finished planning tool might look like.

Core Business Principle

Product-based Business Model Template

Business Description (Sources of Revenue)	Ideal Customer	Market Opportunity	Target Market	Total Customers	Income Opportunity
What	Who	How Many	% of Market	Number	How Much Can I Earn (Gross)

Product Business Model Guide

Use the following worksheet to complete your own business model.

Core Business Principle

Business Description (Sources of Revenue)	Ideal Customer	Market Opportunity	Target Market	Total Customers	Income Opportunity
What	Who	How Many	% of Market	Number	How Much Can I Earn (Gross)
List your primary revenue drivers	Describe your perfect customer	Define your big picture market	What percent of the market can I capture?	How many customers does that represent?	Multiply the product price by the total customers.
	Where does my ideal customer live?		1% 2% 20% ????	Crunch the numbers.	
	To what affinity groups does my ideal customer belong?		What feels reasonable to me?		
	What are the purchasing characteristics of my ideal customer?		Tip: Consider your product development capacity.		

Product-based Business Guide: Example

Use the following completed example to help you complete your own business model if you are stuck.

Core Business Principle

Business Description (Sources of Revenue)	Ideal Customer	Market Opportunity	Target Market	Total Customers	Income Opportunity
What	**Who**	**How Many**	**% of Market**	**Number**	**How Much Can I Earn (Gross)**
List your primary revenue drivers	Describe your perfect customer	Define your "big picture" market	What percent of the market can I capture?	How many customers does that represent?	Multiply the product price by the total customers.
Example: Hand crafted metal garden art for rooftop gardens in Snohomish County.	Demographic: women single/divorced/ professional/some college Geographic: Everett, Bellevue, Seattle/ urban / must have rooftop garden Psychographic: middle class/loves gardening/appreciates hand-crafted crafts/buys local Behavioral: compulsive buyer; will purchase 2 to 5 items at a time for self and gifts; will buy 1 X a year	Total women condo owners, professionals, earning greater than $50,000 a year = 100,000 Total rooftop gardens = 20,000	10% of market	10,000 potential customers Gut check! Can I make 10,000 hand crafted products? No. I can make 200, so I will use 200 as my target.	200 customers Purchasing 2 items a year Each item costs $50 200 X (2 X 50) = 200 X 100 = $20,000 Gut check! I wanted to earn more. So, I will try raising my price or changing another variable.

Core Business Principle

Guide 42: Designing a Service-focused Business

Use this Business Model Worksheet to help you plan for your service-focused business. Notice that the first model is relatively blank. This is your template. Use the template on this page as a guide to help you complete your own business model. Use the guide on the following page if you need a roadmap. There is a completed worksheet in this section so you can see what a finished one might look like.

Business Description (Sources of Revenue)	Ideal Customer	Service = Me	60/40 Rule	Income Goal	Income Opportunity
What	Who	How much will I spend on my business?	40% of my time generates $	How much do I need to earn?	How much can I earn? (Gross)
List the primary revenue driving services I offer	Describe the buying behavior of my perfect customer	I am designing the perfect business. It must be realistic. Tip: This is my total available time.			

Service-focused Business Model Guide

Use this worksheet to help you determine your possible income based on the total hours you plan to dedicate toward your business and the price that you intend to charge on an hourly basis.

Business Description (Sources of Revenue)	Ideal Customer	Service = Me	60/40 Rule	Income Goal	Income Opportunity
What	**Who**	**How much will I spend on my business?**	**40% of my time generates $**	**How much do I need to earn?**	**How much can I earn? (Gross)**
List the primary revenue driving services I offer	Describe the buying behavior of my perfect customer	This is my total available time.	60% of my time is spent on non-revenue generating activities.	List my income goal so I can design the perfect business	
	Demographic	I want to work: _____ Weeks per year _____ Hours per week	Total Available Hours:	Income Goal: $_____	Gross Income $_____
	Geographic Location	How many available hours for work is this?	X .6 = _____	The formula: $_____ Income Goal Divided by _____ Total revenue generating hours	Less Cost of Sales Less Expenses Les Taxes = $_____ Net Income Potential
	Psychographic (Affinity Groups)	_____ Weeks per year X _____ Hours per week = _____ Total Available Hours	Hours supporting my business X .4 = _____	= $_____ Per hour (My hourly rate)	
	Buying Behavior		Revenue Generating Hours	**TIP:** Gut check! Is this rate reasonable in the market?	

Core Business Principle

Bright Idea

Service-focused Business Model: Example

Use the following completed example to help you complete your own business model if you are stuck.

Core Business Principle

Business Description (Sources of Revenue)	Ideal Customer	Service = Me	60/40 Rule	Income Goal	Income Opportunity
What	**Who**	**How much will I spend on my business?**	**40% of my time generates $**	**How much do I need to earn?**	**How much can I earn? (Gross)**
Social media marketing consulting services	Demographic: women small business owners with no employees/ earning $30,000 and up Geographic Location: Greater King and Snohomish Counties, WA; urban and rural Psychographic (Affinity Groups): Middle class/high achievers/ risk takers/garden clubs/women's networking groups like the Women's Business Center and Women Business Owners/ not price sensitive Buying Behavior: Not compulsive/seeking to save time/ready to buy/ 3-6 month contracts after an hourly rate trial	I want to work: 50 Weeks / Year 50 Hours / Week How many available hours for work is this? 50 Weeks per year X 50 Hours per week = 2,500 Total Available Hours	Total Available Hours: 2500 X .6 = 1,500 Hours supporting my business X .4 = 1,000 Revenue generating hours	Income Goal: $50,000 The formula: $50,000 Income Goal Divided by 1,000 Total revenue generating hours = $50 Per hour (hourly rate) To earn $50,000 per year I need to charge $50/hour.	Gross Income $50,000 Less Cost of Sales ~20% = 10,000 Less Expenses ~50% 25,000 = $15,000 (Take home pay) Gut check! I need to change my model so that I can earn $50,000 *after* taxes and expenses.

Guide 43: Making Dollars and Sense

Now that you have designed your perfect business, take a few moments to project your earnings over the year. Consider seasonality, sales cycles, and your customers' buying behavior. You did the work—now it's time to turn your professional business design model into a pro forma income statement. One of the financial statements, a projected income statement is the document that tells you and your investors if this will be a financially viable business.

Core Business Principle

Guide 33: *Show Me the Money* is where you can learn more about financial statements and cash flow statements. However, for the Executive Business Plan, you need to complete only a broad or high-level projected P&L (profit-and-loss statement) for three years like the example below. Jump ahead to Guide 57: *Presenting Projections* for additional tips and templates.

Example:

	Year 1	Year 2	Year 3
Revenue (1)	$ 50,000	$ 60,000	$ 65,000
Cost of Sales (2)	10,000	12,000	13,000
Gross Revenue (3)	40,000	48,000	52,000
Expenses (4)	25,000	30,000	32,500
Net Profit (5)	$ 15,000	$ 18,000	$ 19,500
Profit Margin (6)	30%	30%	30%

(1)Based on your professional business design models, use your expected total revenue for year one, and project your expected increase in sales for a three-year period.

(2) List what it costs you in order to earn that total income. Another way to look at the cost of sales or cost of goods sold is that this is the money you have to spend in order to create your product or offer your service. Use benchmarks in your industry to determine your expected gross margin, profit margin, percent of personnel costs as a percent of total sales, and rent as a percent of total sales. These are typically the biggest expenses for a business. Find this information in the RMA Ratios at your local library, online, or from your business banker.

(3) Your gross profit is the money you have left after your cost of sales to pay for your expenses and fixed costs.
(4) Expenses include all expenses not directly related to the creation of your product or the offering of your service, such as personnel, rent, advertising, networking, bank fees, and taxes.

(5) Your net profit (or loss) is referred to as your bottom line—or what the profit is from your business operations. This number is usually calculated on a monthly and a yearly basis. A projected, versus historical, profit-and-loss statement is commonly referred to by bankers, investment bankers and investors as a pro forma, or pro forma income statement.

(6) Your profit margin is the total net profit divided by the total sales, demonstrated as a percent.

Use benchmarks to help make sure you are on track. For example, you might want to search online for average profit margins for your industry. When I searched for profit margins for home-based business owners, I learned that according to a study by the US Small Business Administration:

The 2011 average home-based business had revenue of $62,523 and a net profit of $22,569. The average profit margin of home businesses was thus 36%. With revenue of $62,523 and net income of $22,569, the average home business had total expenses of $39,958. Included in these expenses: cost of sales, $14,228; average home office deduction, $3,686; travel costs, $4,797; and marketing expenses, $1,054.

My Income Projections

If you feel as if you are on a roll, take some time to project your first year's income and expenses month by month in the template below. This is also a useful guide if you are preparing to project your financial projections using seasonality or other customer buying characteristics you identified in the earlier guides.

Core Business Principle

	Month 1	Month 2	Month 3
Revenue			
Cost of Sales			
Gross Revenue			
Expenses			
Net Profit			

	Month 4	Month 5	Month 6
Revenue			
Cost of Sales			
Gross Revenue			
Expenses			
Net Profit			

	Month 7	Month 8	Month 9
Revenue			
Cost of Sales			
Gross Revenue			
Expenses			
Net Profit			

	Month 10	Month 11	Month 12
Revenue			
Cost of Sales			
Gross Revenue			
Expenses			
Net Profit			

Profit and Loss Projections	Month 1	Month 2	Month 3	Month 4	Month 5	Month 6	Month 7	Month 8	Month 9	Month 10	Month 11	Month 12	Total Year 1
Income													
Source 1													
Source 2													
Source 3													
Total Revenue													
Total Cost of Goods Sold													
Gross Profit													
Expenses													
(Use the model in Chapter 8: Show Me the Money)													
Total Expenses													
Net Profit													

How do your projections compare to your industry averages? If you aren't ready to complete the following projections in dollars, use percentages as placeholders. Know what the Key Performance Indicators (KPIs) are in your industry and the RMA Key Ratios. Here is an example. You would then compare your projections to the industry norms for your business.

Sample Pro Forma Income Statement (%)

Example	Year 1	Year 2	Year 3
Revenue	100%	100%	100%
Cost of Sales	45%	40%	38%
Gross Revenue	55%	60%	62%
Expenses	40%	40%	40%
Net Profit	15%	20%	22%
Profit Margin	15%	20%	22%

My Pro Forma Income Statement

	Year 1	Year 2	Year 3
Revenue			
Cost of Sales			
Gross Revenue			
Expenses			
Net Profit			
Profit Margin			

Professional Business Design

In the *Designing a Perfect Business* section of the *Toolkit*, we introduced you to the business design tool that Fortune 500 companies use for product development.

If you started a business that develops a product, then you were armed with a model to help you determine who to sell to, at what price, and sales quantity needed in order make your business goals a reality.

If your business provides a service, then you were armed with a model to determine you're pricing, hours generating revenue, and earning potential based on your personal time commitment to the business.

Using the professional business design tools and guides, you were introduced to each of the five section of a business model:

1. Business Revenue Description
2. Ideal Customer Identification
3. Market Opportunity
4. Target Market
5. Income Potential

You integrated eight of the Core Business Principles into your business design process including: business model, revenue model, pricing model, customer identification, market opportunity, target market, features vs. benefits, and pro forma financial statement.

Last: Next Steps

Now that you have designed your business, it's time to write your business plan. It will be simple now that you have designed the perfect business. Writing the business plan gives you an opportunity to share your vision and venture in a format understood by investors, bankers—anyone you want to involve in your venture.

Designing Your Perfect Business To Dos

- Check your assumptions through market research
- Compare your income projections and expected expenses against industry averages as a benchmark
- Complete your Income Projections in this section— you will need them for the Executive Business Plan
- Complete the Guide *Customer Buying Behavior* to help identify potential income if you have not already

Still Ahead

- Learn the components of a Marketing Plan
- Complete an Executive Business Plan
- Understand the importance of choosing the perfect banker

Designing a *Perfect* Business Certificate of Completion

You have successfully taken a step toward designing the business of your dreams.

In this section of the *Small Business Toolkit,* we introduced you to the art of professional business design. Business planning is personal planning. You are now armed with the tools and business design process used by Fortune 500 companies—*made simple.*

In this chapter, you mastered Core Business Principles: Business Model Revenue Model, Pricing Model, Market Opportunity, Target Market, Customer Identification, Features vs. Benefits, Components of a Marketing Plan, and Pro forma Financial Statements. *Whoa!* You completed Guides 32 through 43, and now it's time to reward the commitment.

Completed Guides
Guide 32: The Art of Business Design
Guide 33: Show Me the Money!
Guide 34: Selecting Your Ideal Customer
Guide 35: Where in the World?
Guide 36: Target Market
Guide 37: Spotting the Target
Guide 38: Priced to Sell
Guide 39: My Bottom Dollar
Guide 40: Designing My Perfect Business
Guide 41: Designing a Product-based Business
Guide 42: Designing a Service-focused Business
Guide 43: Making Dollars and Sense

Complete your certificate of completion on the following page to memorialize your accomplishments before we move ahead.

Congratulations!

Entrepreneurial Edge

Small Business Toolkit

Certificate of Completion

I certify that I, _____, have successfully completed

Professional Business Design

Including: Core Business Principles– Business Model Revenue Model, Pricing Model, Market Opportunity, Target Market, Customer Identification, Features vs. Benefits, Components of a Marketing Plan, and Proforma Financial Statements

Signature: _____   Date: _____

SPROUTT

Chapter 6: **The Executive Business Plan**

Guides

Takeaways:

Describe the elements of a solid business plan including: organizational structure, management team, value proposition, revenue model, market opportunity, competitive environment, competitive advantage, and marketing strategy.

Explain why every entrepreneur should create a business plan and the benefits of developing a plan.

Guide 44: The Executive Business Plan

The Executive Business Plan is a simple, single-page business plan that "tells the whole story"-it is a more advanced business plan than the Quick Plan in that it paints the whole picture of your business for an investor, banker, or partner. We developed this version of a single page business plan using the major components and format of a formal business plan used by investment bankers to spur investment interest for their clients. Now *you* have the model too!

**Play the Game.
Know the Rules.**

This business plan can be used by both pre-startup businesses—early and development stage businesses—and existing businesses alike. There is a simple way to expand each section to create a formal business plan. All of the key components of a formal business plan are included in the Executive Business Plan.

Who should write an executive business plan?

Any entrepreneur or small business owner seeking funding, from a banker to a venture capitalist, will find this model to be a simple, easy tool to help create a compelling business plan. Use the Executive Business Plan to help you successfully plan to start or plan to grow your business.

Design your perfect business

The business plan your banker wants to see.

Through the guides on the following pages, you will:

- Understand the key components of a business plan
- Learn how to write an Executive Business Plan —the single page business plan your banker wants to see
- Be able to tell your story in a compelling way to friends, family, and fools...or from anyone else from whom you may seek funding!

The Executive Business Plan is a tool that can help any size of business and a business at any stage—from idea stage to expansion. Whether you need a business plan for your banker, a potential partner, or a prospective investor, the Executive Business Plan with its simple and concise format, is the model they want to see. We modified the Executive Business Plan guide in the *Toolkit* from those used by investment bankers to raise millions of dollars at a time for their clients.

How many pages should a business plan be:
- *A. 40 or more*
- *B. 10 to twenty*
- *C. Fewer than 10*

Answer: Bankers want to see a plan between 8-10 pages plus financials.

As an investment banker, we would expand this very same single-page business plan model into a longer—three to 8 pages—to pitch investors and compete for their equity investment on our clients' companies.

We pared down this version of the Executive Business Plan into a single-page template for simplicity. It can also be used as an executive summary.

Guide 45: 10 Steps to an Executive Business Plan

10 Steps to an Executive Business Plan

The following are the components of the Executive Business Plan. Each section has a graphic associated with it. Look for the graphic on the *Executive Business Plan* guides on the following pages as you complete your own business plan.

         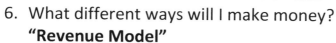 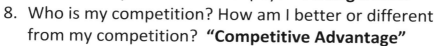

1. What do I do? **"Business Description"**
2. Who is the team that can make this happen? **"Management Team"**
3. How do I know there is revenue potential here? **"Market Opportunity"**
4. What does my ideal customer look like? **"Target Market"**
5. What do I sell? **"Products and Services"**
6. What different ways will I make money? **"Revenue Model"**
7. What will my ideal customer pay? **"Pricing Model"**
8. Who is my competition? How am I better or different from my competition? **"Competitive Advantage"**
9. How will I identify and sell to my target customer? **"Marketing Plan"**
10. Is this company financially viable? **"Income Projections"**

Guide 46: Making an Impression

A plan is your dream on paper.

Remember, it is likely that you will not be the person presenting your business plan to a decision maker when you are applying for a business loan or seeking angel investment capital. Your business plan must reflect your capacity to make your business a success.

What are the most important components of your business plan?
A. Business Description
B. Market Opportunity
C. Management Team
Answer: A, B, and C. All of the above, in that order.

The top three sections of the business plan in terms of importance to investors are:
1. Business Description – Delivers the perfect pitch.
2. Market Opportunity – Shares that now is the right place and time.
3. Management Team – Emphasizes that your team is the best team.

The business description tells the reader your company name, its corporate structure, what you do, and what pain you solve. It will let the reader know that you can describe what you do in as little as a paragraph demonstrating that you know your business. It will let them either want to read more, or take a pass on the plan altogether.

The market opportunity lets the reader know what space your business will play in and that there is a path to make money. An investor invests primarily in a person—you. The management team section of your business plan is that important section that demonstrates to your reader that you are the one to make this project a success and that you have the right team on board. It may also point out your weaknesses and share a plan to fill any management team gaps.

Guide 47: When a Single-page Plan Is *Not* Enough

All components of a formal business plan are found in the Executive Business Plan. Use this guide to help you expand your single-page plan into a longer—more formal—business plan.

Your banker only wants to see an eight-to-ten page business plan plus financials—not a forty page plan created by a software package. The following is a benchmark for expanding your single-page business plan into a longer—yet not too long—business plan your banker wants to see.

Here's how to expand your single page Executive Business Plan into a longer more traditional business plan.

1. Business Description – two to three paragraphs

2. Management Team – two to three paragraphs

3. Market Opportunity – three to four paragraphs; use charts and graphs to help describe the value or major trends in your industry

4. Target Market – three to four paragraphs to define your customer

5. Products and Services –three to four paragraphs; if you have a technical product, such as software or a mechanical design, attach a Technical Specification Document as an addendum. Do not include the "technical spec" in the business plan.

If you have a company in the technology industry (software, microtech, nanotech, biotech, wireless device, disruptive technology, etc.), your investor may have a due diligence team familiar with your technology review your business plan and technical specification document.

The *Entrepreneurial Edge Inventor's Workshop* includes guides on writing a technical specification document and as a part of the Inventor's Marketing Plan.

6. Revenue Model – one to two paragraphs

7. Pricing Model – one to two paragraphs; this section can actually be included in the revenue model section.

8. Competitive Advantage – one to two paragraphs; use a competitive matrix.

9. Marketing Plan – three to four paragraphs; Keep this high level. If you are using vertical or channel sales strategies, specify that. If you are reaching your customer through strategic direct marketing, deep dive into your process. You may be asked for a complete sales plan and marketing plan to support the business plan. Be prepared.

10. Income Projections – Three year pro forma P&L; Keep the financials high level—not detailed. Prepare and have available as an attachment month-by-month P&L and cash flow statements.

Guide 48: The Perfect Pitch

Describing My Business

My Company Name

Use your grounding statement to help you complete the business description. The business description should be a few sentences long. When you are writing a formal business plan, this section can be two to three paragraphs, compared to the four-sentence goal for your executive business plan.

**Business
Description**

What do I do? What pain do I solve?

Moreover, what *pain* do I solve? Does your business solve a problem or a great pain anywhere? What need does your product or service address in the marketplace? The following are examples of concise business descriptions.

Example 1

High Tech Fitness, Inc is a Delaware corporation formed in 2011 to develop market and license its patented global positioning unit for use in the US$6.4 billion sportswear market. The company is seeking $600,000 to bring to market its newest product: a patented, weather-proof, washable micro global positioning (GPS) beacon for use in high-tech fitness gear.

Example 2

Versaly is a Seattle-based mobile media and entertainment company for the always-connected generation. Versaly developed and is marketing a cloud-based multi-channel B2B bulk video delivery platform that reduces the cost and improves efficiency of global video syndication. Our customers include media companies, video distributors, global mobile carriers, independent mobile video portals, and online video destinations.

Example 3 (Merchant Artisan)

Rooftop Garden Art is a Washington State Limited Liability Company founded in 2011 in order to develop, market, and sell hand crafted garden art to the 500,000 condominium owners in the greater Seattle area who have access to a rooftop garden.

Use this space to complete your business description now. Refer to the *Grounding Statement* guide to review your work or to use one of the examples as a model.

My Business Description:

Guide 49: Perfect Players

Management Team

This is where you get to tell the world—or your potential investor—why *you* are the one to pull this business off. Use the management team section of your business plan to describe all the experiences you have had that can directly support your success as the leader of this company. Also, note any missing links. If you need help discovering your strengths and identifying your team visit the *Discovering Your Strengths*, *Engaging Advisors*, and *Identifying Your Dream Team* guides.

Information that can be included in the management team section of the Executive Business Plan are your professional biography, your executive team, key employees, your advisory board, or other business service providers. List your key team in the space below now.

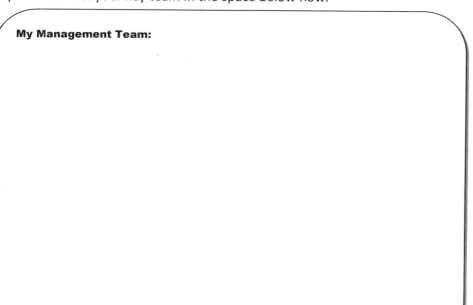

My Management Team:

Bright Idea

TIP: A banker or investor is looking for a 'been there, done that' CEO, president or company founder. If you are not that person, refer to the entrepreneur assessment in the *Discovering Your Strengths* guide to help you uncover your best leadership attributes.

My Management Team, continued:

Guide 50: Right Place, Right Time

**Core Business
Principle**

Get an investor interested using your market opportunity. This section was covered in depth in the *Designing My Perfect Business* guides. If you feel stuck, visit that section of the *Toolkit* to put you back on the right path. You can also review the sample business plan at the end of this chapter. Think big picture. Here are some questions to help you get started down the right path. Consider the following:

- What industry am I in?
- What is the size of that industry?
- Am I in a segment of that industry? Which one?
- What is the size of the overall market?
- Is the market growing or shrinking?
- What factors might contribute to this markets success or failure: legal, government, environment, etc.?

This will likely take some research. Understanding your market will also help you understand your competitive environment.

Bright Idea

TIP: Start by performing secondary research (online, at the library) by identifying your industry and search online for a phrase that includes your industry and market size. For example, using the Example 1 of the business description in Guide 48, we searched for "performance sportswear market" using Google search. The results were an immediate success! We were able to identify the total US market, global market size, percent increase over last year, charts, graphs, pictures, and so much more.

Try a search online first, and then move on to more traditional research tools—like your local business librarian.

210 THE EXECUTIVE BUSINESS PLAN

**Market
Opportunity**

My Market Opportunity

My business is primarily in the _____ industry.

That industry represented $_____ last year and

is expected to grow to $_____ in the current

year representing a _____ percent growth rate.

Key factors affecting this industry include the following:

	Strengths	Weaknesses	Opportunities	Threats
Political Factors				
Environmental Factors				
Social Factors				
Technological Factors				

Guide 51: Piece of the Pie

Target Market

What piece of the pie will you plan to reach? Describe the portion of the market or industry that you will actually reach, that is, sell to. This section is important. To learn how to identify your 'piece of the pie', visit the chapter on *Designing Your Perfect Business* for guides introducing you to this concept and which lead you down the path of identifying your target market.

**Core Business
Principle**

My Target Market:

Target Market

**Products and
Services**

Guide 52: Honorable Prosperity

Products and Services

In the 1950's, earning an income from your own efforts was sometimes called honorable prosperity. So, what's y our honorable prosperity? What does your business provide its customers?

The products and services section of the business plan is your opportunity to describe what you sell, what products or services are expected to become available in the future, their uniqueness, the benefits to the customer, your pricing strategy, and sales channels and vendor relationships, if any.

This is not a place to list the various products or services. It can be three to four paragraphs if you are completing a more formal business plan—but keep it short if you are writing the single page Executive Business Plan.

If you have a technical company, feel free to complete a separate document, like a technical specification document to attach to the business plan. In the *Entrepreneurial Edge Inventor's Workshop,* there are guides to help you complete one.

TIP: Review *Selling Benefits*, *Uniqueness Advantage,* and *Priced to Sell* for detailed guides to help you complete this section.

My Products or Services

**Products and
Services**

Core Business Principle

Guide 53: Profitable Interactions

Revenue Model

A revenue model describes how your business will generate money. Having a planned way to let your clients know what you have that they can use and compelling reasons why you are the best one to solve their problems is a part of your revenue model.

Steps to Profitable Interactions

To create your revenue model, start by listing your revenue streams and cost structure. Are your costs in line with industry norms? Are they better? How and why can you buy at a cost advantage over your competitors?

You make money on the buying—not the selling.

Revenue Model

Of your customer segments, select which of your products or services will be most compelling for the greatest number of customers. Create your value proposition to describe their unique advantages over your competition, and what makes you special, memorable, and stand apart from the customer's perspective. This may include your pricing strategy, values, leadership or other attributes that make you unique.

Identify your sales channels and distribution channels: how and where will your customers find you, buy from you, and know when you have a special offer for them?

Finally, build in sustainable profitable growth. Consider your competitive advantage and design a stream of future customers. Create a sales plan and strategy to make the sale and a marketing plan to reach your perfect customer.

My Revenue Model:

**Core Business
Principle**

Guide 54: The Price Is Right

What will my ideal customers pay? How frequently will they buy? How am I pricing my product or service compared to my competition? This will be especially important. It will drive your financial projections. Use your data from the chapter *Designing Your Perfect Business* and review the *Priced to Sell* guide to help you complete this section. Describe your pricing model and strategy here.

Pricing Strategy

My Pricing Strategy:

Guide 55: The Lay of the Land

Having a competition section in a business plan is not self-defeating. In fact, it lends credibility to your plan and gives you an opportunity to explain the competitive forces that affect your business, share how you are unique and different from the competition, and demonstrate that you are an expert in your industry.

Core Business Principle

In the business plan, you may choose simply to insert your competitive matrix from the *Competitive Matrix* guide, or you may choose to include a paragraph about your competitive forces from the *Profitable Interactions* guide or to summarize your competition and competitive advantage.

My Competitive Advantage: (or summarize your competitive matrix)

Competition

Core Business Principle

Guide 56: Creating Connections

Components of a Marketing Plan

A marketing plan can seem confusing if you haven't written one before. Many think that a promotion plan is a marketing plan. Another common confusion point is that a marketing strategy isn't even a marketing plan. A marketing plan will include your marketing strategy, but the actual marketing plan, is a much broader business-planning document than you might think.

A marketing plan includes a marketing strategy.

In fact, bankers might not ask for a business plan from an existing business that is seeking a business loan. Instead, it is very common for them to ask for a marketing plan instead. The bankers know the business is already up and running. So, they don't need to see how that business got started, what your business goals are, and how you plan to operate your company.

Marketing Plan

Instead, if they are lending you funds for a certain new product development, launch, or expansion of your business, the marketing plan will demonstrate how you plan to execute that expansion strategy and generate cash flow from new customers, increase your volume of existing customers, and create a flow of future customers.

It is the marketing plan that focuses on sales, pricing, promotion, trends in the industry, competition, your strengths and how to plan to implement your strategy—whatever it may be.

A marketing plan is not <u>the</u> marketing strategy.

Target marketing options: broad vs. narrow

- Mass Marketing is when you ignore market segments and try to sell to the whole market with one offer (Undifferentiated Marketing). No micro entrepreneur should try this approach as it is ultra expensive. Think McDonalds.
- Target Marketing (differentiated marketing) Is when you decide to sell to select market segments and have different value propositions for each segment. This is a perfect alternative for inventors and micro entrepreneurs.
- Niche Marketing (concentrated marketing) is when you target a large share of a small market vs. small share of a large market.
- Micro-Marketing (local and individual marketing) includes one-to-one marketing, customization, and personalization.
- Strategic Direct Marketing is a combination of Target Marketing and Micro-Marketing, and is a best practice taught through the National Business incubation Association.

Marketing Mix

Your marketing mix helps you define the marketing elements for successfully positioning your product or service to your customer or strategic partner.

Marketing mix refers to the "4 Ps" of marketing originally developed in 1964. The model remains one of the most popular standards in business marketing training. The 4Ps help you define your marketing options in terms of product, place, price, and promotion. The model is a useful tool to help you plan a new venture, launch a new product or service in an existing company, or evaluate an existing promotion plans to optimize the impact with your target market.

Whether you are an inventor or a business owner, the marketing mix is an important tool in your business toolbox. The four components of the Neil Bordon's Marketing Mix are:

- **Product:** The right product to satisfy the needs of your ideal customer.
- **Price:** The right product offered at the right price.
- **Place:** The right product at the right price available in the right place or through the right distribution channel.
- **Promotion:** Informing potential customers of the availability of the product, its price, and its place.

**Core Business
Principle**

The following are the components of a strategic marketing plan. Use this as your marketing plan outline.

Marketing Plan Outline

1. Executive Overview
2. Market Review
   a. Trends Overview
   b. Market Segments
   c. Target Market (Primary and Secondary)
3. Competitive Overview
4. Product and Business Overview
5. Strengths, Weaknesses, Opportunities, Threats
6. Goals and Objectives
   a. Sales Objectives
   b. Marketing Objectives
7. Strategies
   a. Positioning
   b. Product
   c. Pricing
   d. Promotion
8. Action Plan and Implementation
   a. Media Mix
   b. Schedule
   c. Budget
   d. Assignments
9. Tracking and Evaluation
   a. Response Tracking Procedures
   b. Sales Reviews

6 Steps to Market Making

1. Set Market Making Goals
2. Identify Your Top 20 Targets
3. Determine Market Comparables
4. Identify Your Value Proposition
5. Mobilize Your Resources
6. Customize Your Messaging

Marketing Strategy Checklist

Use the following checklist to help create pull together your own marketing strategy. Check off the sections you have completed or assign yourself a drop dead date.

	Due Date	☒ Done!
Describe your company		
Describe your new product, service, or invention		
Identify your target buyers/end users		
Determine your marketing channel or segment		
Identify competition and potential strategic partners		
Determine whether your company will be a market category leader, follower, challenger, or niche player		
Describe your inventions value proposition for each unique channel or segment		
Identify the distribution channels (specific companies) through which your products/services will be made available to the target market/end users		
Define whether your pricing will be above, below, or at parity with your competitors and establish whether you will lead, follow, or ignore changes in competitors' pricing		
Describe how advertising, promotions, and public relations will convey the unique characteristics of your products or services		
Describe any research and development activities or market research plans that are unique to your business		
Develop your business development strategy		
Create a marketing schedule, budget and timeline		

Guide 57: Presenting Projections

Income Projections

There is a specific format an investor is used to seeing when looking at a business plan. Ideally, you should complete a projected income statement for three years. The first twelve to eighteen months should be broken down month-by-month. That way you will be able to show an investor the first year's income and expenses month by month with a total at the end of year one, or projected out until the numbers start to stabilize. Most businesses are cash heavy during the first several months of operation and ramp up income slowly.

Financial Projections

Most bankers and business counselors support certain benchmarks. The best way to determine what the financial benchmarks should be for your specific business is to ask an expert.

Ask a banker to compare your business, based on your NAICS code, to others in your industry and income size.

Bright Idea

TIP: The RMA Manual has this information and is available at a library in the business reference area. Also, talk with a SCORE counselor. He or she see dozens of businesses each month, from varying industries. It is likely the counselor has come across a business in your industry and could share with you the information they have gleaned about benchmarks.

Further, there are financial ratios that are standard across all business industries. Become familiar with the key financial ratios that make a difference to your profit mastery. There are several templates available free and online that have working formulas to help you complete a profit and loss statement of your own.

The US SBA SCORE counselors have developed several free online tools. Visit the Business Resources section of the *Toolkit* for links to the SCORE website.

TIP: Use your data from the chapter *Designing Your Perfect Business* and specifically the *My Bottom Dollar* and *Making Dollars and Sense* guides to help you create a projected income statement. Use the template in this section to start.

Bright Idea

Here are some examples of actual financial projections presented in the Executive Business Plan single-page format. Notice there is no single correct way to present financial data in a concise manner.

Sample Financial Summary 1
This example is from a company that designed, developed, and marketed a new toy that was sold in major retailers and online hobby stores. It projected to sell over one million of their toys at a $110 price point. The business was a success—but they did not meet their revenue projections.

	Year 1		Year 2		Year 3	
Total Revenue	$ 2,777,185	100%	$ 6,942,963	100%	$ 13,885,925	100%
Indirect Costs	$ 675,400	24%	$ 700,400	10%	$ 882,400	6%
Direct Cost to Mfg /Buy	1,944,030	70%	4,860,074	70%	9,720,148	70%
Total Cost of Doing Business	$ 2,619,430	94%	$ 5,560,474	80%	$ 10,602,548	76%
Net Profit	$ 157,756	6%	$ 1,382,489	20%	$ 3,283,378	24%

Sample Financial Summary 2
This example is from a high-tech fluid-control company that was successful in securing government grants and investment capital, and eventually went public. This was its actual financial presentation to investors. Note that it was considered appropriate to demonstrate that the company intended to lose money for the first three years. Most businesses will lose money before they earn it. (Total S.G.& A means Total Expenses)

INCOME STATEMENT (000's)	2002	2003	2004	2005	2006	2007
Sales	$ -	$ -	$ 6,250	$ 37,500	$ 180,000	$ 524,250
Total Costs	$ 1,594	$ 1,927	$ 6,419	$ 25,240	$ 104,212	$ 276,915
Gross Profit	$ (1,594)	$ (1,927)	$ (169)	$ 12,260	$ 75,788	$ 247,335
Total S.G.&A.	$ 364	$ 1,338	$ 2,497	$ 5,304	$ 12,103	$ 29,822
Operating Profit	$ (1,958)	$ (3,265)	$ (2,666)	$ 6,956	$ 63,685	$ 217,513
Net Income	$ (1,958)	$ (3,265)	$ (2,666)	$ 6,956	$ 39,839	$ 134,858
% to Sales				19%	22%	26%

Profit and Loss Template

INCOME	
Gross Income from Sales or Service	
Less: Returns and Allowances	
Gross Sales	
COST OF SALES	
Inventory – Beginning of Period	
Purchases, Labor, Materials and Supplies	
Freight-in, Other	
OTHER COSTS OF SALES	
Other:	
Sub Total	
Deduct Inventory – End of Period	
Total Cost of Sales	
Gross Profit	
COST OF DOING BUSINESS	
Advertising, Marketing and Public Relations	
Automobile Expenses	
Bad Debts	
Bank Fee,	
Credit Card Fees	
Delivery Expenses	
Depreciation	
Dues and Subscriptions	
Insurance	
Interest	
Labor (misc.)	
License Fees	
Office Supplies & Expenses	
Operating Expenses	
Payroll Taxes	
Postage	
Professional Fees	
Rent	
Repairs & Maintenance	
Telephone	
Travel and Entertainment	
Utilities	
Wages	
Web Hosting & Internet Fees	
OTHER COSTS OF DOING BUSINESS	
Total Cost of Doing Business	
Operating Profit or Loss	

Guide 58: Executive Business Plan Template

Business Name:
Contact Information:
Investment Needed:

Business Description
Grounding Statement OR Business Description

Management Team
Professional Biography – or list your team

Market Opportunity
This is where you talk about the "big picture". How big is the market overall?

Target Market
This is where you talk about your ideal customers and how you plan on reaching them.

Description of Products or Services
This is where you describe what you are selling, creating, or re-selling.

Revenue Model
This is where you talk about how you will make money.

Competitive Advantage
This is where you talk about how you are better and different from the competition.

Income Projections

	Year 1	Year 2	Year 3
Sales/Income			
(less) **Cost of Sales/Goods**			
(equals) **Gross Profit**			
(less) **Expenses**			
(equals) **Net Profit/Earnings**			

High Tech Fitness, Inc.
Jane Doe, Owner
Jane@hitechfitness.com
888-888-8888
wwww.hitechfitness.com
Seeking $600,000

Guide 59: Executive Business Plan Sample

Business Description

High Tech Fitness, Inc is a Delaware Corporation formed in 2011 to develop, market and license its patented global positioning unit for use in the sportswear market. The company is seeking $600,000 to bring to market its newest product: a patented, weather-proof, washable micro global positioning (GPS) beacon for use in high-tech fitness gear.

Management Team

Jane Doe, founder, has been a technologist and mechanical engineer for 20 years. She invented the XYZ system now used in all police uniforms to help detect their location. She has an experienced team, but is seeking a VP Sales with experience in the sportswear industry.

Market Opportunity

GPS technology has recently been successfully integrated into telephones, iPods, and chips implanted into animals for location detection. The market for integrated GPS systems is $2 billion worldwide. The market for high-tech clothing is $1 billion worldwide. The market for high-tech clothing in the US is $500 million, and is the fastest growing market segment.

Target Market

The target customer for the newly developed technology includes existing leaders in the outerwear and fitness wear markets, such as: Nike, Columbia Sportswear, NorthFace, REI, and others. In addition to companies that are their own brand, the Company intends to market directly to clothing manufacturers.

Description of Product(s) / Services

The product is a micro GPS unit that works with all satellite and cellular systems. The patented product is unique in that it is able to be woven into a fabric, is washable, and has an unlimited life span.

Revenue Model

The Company will generate income through two main sources of revenue: licensing its technology to fitness wear manufacturers on a limited basis and through royalties or profit-sharing agreements based on sales of the high tech garments.

Competitive Advantage

The company has several direct competitors including Garmin and other GPS system developers. However, no existing GPS system has the 'wearable' characteristics of ours. Further, we are the first company to market the product to the sportswear industry.
These competitors my be seen as acquisition targets in the future.

Income Projections

	Year 1	Year 2	Year 3
Revenue	$500,000	$2,000,000	$10,000,000
Cost of Sales / Goods	$750,000	$1,000,000	$4,000,000
Gross Profit	($250,000)	$1,000,000	$6,000,000
Expenses	$300,000	$500,000	$1,000,000
Net Profit / Earnings	**($550,000)**	**$500,000**	**$5,000,000**

Last: Next Steps

The Executive Business Plan is a simple solution for creating your business plan—the plan your banker or partner wants to see. You designed your perfect business—take the time to turn that planning into a business plan.

It can be daunting when you are asked for a business plan—usually by a banker, partner, or spouse—and you aren't sure where to start. Most business owners dive into their business without taking the time to prepare a plan, others used a software package to create one for them. A business plan is an ever-changing document so don't wait to start. Here are some takeaways to help keep you on track and a preview of what's still to come.

Executive Business Plan To Do's

- Write a concise business description
- Present my management team
- Identify the market opporuntity
- Refine my target market
- Determine my competitive advantage
- Present my projections
- Complete my Executive Business Plan

Still Ahead

- Gain knowledge about financial statements
- Create a cash flow projection that tells me when I can start taking money out of my business and stop putting it in!
- Learn about capital investment options

The Executive Business Plan Certificate of Completion

You are now armed with business plan your banker wants to see—the Executive Business Plan.

The Executive Business Plan might be considered an executive summary of a traditional business plan. However, it is the executive summary version of a business plan that investors, bankers, and advisors first want to see.

We practiced the following Core Business Principles: Business Model, Revenue Model, Pricing Model, Customer Identification, Competitive Advantage, Market Opportunity, Target Market, Strategic Direct Marketing, and Pro Forma Financial Statements. You completed guides 44 through 59 and now it's time to reward the commitment.

Completed Guides
Guide 44: The Executive Business Plan
Guide 45: Components of an Executive Business Plan
Guide 46: Making an Impression
Guide 47: When a Single-page Plan Is *not* Enough
Guide 48: The Perfect Pitch
Guide 49: Perfect Players
Guide 50: Right Place, Right Time
Guide 51: Piece of the Pie
Guide 52: Honorable Prosperity
Guide 53: Profitable Interactions
Guide 54: The Price Is Right
Guide 55: The Lay of the Land
Guide 56: Creating Connections
Guide 57: Presenting Projections
Guide 58: Executive Business Plan Template
Guide 59: Executive Business Plan Sample

Complete your certificate of completion on the following page to memorialize your accomplishments before we move ahead.

Congratulations!

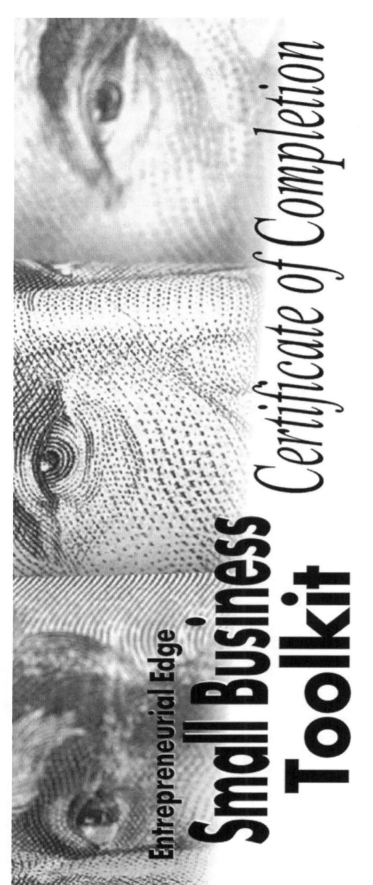

Entrepreneurial Edge

Small Business Toolkit

Certificate of Completion

I certify that I, _____, have successfully completed

The Executive Business Plan™

Including: Core Business Principles™ Business Model, Revenue Model, Pricing Model, Market Opportunity, Target Market, Customer Identification, Competitive Advantage, Features vs. Benefits, Components of a Marketing Plan, Strategic Direct Marketing, and Proforma Financial Statements.

Signature: _____   Date: _____

Chapter 7: **Money Rules**

Guides

Putting you in control of the flow of cash!

Takeaways:

Explain the importance of cash management for a new venture.

Describe how to create the basic financial statements and use them to manage a small business.

Create projected (pro forma) financial statements.

Conduct a break-even analysis for a small business.

Guide 60: Money Matters

The number one reason businesses fail during the first three years is:

UNDERCAPITALIZATION

When I ran business assistance programs funded by the US Small Business Administration (SBA) and US Department of Agriculture (USDA), this was a favorite quote professional business counselors would use to emphasize how important access to capital is for every early-stage entrepreneur.

We believe that access to capital, and projecting with accuracy your cash needs are important, if not critical to a leader's control of his or her business.

Putting you in control of your cash.

However, let's dig deeper. Undercapitalization implies that you didn't start your business venture with enough money, or that you don't have enough capital to keep the business operating. This diagnosis is a symptom, and not the true top reason that new businesses—and some long standing ones—fail.

This segment of the *Toolkit* is all about money matters. Finding funds is one issue, but what about the money rules?

Finance is an art, not a science.

Finance is an art, not a science. Your financial projections will be as sound as you can make them based on other companies' past performance, industry best practices, and your personal business design. But there are some rules. Unless you know the rules of the finance game, you can't play. You won't even make it in the door.

Finance is an art, not a science.

How do I know? From experience in the finance world from angel investing to small business and international banking. And this section of the *Toolkit* will arm you with the knowledge you need to own the money rules.

As a member of the investment due diligence committee of Seraph Capital, the all women angel investment group, I and my fellow members screened forty business plans a month for two or three that would gain the opportunity to present for possible investment.

As an international and small business banker for the largest financial institutions in the world I was responsible for qualifying and assessing risk of small business borrowers from twenty-five thousand to $5 million per project. And as a microloan fund manager for a Community Development Financial Institution and business incubator, I have had the opportunity to act as the actual loan committee, the banker on the other side of the table, determining your access to capital.

Through these experiences, I learned the rules. I can tell at a glance whether or not you have. Get to know the money rules.

Money Rules
1. Project It*!*
2. Present It*!*
3. Access It*!*
4. Control It*!*
5. Manage It*!*

Money Rule 1: Project It*!*
Projecting your income, expenses, profit, and cash flow break-even is a part of your perfect business design.

Money Rule 2: Present It*!*
In order to access OPM—other people's money—whether it is a capital investment from a friend or family member or securing a business line of credit from your favorite banker—is all about presentation. You will likely not be the one to present your loan request to a loan committee. Your presentation will speak for you. Lean how to present properly—to a banker, angel investor, or even your spouse.

Money Rule 3: Access It*!*

Knowing how to access OPM—and your own—is a part of understanding your options—a *Key to Success.* In this section of the *Toolkit*, you will learn what the difference between equity and debt financing looks like, where to get it, and the rule of the capital investment game. We even prepare you for the perfect ten-minute angel investment presentation.

Money Rule 4: Control It*!*

When you control your cash, you control your future. Learn to set up a chart of accounts from the start, put in place financial controls for your business, understand cash management options, and learn to leverage before you need to.

Money Rule 5: Manage It*!*

We are not our business—we need to manage our business. Managing money is all about knowing the rules of the financial game—putting you in the driver's seat. Learn to orchestrate your future through profit mastery.

If numbers scare you—or if you are great at them, but you haven't ever put together a cash flow statement—then look no further. Money Rules takes from, and adds to, the forth guidebook in the *Entrepreneurial Edge Incubator Toolkit*. The *Incubator Toolkit* is used by microenterprise development centers and business incubators in five countries to help their clients succeed.

These tools were also presented as a best practice at the National Business incubation Association and were made a requirement of the international Association's Professional Incubator Manager Certificate program in the Client Funding Category.

This section of the *Toolkit* includes strategies and solutions for putting you in control of your cash. You will learn how to create a cash-flow projection, and how to monitor cash and set up financial controls for your business, borrow better, and understand the differences between debt and equity as funding solutions for your venture.

Money Rules will guide you on your path to uncover where your money is going—or *where it went*.

Core Business Principle

Guide 61: Fast Financial Statements

Understanding Financial Statements in 10 Minutes or Less

We introduced these fast financial statements to participants in the US Navy, US Small Business Administration, IRS, Women's Network for Entrepreneurial Training (WNET), and SBA Lenders Roundtables over the past decade. If you need to get a handle on what financial statements mean to you and your business, start here.

Did you know your business financial statements could answer these questions:

- *How much will I make?* – The income statement (also called a profit & loss statement, but more on that later!) answers this question.

- *How much will I need to start?* – Your cash flow statement tells you this.

- *When can I stop putting money in, and start taking money out?* – Again, your cash flow statement lets you know this.

- *Will the business do for me 'financially' what I want/need it to do?* – The income statement answers this question.

We created the five money rules to arm you with the rules of the financial game. In order to secure investment capital, you need to know the basic rules. Here are some basics to get you started on the right track.

First, we present fast financial statements and a simple concept to help you get to know the banker's language. Upon completion of this guide, you should feel confident that you understand concepts and solutions including:

1. The three documents that make up a set of "financial statements"

2. The concept of "Cash In", "Cash Out", "Cash Left Over" and how it fits into the three financial documents, a balance sheet, income statement, and cash flow statement. There is a guide to help remind you the "cash in ~ cash out" concept to guide you through the process of developing your own set of business financial projections.

3. You will gain insider tips on each of the components of the fast financial statements and understand the various names for a profit-and-loss statement.

Takeaway 1

What three documents make up a set of financial statements? Test your knowledge:

1. B_____ S_____

2. P_____ & L_____

3. C_____-Flow Statement

So what do make up a set of financial statements?

TIP: Answers on the following page.

Takeaway 2

Now that you know what makes up a set of financial statements, the next step is to figure out what information each statement captures so you can create your own.

Each statement paints us a picture of sorts, of the
- Money coming into the business
- Money going out
- Money left over

Each statement shares this information in a different way; each has different names or titles for the same concept.

However, the concept of money IN, money OUT, and money LEFT OVER remains the same.

> One key concept to take away from this guidebook is:
>
> _____ **IN** _____ **OUT** _____ **LEFT OVER**

TIP:
$

To help us understand what these unique statements tell us and how to understand their differences, in this *Toolkit*, each financial document has a picture associated with it. Take a look at the key on the following page.

Answers
1. Balance Sheet *
2. Profit-and loss Statement *
3. Cash-flow Statement *

* For the same time period.

Financial Statements Matrix

$ In	**Income Statement** ~ also called ~ -Profit & Loss Statement -P & L -Operating Plan -Earnings Statement	**Cash-flow Statement**	**Balance Sheet**	**Personal Financial Statement** ~ not a business financial statement — but it acts the same ~
$ In	Income	Cash On Hand and Sales Income and Proceeds from Financing Activities	Assets	Assets
$ Out	Cost of Goods Sold and Expenses	Expenses	Liabilities	Liabilities
$ Left Over	Net Profit (Loss)	Cash Available	Owner's Equity	Net Worth

Remember the formula! Money in minus money out equals money left over. What each category is called will change from one financial statement to the other but the formula remains unchanged.

Income Statement

The income statement uses a camera as its representation, because we can look at a month, or a year, or even compare a specific period to another using this statement. It shows us how we are doing financially at a given moment in time. The income statement is a *snapsho*t of your business at a single point in time.

Money Wise

TIP: Compare the income statement from the prior month to the current month to look for any unexpected variances. Do this on a monthly basis or more frequently if you are in need of better cash management and financial control. This simple tool has uncovered for my clients everything from out-of-control travel expenses in a software company to a pilfering bookkeeper in a wellness center and more.

Cash-flow Statement

The cash-flow statement uses a piggy bank symbol with a Band-Aid on it as its representation. Cash flow tracking or lack thereof typically gets you into the most trouble. The cash flow statement acts like a piggy bank or a cash register in the sense that the cash left over at a given period, like a month or year, is available for the next day. This financial statement tracks real cash. The cash-flow statement demonstrates the revolving nature of cash, its in-flow and out-flows, month- to-month.

Money Wise

TIP: Use a cash flow projection to better control your accounts receivables or determine how much capital will be required for a new project, such as launching a new retail store or product line.

Balance Sheet

The balance sheet is associated with a level, because the balance sheet must do exactly that, balance. It is a precise financial document that business owners typically do not pay much attention to but can literally turn off your access to capital opportunities if not managed and understood. This is the document bankers pay much attention to, while business owners don't. The balance sheet is like a personal financial statement for your business. Let's level the playing field with an understanding of this important and useful tool.

Money Wise

TIP: Pay attention to the owner's equity section of the balance sheet. Banker's do!

Personal Financial Statement

The personal financial statement is not a part of your business financial statements. However, this important document is included in this section of the *Toolkit*. Why? This document tells someone the same thing as your business balance sheet, but for you, the individual business owner! Because a banker usually needs this information when we borrow money, we use a picture of a wallet to represent this personal financial document.

TIP: A personal financial statement demonstrates your net worth: what you have less what you owe as well as a detailed description of your outstanding and available credit, e.g. credit cards. This can affect your ability to secure debt financing for your business if not managed.

Money Wise

Financial Statement Formulas

Profit and Loss Statement

Income minus (-) Cost of Goods Sold equals (=) Gross Profit
Gross Profit minus (-) Expenses equal (=) Net Profit or Net Loss

Cash-flow Statement

Cash on Hand plus (+) Sales equals (=) Cash Available
Cash Available minus (-) Expenses equals (=) Cash Position at Month-end

Balance Sheet

Assets minus (-) Liabilities equals (=) Equity

Personal Income Statement

Assets minus (-) Liabilities equals (=) Net Worth

Test Your Knowledge

Test your understanding of the main components of the financial statements by filling in the blanks below.

	Income Statement ~ also called ~ -P_____ and Loss Statement -P & L -O_____ Plan -Earnings Statement	C_____-flow Statement	B_____ Sheet	Personal Financial Statement ~ not a business financial statement – but it acts the same ~
In	I_____	Cash On Hand and Sales Income and Proceeds from Financing Activities	Assets	Assets
Out	C_____ of G_____ Sold and Expenses	E_____	Liabilities	Liabilities
$ Left Over	Net P_____ or Net Loss	Cash Available	Owner's E_____	N_____ Worth

Guide 62: Startup Expenses

Building Blocks for Your P&L

The cash-flow statement can help you figure out how much money you have put into our business—even before you start. It can also help determine when you can take money out (e.g., pay yourself). It can also help determine your initial costs of starting a business.

When creating a cash flow statement for the first time, it can be helpful to start with the cash out (expenses) before diving into the cash in. So, let's start with your basic startup budget. Once you know your one-time expenses and you document your expected ongoing monthly expenses, you can create a business budget. That budget can be the building block for your formal projected profit and loss statement—or pro forma P&L. It is simple to turn your P&L into a cash flow statement. We are all about simple!

**Core Business
Principle**

Instead of starting with the cash in of your business—let's start with cash out!

This tool is helpful whether you have already invested startup capital into the business or if you are just starting the planning process. You will not calculate and give value to your time already spent on starting the business to include in this worksheet. This expense guide is for actual cash expenditures only.

TIP: Only include cash expenses—not your time.

Money Wise

You may have expenses other than those listed in this guide. Create your own expense worksheet, or use the templates and tools you may find online free. No single model is perfect for every business.

One-time Expenses/Costs

Start by completing the one-time expense guide here or create one using Google Docs or Excel. If you are visiting a SCORE Counselor, ask him or her for a profit and loss template or cash flow projection worksheet.

Use this guide to help you determine what you have already spent on your business and what you still need to spend this year in order to reach your financial goals.

Core Business Principle

Assumptions are footnotes to every financial statement

My One-time Expenses/Costs	Already Spent	Need to Spend
Mortgage or Lease Deposit		
Inventory		
Store Fixtures, Signs & Equipment		
Office Supplies & Store-use Items		
Professional Fees (Legal & Accounting)		
Licenses, Permits & Registration Costs		
Insurance		
Utilities Deposits/Connection		
Website Development		
Telecommunications		
Networking / Computer / Printers		
Software / Other		
Other Fixed Start-up Costs		
Total:		

Assumptions: (Notes of Explanation to the Above.)

Guide 63: Business Budget

Business Budget Guide

Each business will have different profit-and-loss statement and cash flow categories, just as each business will have different record-keeping requirements. This simple guide should get you off to a start. You may not need all the categories of expenses represented. You may have others— just add them.

Core Business Principle

Sample Expense Categories

CASH PAID OUT
Purchases (merchandise)
Purchases (specify)
Purchases (specify)
Gross wages (exact withdrawal)
Payroll expenses (taxes, etc.)
Outside services
Supplies (office & oper.)
Repairs & maintenance
Advertising
Car, delivery & travel
Accounting & legal
Rent
Telephone
Utilities
Insurance
Taxes (real estate, etc.)
Interest
Other expenses (specify)
Other (specify)
Other (specify)
Miscellaneous

Recurring / Monthly Expenses

	Monthly	Annually
Lease Payment:	$500	$6,000
Total:		

Core Business Principle

Guide 64: The Timing of Cash

Cash In Worksheet

You may have several ways to bring in money. Many businesses have multiple sources of income. For example, a landscaper may earn money doing yard maintenance, design, and wholesale of plant material. Consider revisiting the *Designing Your Perfect Business* guides to help you plan and project your income projections.

Specifically the guide *Show Me the Money!* Includes worksheets and tools to help you uncover both primary and secondary income, and leads you through a process of allocating time to the various sources of revenue to help you plan, design, and project how you spend your valuable time and financial resources.

Take your information from those worksheets and summarize it in this section of the *Toolkit*. You already did the planning work. Now you're putting it into a format your banker or accountant can understand.

Use a worksheet like the *Cash In Worksheet* on the following page to help you document your sources of income and the expected timing of the income to hit your business account.

"Cash In" Worksheet

Sources of Revenue (Sales Income)

Use this space to list the **Ways** you will generate income from your business activities here.

	Monthly Amount	Annual Amount
Income Source 1:		
Income Source 2:		
Income Source 3:		
Other income?		

Timing of Income

Don't forget the "timing" of payments from clients and customers! The U.S. Government may pay net 90 (90 days after you send them an invoice), while a different customer may pay within 30 days! Retailers may collect cash and credit payments right away, while 10% of their checks may come back with "insufficient funds".

Of the Above income, what is the timing of cash?

	1 month Net 30	2 months Net 60	3 months Net 90	More? Other
Income Source 1:				
Income Source 2:				
Income Source 3:				
Other income?				

Other Income

Do you have other sources of income that should be included in your Cash Flow Statement? (Interest income, Investment income, etc.) List them here.

**Core Business
Principle**

Money Rule

Guide 65: Your Proforma P&L

Presto Change-o!

You will notice how your business budget can easily be turned into a Profit-and-Loss statement. Your budget categories are complete, your monthly-anticipated expenses are projected for each month, and you have an annual expense expectation per line item.

Converting your budget, one-time expenses, and cash-in worksheets into a P&L is a two-step process.

First, take the information from the cash-in worksheet and summarize the information in the form of revenue.

Next, gather the data from your business budget and place that information in the expenses category of your cash-flow statement template. This is the beginning of your P&L. Change line item titles to meet the needs of your business. No business P&L is exactly the same!

TIP: Instead of bulking all your expenses together, remember to separate your ongoing expenses (operating expenses) from the money you have to spend to create your product (called your cost of goods sold or COGS).

Revisit the guides *Presenting Projections* and *Making Dollars and Sense* for help about the P&L and how to design a perfect P&L for your business.

Basic P&L Model

	Monthly Budget	Annual
Revenue		
Revenue 1		
Revenue 2		
Revenue 3		
Revenue 4		
Revenue 5		
Total Revenue		
Cost of Producing Goods		
Purchases 1		
Purchases 2		
Purchases 3		
Purchases 4		
Total Cost of Goods Sold		
Total Revenue - Total Cost Production		
Operating Expenses		
Salaries & Wages		
Office Expenses		
Rent Expense		
Travel Expenses		
Maintenance Expenses		
Other		
Other		
Other		
Other		
Other		
Other		
Total Operating Expenses		
Net profit or Loss		

The P&L Example

	January	February	March		December	YTD
Revenue						
Sales	$ 50,000	$ 52,500	$ 55,125		$ 85,517	$ 693,356
Sales Returns	-	-	-		$ 85,517	$ 693,356
Net Sales	$ 50,000	$ 52,500	$ 55,125		$ 34,207	277,343
Cost of Goods Sold	$ 20,000	$ 21,000	$ 22,050		$ 51,310	$ 416,014
Gross Profit	$ 30,000	$ 31,500	$ 33,075			
Operating Expenses						
Salaries & Wages	$ 7,500	$ 7,875	$ 8,269		$ 12,828	$ 104,003
Depreciation Expenses	500	525	551		855	6,934
Office Expenses	475	499	524		812	6,587
Rent Expense	1,500	1,575	1,654		2,566	20,801
Travel Expenses	250	263	276		428	3,467
Maintenance Expenses	100	105	110		171	1,387
Advertising Expenses	200	210	221			
Total Operating Expenses	$ 10,525	$ 11,051	$ 11,604		$ 17,659	$ 143,178
Income From Operations	$ 19,475	$ 20,449	$ 21,471		$ 33,651	$ 272,836
Interest Income (Expense)	(100)	(105)	(110)		(171)	(1,387)
Income Before Income Taxes	$ 19,375	$ 20,344	$ 21,361		$ 33,480	$ 271,449
Income Tax Expense	750	788	827		1,283	10,400
Net Income	$ 18,625	$ 19,556	$ 20,534		$ 32,197	$ 261,049

Guide 66: Cash Is King!

Every entrepreneur needs to be able to tell when he or she can start taking money out of the business and stop putting it in by creating a cash flow projection.

You should feel comfortable—as will your investors partners or spouse—with how much more cash your business will take before it turns the corner and starts paying contributing to your personal bottom line.

The cash-flow statement is the document that helps you answer the question:

"When can I stop putting money into my business and start taking it out?"

Many banks, including the US Small Business Administration government guaranteed lending programs, look to cash flow to determine one's ability to repay a new business loan. The cash-flow statement is especially important for a business seeking other people's money—OPM.

A cash-flow statement is one of three financial documents that make up your business financial statements. The cash-flow statement is a great planning tool to help you start—and stay—on track in your business.

Core Business Principle

Design your perfect business

Pulling It All Together

One-time Expense Worksheet

Gather the data from the one-time expense worksheet you already completed and complete the first column of the cash-flow statement listed "Pre Startup". If you are seeking outside capital, you can title this column "Pre-Loan" or "Pre-Investment". There is a section of the cash-flow statement labeled cash infusion, investment, or loan amount. List any expected new cash infusion into the company using this row in the month you plan for the investment to land.

Business Budget / Expense Worksheet

Gather that data from the Business Budget/Expense Worksheet
That you completed earlier in this section of the *Toolkit*. Use this information fill in the "Cash Out" section of the cash-flow statement.

TIP: your monthly expenses in this section should be very consistent. Your salary as owner, however, may start small and increase over the year as the company becomes more stable and profitable.

Bright Idea

Cash-In Worksheet

Finally, gather the data from your complete cash flow worksheet called "Cash In: and use it to fill in the "Cash In" section of the cash-flow statement. This section is only looking for the "total" cash in for any given month. Start the section with the cash position you had after all the one-time expenses in column one.

The Flow of Cash Formula

On the following page is an example of a blank cash flow statement template. Ending cash in month one becomes beginning cash or cash available to start month two. And so on. And so on. And so on.

Starting cash (Cash on hand)
plus (+) income
plus (+) cash infusion
minus (-) expenses
equals (=) ending cash
ending cash equals (=) next month's cash on hand

Cash-flow Statement Example

Cash Flow (12 months)

Enter Company Name Here   Fiscal Year Begins: Jan-06

	Pre-Startup EST	Jan-06	Feb-06	Mar-06	Apr-06	May-06	Jun-06	Jul-06	Aug-06	Sep-06	Oct-06	Nov-06	Dec-06	Total Item EST
Cash on Hand (beginning of month)			0	0	0	0	0	0	0	0	0	0	0	0
CASH RECEIPTS														
Cash Sales														
Collections fm CR accounts														
Loan/ other cash inj.														
TOTAL CASH RECEIPTS	0	0	0	0	0	0	0	0	0	0	0	0	0	0
Total Cash Available (before cash out)	0	0	0	0	0	0	0	0	0	0	0	0	0	0
CASH PAID OUT														
Purchases (merchandise)														
Purchases (specify)														
Purchases (specify)														
Gross wages (exact withdrawal)														
Payroll expenses (taxes, etc.)														
Outside services														
Supplies (office & oper.)														
Repairs & maintenance														
Advertising														
Car, delivery & travel														
Accounting & legal														
Rent														
Telephone														
Utilities														
Insurance														
Taxes (real estate, etc.)														
Interest														
Other expenses (specify)														
Other (specify)														
Other (specify)														
Miscellaneous														
SUBTOTAL	0	0	0	0	0	0	0	0	0	0	0	0	0	0
Loan principal payment														
Capital purchase (specify)														
Other startup costs														
Reserve and/or Escrow														
Owners' Withdrawal														
TOTAL CASH PAID OUT	0	0	0	0	0	0	0	0	0	0	0	0	0	0
Cash Position (end of month)	0	0	0	0	0	0	0	0	0	0	0	0	0	0

CASH IN

CASH OUT

$

**Core Business
Principle**

Steps to a Cash-flow Statement

As a recap, your P&L demonstrates the financial viability of your business—it helps you answer the question "will this business generate a significant enough profit in a reasonable timeline to meet my goals?"

Your cash-flow statement acts like a cash register for your business and shows the timing of your actual cash needs. A company might look good in the P&L, and then fail due to lack of operating cash.

The cash-flow statement can help you: identify how much money you need to start your business or a capital project, show you when you can start paying yourself and how much, and helps you project for future onetime expenses like a marketing campaign, or business travel. It can also be used to track the timing of cash flow.

Remember that a cash-flow statement is starting at the beginning of a given month with the actual amount of cash you have in your business accounts, at that moment. It is not a projection of what you might have in the future or what you expect to raise through a fundraising effort. The cash-flow statement acts like a cash register for your business. It tracks the flow of actual cash.

In business—cash is king.

The great thing is that once you have created your P&L, you are 90 percent to having a cash-flow statement. Notice the format of a P&L compared to a cash-flow statement. Similar—right? There are three steps to change your P&L into a cash-flow statement. A cash-flow statement is your P&L, with the following changes:

Revenue becomes dynamic cash-in.
Create a "total" for the new cash-in section of your spreadsheet. Use the template on the preceding page as an example. Typical Cash-In categories include:

- ☐ Cash on Hand
- ☐ Cash Sales
- ☐ Cash from Accounts Receivable or Collections
- ☐ Cash from Outside Investment
- ☐ Cash from Bank Financing
- ☐ Total Cash Available

Did you add cash received from a bank loan or other capital investment in the cash in section?

Include the timing of your cash in. If your business is seasonal, distribute cash in the appropriate month you expect it to hit. If you collect invoices thirty days after you send them out, project the cash thirty days from your sent invoice. Revisit Guide 64: *The Timing of Cash* to help with this process.

Money Out = Cash Out
In the cash-flow statement, all the expenses of your business are bulked together in one section. The *cost of goods sold* and *operating expenses* join into one category called "expenses".

If you expect to make loan payments or interest payments to your investor or bank, add a category for those cash expenditures in your expenses category in the cash-out section of the cash-flow statement. The cash-out section of the cash-flow statement, in addition to your expenses, might include:

- ☐ Loan Repayment
- ☐ Capital Expenses
- ☐ Startup Expenses
- ☐ Owner's Withdrawal

Make it flow
The trick to making your cash-flow statement flow is to use these formulas to start tracking your cash like a cash register:

Total Cash In – Total Cash Out = Total Cash Available
Total Cash Available = Starting Cash the next month

Now that you have your financial statements in order, let's project some profit!

Core Business Principle

Guide 67: Profit Mastery

There is a set of core business concepts, according to the National Business Incubation Association, that attributes to an entrepreneur's success. We call them our Core Business Principles and break-even analysis is one of them.

Understanding profitability and break even for your business and capital investment is a critical for each business owner. Break-even analysis is useful because it helps recognize the chances of a new venture succeeding. Break-even for your business means to make neither a profit nor loss.

Definition of Break-even:

Make neither profit nor loss

Break-Even Point (BEP) or (BE)

In cost accounting, the break-even point (BEP) is the point at which cost or expenses and revenue are equal: There is no net loss or gain, and one has broken even.

Break-even is also the level at which an investment project recovers all of its costs and starts making profit.

You can also use break-even to determine how many units of a product your business needs to sell before it starts earning profit on that particular product. This keeps cost accountants very busy—especially in large companies. Small business owners need to use this tool too! Use this profit mastery tool throughout your product and business lifecycles. You are the master of your profit.

Consider this example for a product based business—a merchant artisan who makes wood bowls. If this business owner sells fewer than ten bowls each month, he will lose money; if he sells more than ten, he will generate a profit.

With this information, the business owner or manager will determine how to create and sell ten bowls per month—more if he actually wants to make a profit.

If he thinks he cannot sell that many, to ensure viability he could:

- Try to reduce the fixed costs (by renegotiating rent for example, or keeping better control of telephone bills or other costs)

- Try to reduce variable costs (the price he pays for the wood or oil by finding new suppliers or renegotiating purchase price).

- Increase the selling price of his bowls.

Any of these would reduce the break-even point. In other words, the business would not need to sell as many bowls to make sure it could pay its fixed costs.

TIP: You make money on the purchase of your goods, materials or inventory—more so than on the actual sale. Pay attention to variable costs and renegotiate often.

Money Wise

Example of Contribution Margin:
Say your business makes blown glass bowls and sell them for one hundred dollars each through a coop. There is no shipping.

Sales Price	$100.00
Minus (-) Purchase Price of Glass per unit	$ 20.00
Minus (-) Packaging	$ 2.00
Minus (-) Coop fee (50% of retail sale)	$ 50.00
Equals (=) Contribution Margin	$ 28.00

This calculation shows that each time you sell a glass bowl you have twenty-eight dollars left to pay for your other expenses. This amount is called the contribution margin or gross profit. Most businesses refer to their gross profit simply as gross, as in "what did your business gross this year?"

Your business budget will be tracked by you or your accountant or bookkeeper using a software tool like QuickBooks®.

Money Wise

TIP: Consider creating a chart of accounts once and sticking with it! This is a best practice by serial entrepreneurs. In fact, when you have a single chart of accounts for the entire lifespan of your business, you position yourself to sell the business down the road.

The majority of micro-enterprises simply shut down, close their doors, and cease operations when the business owner is tired of the business—or can't manage it due to economics or health. When you plan the future in mind, you create a financial model that is traceable over the years. When you have a single budget, or chart of accounts, your future self (or potential buyer) can assess how the business did month over month or year over year with the same metrics. Simple as that sounds, it can mean the difference between your ability to sell your business for a value that makes sense to you—and shutting down because an outside party can't figure out the numbers.

Your gross profit can also be reflected as a percentage and is then called your Contribution Ratio or Profit Margin. Here is an example based on the glass bowl scenario.

Contribution Ratio:

Contribution Margin ÷ Sales Price = Profit Margin
$28.00 ÷ 100 = .28 or 28%

Example of Break-even:
The break-even point in number of units sold is:

$$\text{fixed cost} \div \text{contribution per unit}$$

or in revenue terms:

$$\text{fixed costs} \div (1 - \text{contribution margin})$$

In this example, the following would be true. When the merchant artisan sells three bowls, he will have covered his fixed costs.

Purchase Price of Glass per unit	$ 20.00
Packaging	$ 2.00
Coop fee (50% of retail sale)	$ 50.00
Fixed Costs	$72.00

$$\$72.00 \div \$28.00 = 2.5$$

Gut Check
If the business owner breaks even after he creates three bowls a month – or 36 bowls annually (3 X 12 = 36), and he wants to earn ten thousand dollars a year from making and selling his bowls, then he would need to sell 358 bowls additional bowls ($10,000 ÷ $28 = 358).

That would mean the artist would have to be able to create and sell over thirty bowls a month. Or, considering seasonality, perhaps three hundred bowls during the winter holidays and the remainder during the rest of the year.

TIP: When you determine your break-even for your product, take the second steps to determine if the income you can earn from the business based on your current inputs or assumptions makes sense for you.

Bright Idea

Making thirty bowls might not be viable (based on the time to make each bowl for example). If making fifteen bowls a month is more realistic, he must consider his alternatives. Can he increase the price of the bowls? Can he decrease his cost of materials? Can he negotiate a better deal with the Coop where he sells your products?

Money Rules

Money rules put you in control of your cash. You are armed with the rules of the finance game—so you can play. In this section of the *Toolkit,* you were first introduced to the money rules:

- Project It*!*
- Present It*!*
- Access It*!*
- Control It*!*
- Manage It*!*

Cash is king! Undercapitalization is the number one reason a new business fails within the first three years.

Now that you understand what makes up a set of financial statements and the differences between these important financial management tools, and you understand how to project, present, control, and manage your cash, you are on the fast-track to sustainability.

Up next are some of the Access It*!* money rules. *Show me the money!*

Last: Next Steps

This section of the *Small Business Toolkit* was all about introducing you to the financial language of your business plan. Some entrepreneurs are more comfortable with financials, budgets, and monitoring the flow of cash than others. Financial statements are "banker talk" for your business. Once you know what comprises a set of business financial statements and how to create your own, you are armed with the language you need to speak when seeking OPM.

Money Rules To Do's

- Create a one time expense budget
- Complete the Cash-In Worksheet
- Turn my budget into a Cash Flow Projection
- Practice break-even often to project when my business will be break even
- Know how many units of product I need to sell each year to reach profitability

Still Ahead

- Get on the inside track of your financial institution
- Discover the rules of the fundraising game
- Learn to mobilize resources to support your business

Money Rules
Certificate of Completion

You have discovered the money rules.
When you know the rules, you can play the game.

In this section of the *Entrepreneurial Edge Small Business Toolkit* you were introduced some financial basics that are at the core of your business success.

You completed guides 60 through 67 and were introduced to the concept of pro forma—or projected—financial statements. You completed a startup budget, profit-and-loss statement, and cash-flow statement. You learned how to determine which of your products will be profitable and when—critical tools for your financial success.

Completed Guides

Guide 60: Money Matters
Guide 61: Fast Financial Statements
Guide 62: Startup Expenses
Guide 63: Business Budget
Guide 64: The Timing of Cash
Guide 65: Your Pro Forma P&L
Guide 66: Cash Is King!
Guide 67: Profit Mastery

Complete your certificate of completion on the following page to memorialize your accomplishments before we move ahead.

Congratulations!

Entrepreneurial Edge

Small Business Toolkit

Certificate of Completion

I certify that I, _____, have successfully completed

Money Rules!

Including: Business Budgeting, Fast Financial Statements, Break-Even Analysis and Profit Mastery

Signature: _____ Date: _____

Chapter 8: **Show Me the Money!**

Guides

Guide 68: Better Borrowing
Guide 69: Get Noticed!
Guide 70: 5 Money Raising Questions
Guide 71: Debt vs. Equity
Guide 72: Finding Funding
Guide 73: Business Loan Checklist
Guide 74: When a Bank Doesn't Feel Right
Guide 75: Scoring an A+ with the Five Cs of Credit
Guide 76: Credit Worthiness Assessment
Guide 77: Structure of Debt Financing
Guide 78: Introduction to Equity
Guide 79: Show Me an Angel!
Guide 80: The Perfect 10-minute Pitch
Last: Next Steps
Certificate of Completion

Positioning You for Success!

Takeaways:

Understand the various types of financial institutions and identify the right fit for your new venture.

Explain the importance of planning for your company's capital requirements.

Describe the differences between equity capital and debt capital and the advantages and disadvantages of each.

Describe the various sources of debt capital and advantages and disadvantages.

Assess your credit worthiness based on the 5 Cs of credit.

Develop an investment presentation for an audience of angel investors.

Guide 68: Better Borrowing

Choosing the right financial institution is a strategic business decision. So many times we choose to open our business banking accounts with the bank we used as children or students. This chapter will provide you with the pros and cons of all the various types of financial institutions and share some tips about types of OPM—other people's money.

Get to know your banker—
before you need them!

If you don't have a business banker yet, find one. Performing informational interviews with business bankers, sometimes called business relationship managers, at the various banks will give you a better sense if that particular institution will be a good fit for you.

Get to know your banker! Before you feel that you may need a business loan, have a relationship with your banker. Even if you hire a CFO-to-go to help you find the right bank or the right sources of capital investment, as the business owner you must talk the talk, remain in control, and be able to direct that hired gun. The following section on *Choosing the Right Lending Institution* should help.

Choosing the Right Lending Institution

There are several types of banks. Choose wisely!

- Large Institutions (Big Box Banks)
- Community Banks
- International Banks
- Investment Banks
- Credit Unions
- Alternative Lenders
- Hard Money (Sometimes Called Predatory) Lenders
- Peer-to-Peer Lenders

Large Institutions

Big Banks

Big banks, sometimes called "big box banks", refer to the monster banks like Key Bank, Bank of America, JP Morgan Chase, US Bank, and others, depending on the latest headlines. They are the largest banks in the nation based on assets under management. There are some major benefits to choosing a large institution as your primary service provider

Pros: Location, location, location. Namely location of branches. The large banks have more ATMs and service locations than any other type of financial institution. They often have a simplified loan application for small business loan requests under certain thresholds, like $100,000, $50,000, or $2,000, and application requirements may be more lax. Be sure you know the bank's lending limits for your size of business and the loan application requirements.

Cons: Some refer to large banks as box banks, because you may have to fit perfectly into their "boxes" in order to secure business financing. At the branch level, they also often lack decision-making power, business experience, business savings, cash management and loan products, trade banking, or finance experience.

Not all small or early-stage companies will be a good fit for a large institution due to the limited access to capital options. However, the more you know about banking, finance, your business, and the role your banker can play will allow you to manage any financial institution relationship.

Community Banks

A community bank is typically a smaller, regional bank with sometimes several branches in an area. Some community banks in Western Washington include Whidbey Island Bank, Cascade Bank, Columbia Bank, Umquah Bank. Some ways to identify a community bank in your neighborhood include:

- local bankers or branch managers attend Chamber of Commerce luncheons
- bankers are active in the community
- they may coach the local youth teams
- they may only have one local branch
- the business loan officer is also on the local committee
- the business loan committee is comprised of representatives of the bank's board of directors, and they live in your community.

Pros: Community focus. Local engagement and involvement. Local decision-making authority. Most often, the loan committee is a segment of the bank's board of directors. You may even know them and have a personal relationship with them. Relationships matter. Local community banks tend to be extremely relationship focused.

Cons: Watch their cash management, lending authority, assets under management and leadership. These smaller banks tend to go out of business in today's difficult financial climate. Hundreds of community banks have failed in recent years. This does not necessarily mean you would have lost your money if you were with one of these failed banks, but the transition to a new institution that you did not choose could be a hassle.

International Banks

An international bank, like HSBC Bank, is one that can help you conduct business in other countries. We differentiate between a true international bank, one that operates its own banks or branches in countries other than the United States, and a *want-to-be* international bank, one that has a corresponding banking relationship with other banks in countries other than the United States. These banks will call themselves international banks and may be able to offer you many of the services of a true international bank. However, their systems will not connect, transactions may take longer than customary, and the service may be inconsistent from bank to bank, branch to branch, and country to country.

Community Banks

International Banks

Corresponding banking relationships between banks is a great thing. It will let you identify, before you choose a financial institution in a given country, which banks in the other country your bank is comfortable doing business with—banks do need to get along.

Banks with a corresponding banking relationship are like business partners. They have the same goals in mind, they find a way to work together, and they support the same mission—serving you, the customer, in the country in which you intend to do business. Bank of America, for example, uses corresponding banks in some countries. When you work with a Bank of America branch in China, you area actually at a corresponding bank, and not the US based Bank of America. Sometimes banks operate using the corresponding bank's name. So do your due diligence and know with whom you are banking.

As a business working internationally, you will want to learn in which countries the bank has actual offices and which are their corresponding banks in the countries where you wish to conduct business.

When a new customer or business relationship develops in that country, request that the customer or business transaction use the bank with which your primary bank is comfortable. If you do this, your transactions will be more streamlined, you will save money in fees, and your local banker will have the ability to serve you in his or her best capacity.

Pros: Many countries. Great cash management solutions. Currency exchange. Good foreign exchange rates. Control of your international banking relationships. Knowledgeable in trade finance and trade finance options, alternatives, and best-fit options for small business. International access to capital. International personal banking, including mortgages and personal credit.

Cons: If you are not an international business, like a wholly owned subsidiary of a company in another country, or a frequent international business traveler or doing international trade, you may not get the best attention from your business banker in an international bank. An international bank is a specialized bank that is good at assisting businesses transact, control, and manage their cash and credit all over the globe. They may not pay as much attention to a business that is not utilizing its expertise.

Other Banks

Trade Banks

Some banks are purely trade banks. A bank that focuses on international trade—import and export finance and cash management. Sometimes a trade bank will have limits on the size of company or transaction it can handle. Usually the small business owner or solopreneur will not have large enough transactions to require the services of a trade bank. However, for a middle market business—one generating gross income greater than ten million dollars but still less than $100 million—a trade bank might be a perfect fit.

Investment Banks

Investment banking—also known as corporate finance—traditionally involves helping clients raise funds in capital markets and giving advice on mergers and acquisitions (M&A). They also offer investment management—like stocks and real-estate—and cash management solutions that may be more sophisticated than that offered by a community bank or other another more friendly option.

Consider having an investment banking account. However, we don't recommend engaging an investment bank as your primary banking institution—unless it offers small business banking services.

When it comes to long-term cash management, a traditional bank's financial advisor may be more expensive than others for stock, bond, CD's, and other cash-management solutions. Investment banks include JP Morgan, Goldman Sachs, Morgan Stanley Smith Barney, UBS and others. For retirement, cash management, and investment solutions, companies include Charles Schwab, Fidelity, Edward Jones and others.

Pros: Good for mid and long-term cash management. Investment offerings include do-it-yourself options to hands on management for a fee. Checks and deposits (even by mail, if needed). Simple fund transfers. International reach in many instances. Good long-term cash management options (especially if they allow international transactions and investments).

Cons: Use your primary bank's cash management or treasury team for short-term to mid-term cash-management needs. The lack of locations and access to branches, especially in small cities and rural areas, limit your access to capital and transactions options to Internet-based options.

Trade Bank

Investment Banks

UBS

Goldman
Sachs

Credit Unions

Credit Union

Credit Unions

Credit unions are membership-based financial institutions that operate like REI, the famous coop headquartered in Seattle, Washington. A credit union is typically a great option if you are a member of a specific community, like a US Navy veteran, or large company employee like Boeing. There are very good credit unions that serve specific communities of members. Some have broadened their membership base just so they can serve more people, and generate a greater deposit base.

Experience lends that coop banks or credit unions are typically not good choices for use as your primary business bank. Their business bankers may not have real business experience (which is important) and they may not have access to competitive rates, products, and offerings that more traditional business banking institutions and small business alternative banks can offer.

That said they have great offerings for personal banking like competitive auto loan rates and competitive home mortgage rates.

Pros: Community focused. Customer focused, membership focused. Specialty services for the members they serve. Solid at offering personal financial services. Members are also owners.

Cons: Not typically business banks. Typically will not understand or have the capacity to offer international banking, trade finance, cash management, or treasury services—all financial products a small business may need.

Alternative Lenders

Alternative lenders may not be a bank at all. Many alternative lenders are nonprofit organizations or something called a Community Development Financial Institution (CDFI).

There are several community development financial institutions in each state and they tend to be a perfect first step for any small business owner when he or she needs a business plan, financial assistance, business education, and access to capital for their startup, early stage, or difficult-to-fund business. Sometimes they are the only option.

Interestingly, the CDFI traditionally gets its funding from the large financial institutions. In that the large, big-box, banks are not able to support small and very small (micro) loan requests, they are required by the federal government, through an act called the Community Reinvestment Act or CDR, to lend the CDFI's money at a very low or no interest rate. The CDFI's then lend the money to businesses in the form of small or micro loans.

The CDFI must not compete with the traditional bank in terms of loan rates. (Recall they get their money from the banks. The banks would not fund them if they were competitors.) So, a business loan from an alternative lender will have a higher interest rate than the market would normally bear. The loans they offer are typically: more time intensive, difficult, creative, or more risky than those a traditional financial institution would be able to approve. Therefore, the interest rate goes up. Higher risk equals higher rate.

Sometimes an alternative lender will even require that you have received a decline from a bank before it can offer you a business loan.

**Community
Development
Financial Institutions**

Community Development Financial Institutions (CDFI)

The United States Department of Treasury governs both CDFIs and banks. They are all working in concert to provide access to capital to all sizes of business, micro, small, traditional, and international. A CDFI serves those who are creating jobs, building assets for the entrepreneur, retaining jobs, or traditionally unbankable due to credit, capital, or collateral deficiencies.

Pros: We love CDFIs! Traditional banks must maintain an arm's length distance from the client to help protect them from liability. For example, a traditional banker would not offer, or even be able to, help you create a cash flow projection after sitting with you for hours getting to know your business and your personal entrepreneurial goals.

What would happen if your business failed? You might be able to point the finger at your banker, and the bank he or she worked for as having some sort of responsibility for helping you create the model that contributed to your downfall. Traditional banks simply cannot help like a CDFI can.

A CDFI may have a business technical assistance unit, or division, to assist entrepreneurs through the business-lending process. Sometimes when the CDFI secures funding to do what they do, from the Department of Treasury, for example, they have access to financial assistance funds in the form of a very low interest loan to them so that they can re-lend it to you. However, they also might have access to technical assistance funds, a grant that pays the CDFI to provide you with training and/or one-on-one business counseling and coaching to help increase your success in repaying the loan.

With a CDFI, you get the best of both worlds, a banker, mentor, and business coach all in one organization.

Cons: A CDFI is not a bank. Most times they cannot accept deposits, they only give loans and help you with your business planning and growth. You will still have to find a bank to work with for deposits, business credit cards, cash management, and investments, etc.

Short-term Lenders

Watch out entrepreneurs! We are pro OPM. However, know what you are getting into before using a short-term loan to tide your business over until cash flow is strong again. You need to have a solid exit plan before you opt to use a short-term lender (sometimes called a hard-money lender or predatory lender) or a bank to help factor your receivables (pay you in advance of you being paid for services rendered once you sent the bill or invoice). More on factoring later in this section.

Hard money, cash advance, payday lenders, and sometimes factoring companies or receivable financing programs do offer a unique and sometimes valuable service for the entrepreneur. These companies and programs have the resources and ability to give you cash when you need it. At a price.

Sometimes that price might be as high as 300-plus percent when all the fees are included. However, these loans are meant to be short term. Very short term. Like a day, a week, or maybe a few months until your client pays you. Just be aware of what you are getting into, and be sure you can re-pay the loan when you intended to.

Do all you can to force your late-paying client to pay early using accounts receivable collection strategies before choosing to let someone collect for you, or worse yet, charge you an above-market percent of capital to loan you money when you're in a less-than powerful position.

Hard Money Lenders

Accounts Receivable Financing

Accounts receivable financing can be a lifesaver when your company has a government contract that may pay ninety days or more after you invoice the organization (terms of Net 90). This is typical with Department of Education contracts, Department of Defense contracts, and others. Companies that bill hospitals and medical-insurance providers also tend to get into a cash crunch due to late receivables. If there is a cash management reason to access short-term (aka: expensive) capital, then know your options.

Accounts Receivable Financing

Factoring

Factoring

Factoring is a little different than accounts-receivable financing, but many people, even bankers, will confuse the two terms and intricacies. Both options provide advance short-term cash in exchange for fees, interest, and the future repayment of the loan based on the contract or invoice for services rendered or products sold and delivered. With factoring, the company that is providing the capital takes ownership of your invoice.

It has the right to call on it and to collect directly from the client. This might seem like a great concept. No longer are you responsible to collect on this late-paying receivable.

However, think twice. How would you feel if your client felt if he or she had a collection company, instead of you, call to collect payment? First, a lack of trust. Second, a fear that you might be in financial trouble. Usually, only a company in financial trouble needs to use the services of a factoring company. This is true for a hard-money lender. If you need one, you probably don't want to announce to your clients that you need this type if financial assistance.

Money Wise

TIP: Get a referral. Factoring companies are very particular about their clients. They want to be able to collect just as you do. Get a referral to an upstanding factoring company. It may be hard to find, but there are likely a few good factoring companies in every city. Check with your local bankers, CPAs, and even college business professors.

Factoring Example: A former professor of mine happened to work for a factoring company. One of our Edge Entrepreneurs had a contract with the US Department of Education that paid with terms of Net 90. The client ran into a cash crunch. Payment in ninety days for services rendered was not workable for this small business. However, the contract represented good income. The best cash advance scenario for this client, in that he could not reduce expenses, or improve cash flow in another way at this time, was to factor his receivables. A relationship with the professor helped secure the factoring relationship. The extra fifteen thousand dollars a month allowed the business to retain all of its employees and continue operations until the client paid what was due.

Equipment Leasing

Equipment leasing is a form of short-term financing and is an interesting one. Some banks, like Key Bank, offer it while most small and community banks do not. Equipment financing is just that. When you purchase equipment—for startups this can sometimes include the mundane like office equipment—and within a certain time period, say six months, run out of cash and need some OPM, consider re-financing your newly purchased equipment.

Say you started the company, bought computers, printers, office furniture to the tune of one hundred thousand dollars. Then, due to a client not paying you in time, you find yourself in a cash crunch.

An equipment-leasing company or bank might consider loaning you a percent of what you originally spent, based on your receipts, with fees and interest payment attached. You get some cash up front, usually 50 to 70 percent of the value; the leasing company takes ownership of the equipment you just financed; and you pay the bank a monthly interest payment. At the end of the lease, you may pay off the loan and own the equipment, or not. There are several options.

Talk to a bank that provides this type of financing first. Then compare rates, fees, and experience with equipment leasing companies. There are literally thousands out there. Short-term financing is available in many shapes and forms and with different fees, depending on the lender.

Pros: Money when you need it. Short-term, asset-backed financing. Possible last-resort financing.

Cons: Higher interest rate–the greater the risk, the higher the price of capital. Possible loss of the asset on your balance sheet is your owned equipment becomes a leased item. Possibly give up of control over your customer. Possible loss of your asset in the form of accounts receivable (AR) from your balance sheet as the factorer takes control of the AR and leaves you with only a liability.

Possible cycle of reliance on cash advances for services rendered or products delivered that is difficult from which to emerge. Possibility of loss of the business if you are not careful.

Equipment
Leasing

Peer-to-Peer Lenders

Peer-to-Peer Lenders (web-based)

Peer-to-Peer Lenders is new definition for a website that will facilitate a match or connection for an individual or a business to another business or individual who is interested to making a loan. There are many new peer-to-peer lenders popping up. Depending on the federal and state regulations, the options in this space of accessing OPM may continue to increase as it has been, or disappear altogether. The pros and cons are different for investors than they are for the business seeking capital. Let's focus on the business seeking capital and not the community organization seeking to invest and support the business.

Pros: Depending on your business industry, type of business, capital need, credit history, and the person's marketing ability who is actually making the request, the results can vary. The savvy marketer, with a good pitch, good credit, several years in business, and a former credit repayment history will rate stronger than a business owner who is not as strong or credible in those areas. In short – if you can make a good pitch, funding is more likely.

Cons: Time to funding. This is the biggest negative. If you need OPM, the interest rate might not be as much of a consideration as the timing to access the capital. Time to access your fully requested dollar amount is not guaranteed, may not happen, or may happen so late, that the funds are no longer needed – or no longer needed for the purpose for which the investment was initially requested.

Alternative Lenders can be an incredible resource for the small, emerging growth, and microentreprenreur. The key is to know your options, know who you are talking to, and know their primary function. Arm yourself with the ability to make the best possible decision regarding accessing capital for your business, project, acquisition, or expansion. So many options! You need only know the rules of the game to play!

Guide 69: Get Noticed!

Making the Most of Your Banking Relationship

Access OPA

1. Have more than one bank. Keep an account at two or more banks. You never know when one might fail or have a problem. I was a business banker with WaMu when it failed. Diversification of cash and financial institutions is a sound cash-management strategy.

2. Know your bankers. Develop a relationship with them. Let them know well in advance of your capital requirements.

3. Meet with your bankers frequently, at least every six months, as well as in advance of submitting any type of loan request.

4. Identify a specialty group within the bank. For example, Key Bank offers a Key for Women program. This might help you stand out. Chase when it was WaMu offered a Spotlight on Small Business program that allowed me, as a business banker, to highlight my clients in local branches or in a market they were trying to reach.

5. Get noticed! Banks often highlight their special clients in newsletters or internal marketing collateral. Find out how to get involved in any of these programs. Become a preferred client by having a relationship with your bank and your banker—before you need them for anything.

Access OPA

Guide 70: 5 Money Raising Questions

Five questions to ask your banker before you need the cash.

1.

Learn what they are investing in currently by asking questions like:

"Considering your last three or so business loans, in what types of businesses were the investments made?"

OR

"What are the top three industries your bank credit department has the most experience, and comfort level in, making business loans to?"

OR, best yet:

"I am considering my banking options. What types of businesses do you invest in?"

Then let them know what you are looking for—short -term capital, long-term financing, debt restructure or consolidation, or a capital investment for: construction, business purchase, business acquisition, partner buyout, equipment, employees, etc.

See what they say and how fast they are to answer. Do they get excited with you about your project? Do they want to meet right away? Or do they have a referral for you to another banker or financial institution? An unsure banker will not serve you as well or as fast as a confident one!

2. Learn the average size loan they approve by asking questions like:

"What size loan gets approved fastest at your bank: under $50,000, under $100,000, or over a certain level?"

"When you think about your most recently approved business loans, what dollar amounts have they been?"

3. Uncover how many loans they do a month in the branch you are visiting. This could be a soft discussion with the bank's relationship manager or branch manager. He or she may even share the bank's goals or branch's expectations with you. Some banks simply are not lending to new clients. You need to know if that is the case.

4. Ask which banker in the institution in your region has the most approved loans. You want that person to be your business-lending banker! Get his or her name and number and call the them!

5. Learn what loan criteria the bank has for the size loan you are thinking about. Ask for a loan application and business loan checklist. Ask what ratios the bank looks at and what it is looking for or hoping to see in your cash-flow projections, your profit-and-loss statement, and your taxes.

TIP: If you are filing a tax extension—or if you owe back taxes and are working with the IRS on that situation—get a letter from the IRS or your accountant to that effect. Your banker will want to see it.

Money Wise

Watch the Credit

Your business and personal credit go down roughly 60 points each time a bank pulls your credit report in order to review your business loan request. Your credit score will pop back to its former level, on its own, in up to six months time.

Money Wise

TIP: If you expect to be declined for a business loan from a traditional bank, and want to go to an alternative lender, ask a banker at a large bank to review your *non-signed* business loan application to assess its interest and ability to provide you funding.

When the banker comes back and says, *"Sorry, we are not likely to help you because of x, y, and ,"* ask for that decline in an email or a note.

Once a traditional lender has declined you in this way, you will have preserved your credit, and will be able to work with an alternative lender. If the traditional lender doesn't want to write anything down (this can be expected due to liability in that the bank actually doesn't have a signed business loan application and thus could not have performed an actual credit check or made a decision on credit), then simply tell the alternative lender who declined you and what the lender said.

This will likely be enough information for the loan officer from an alternative lender, or CDFI, to feel comfortable that it is not stealing a loan opportunity from a traditional bank—which would go against its lending policy and guidelines.

Guide 71: Debt vs. Equity

Access OPA

Raising Money

Capital requirements are a measure of how much capital a firm needs to stay in business, expand its business, or complete a project that is outside the day-to-day scope of its existing business.

OPM comes in two generic forms: equity or debt.

Learning to navigate the maze of funding options for your business can be daunting. This section of the *Toolkit* offers the existing business owner as well as the potential entrepreneur the information they need to secure equity or debt funding for their business and to improve their loan application.

> *Have you used up your savings to start or expand your business?*
> *Do you wonder what lenders look for when approving loans?*
> *Are you unsure of where to get capital to expand your business?*

Whether you need funding to expand operations or to start a new venture, *Show Me the Money* will shed some light on some of the rules of the game.

According to many, the final element that determines whether you are ready to become an entrepreneur is if you are able to raise significant amounts of money from investors. If you can make other people believe in your dream and share your goals so that they are willing to invest hard-earned cash in your venture, chances are you have what it takes.

Debt versus Equity

Typically, financing falls into two fundamental types: debt financing and equity financing.

Debt Financing

Debt financing is when you borrow money that will be repaid over a period of time, usually with interest. Debt financing can be either short-term—full repayment due in less than one year—or long-term where—repayment is due in five to seven years or more. The lender does not gain an ownership interest in your business and your obligations are limited to repaying the loan. Some loans can convert to equity. These are called convertible notes.

Equity Financing

Equity financing describes an exchange of money for a share of business ownership. This form of financing allows you to obtain funds without incurring debt. In other words, you are not required to repay a specific amount of money at any particular time. The investor still expects a return for his or her investment—just not in the form of loan payments.

Money Wise

TIP: The major disadvantage to equity financing is the dilution of your ownership interests and the possible loss of control that may accompany a sharing of ownership with additional investors.

Debt Versus Equity: What Is It Anyway?

Essentially, the entrepreneur has two basic choices when considering financing:

*Pledging a part of one's soul
or giving a piece of it away*

In terms of OPM and business financing the following are some differences between debt and equity.

Typical Return on Investment (ROI)

Investors who capitalize your business will expect very different returns on their investment, depending on whether they are lending you money (debt) or taking a part of your business in exchange for the cash (equity).

The following is a typical breakdown of expected returns on investment and what you might expect as a business owner from each of the types of capitalization.

Debt	Equity
Repaid	Not repaid
No ownership dilution ROI ~ 2 - 20% ROI within 5 – 10 years Personal guarantee 30 - 120 days to funding	Dilutes owners equity ROI >20% (3 - 10X Return) ROI within 3 - 5 years No personal guarantee 6 months to 1 year for funding

Loans and Patient Capital

Debt is repaid to the lender with interest. There is patient capital— investors who may be interested in your well-being or the mission of your company or who just, for some reason or another, are not interested in getting their money back any time soon. There are patient investment groups, like Investor's Circle out of California. This group seeks to invest in companies that are eco-friendly and make socially responsible or triple bottom line investments. They are interested in a return, just not in as short of a period as a non-patient capital lender. They also may invest in equity or quasi-equity, an equity investment with some interest paid or that which may turn into debt.

Loans that Turn Into Equity

There is also a combination of debt and equity that looks like debt, but that may convert into equity. This capitalization option is called a convertible note. This is a very common type of investment today and more micro and small businesses, social enterprises, and even fast emerging growth companies use this investment vehicle.

Access OPA

Guide 72: Finding Funding

Have you ever wondered where to find a business loan? Look no further. The following are some common places to look if you are seeking debt financing for your small business.

Personal Loan to the Business

This is where you loan your business money, document that fact with a promissory note, and repay yourself on a schedule, as needed or upon exit from the business.

If you have been using your personal cash flow to operate the business, it can only be considered capital investment in your business if you document such as either debt or equity. Debt = personal loan. Equity = ownership interest. Your equity investment increases the value of the business and increases your potential leverage—or access to capital—into the future.

Friends and Family Loan to the Business

See above. Document. Document. Document.

Traditional Debt: Bank Loans, Lines of Credit, Home Equity Loans, Equipment Financing, Some Accounts Receivable Financing

Traditional debt financing is found at traditional financial institutions. Revisit the guide *Better Borrowing* for an overview of traditional and alternative financial institutions and the guide *Money Raising Questions* to learn what to ask a banker to assess a good fit for your business.

Alternative Financing: Short Term Financing (Cash Advance), Factoring, Patient Capital, Community Development Financing, Microlending, Peer Lending

Alternative debt financing is found at alternative financial institutions and even non-financial institutions. Revisit the guide Better Borrowing for an overview of traditional and alternative financial institutions.

TIP: Alternative financing is more expensive to the borrower than traditional financing. Check with the big guys first. See if you qualify for traditional financing, and then seek alternative financing to bridge the gap until you can qualify.

Money Wise

Equity: Personal Investors, Angel Investors, Partners, VC's, Banks, Family Offices, Angel Investment Clubs, Institutional Capital

To learn all about equity financing in your area find a club or association that serves fast growth entrepreneurs. Some such organizations are the MIT Forum, Northwest Entrepreneur Network, or a similar network in your region, college business plan competitions. The business plan judges are typically local investors and bankers, college business instructors, business attorneys, securities attorneys, angel investment clubs, and associations like Kieritsu Forum and Alliance of Angels.

TIP: Get involved in the community. You will learn a ton, make connections, and develop relationships. Equity financing is much about relationship building.

Money Wise

Strategic Partners, Joint Ventures, Partnerships

This is the fun part! Visit the guides *Strategic Coopetition* and *The Quick Plan's Getting Direct with Strategic Direct Marketing* to put you in the right mind set to begin to do this in a strategic manner. To secure funds—debt or equity, some combination of the two, or a new model altogether—one must think outside the box. In fact, who said there is a box? There is no box when it comes to strategic funding through partnerships or joint ventures.

Access OPA

Guide 73: Business Loan Checklist

What information does my banker want to see?

Money Wise

Typical Bank Financing Checklist

_____ Bank Loan Application

TIP: Don't sign yet! But do complete it. Signing authorizes credit check and processing which may be pre-mature until you know that you are choosing this banking institution.

_____ 3 Years of Business Financial Statements
(Profit-and-loss statement and Year-end balance sheet)

_____ 3 Years of Business Taxes (signed, executed, and current)

_____ Personal Financial Statement

_____ 3 Years of Personal Taxes (signed, executed, and current)

_____ Market Capitalization Table
List of owners with over 10 percent and their percent of ownership. They may need to sign loan and bank-related documents.

_____ Business License / Proof of Ownership

TIP: The banker may pay a visit to your state's Secretary of State website and or the Department of Revenue to see whom you have listed as board members and/or owners. Any of these individuals listed there may be required to provide personal information in order for the bank to consider a loan request.

Money Wise

Be aware of the bank's policies and procedures regarding minority shareowners and or investors. What you consider a *silent partner* may not be so silent to the banker.

_____ Cash Flow Projection for 12 to 18 Months (or more depending on the business)

TIP: The Cash-flow projection lets the banker know that you have free cash flow to cover: 1.) loan expense (interest and/or principle) of the new loan request, 2.) owner's salary, 3.) employees, and 4.) general operations of the business.

Money Wise

In your projections, cash flow, and income, don't forget to pay yourself. Banks and government guaranteed lenders don't like owners to bootstrap for more than a few months. They fear your business may fail due to the owner (you) getting tired of not being paid.

If you, as the owner do not need income from your business—at least initially—you may need to show that your other income: from investments, savings, another day job, or inheritance, can cover your day-to-day bottom line.

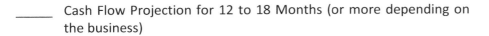
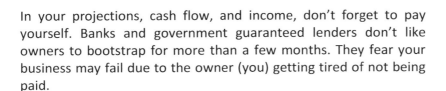

Access OPA

Guide 74: When a Bank Doesn't Feel Right

But you still need OPM (Other People's Money)

Alternative Lender FAQ

What is an Alternative Lender?

An alternative lender can be a loan fund associated with a non-bank entity. The fund could be administered by a nonprofit organization or government agency with a specific mission. Applicants must meet criteria to be eligible for their lending programs.

Loan funds may focus on supporting economic development, job creation, business retention, or helping underserved populations to access capital.

There are several in every state. On the Entrepreneurial Edge Series website (www.EntrepreneurialEdgeSeries.com), you will find a list of all Community Development Financial Institutions (CDFIs) in each state. Check yours out. They may offer both access to capital investment as well as free business help.

Be Prepared to Access Capital Before You Need It

You will need to collect much the same data and due diligence for an alternative lender as you would for a bank. In addition to the requirements in a business loan application, an alternative lender might ask for the following information. Most will have their own loan checklist. Ask for it.

1. Business Plan Information

   In addition to your executive business plan, and marketing plan, an alternative lender will want to know how your business skills have prepared you for success in your venture. For each person owning 20 percent or more of your business, describe the business skills acquired from previous work experience, training, and education with a focus on skills necessary to successfully operate your business. Use the entrepreneur assessment tools in the *Startup Success* guides to help. Talk about your strengths. You have them. Now get them on paper.

2. Business Assets Requirements

   List your business asset requirements. Include the answers to the following questions: How much cash do you need to cover six to twelve months of operating expenses? What are your inventory needs? What equipment, furniture, fixtures, leasehold improvements, or vehicles do you need? Are you buying property? Are you building something? What about new hires? Think about everything for which you need cash. You may not include it all, but at least do the big picture planning.

3. Personal and Business Assets

   List all of your personal and business assets that are available to secure your loan request. Yes, personal too. Alternative lenders can use personal assets to secure a business loan, unlike a bank. However, banks like to see marketable securities (your stocks and mutual funds not in a retirement account). They can sometimes use those as collateral.

   An alternative lender can get creative. Do you have a car, a second car, a boat, jet skis? What else? Include all business assets at cost and all personal assets at market value. Include the latest appraised value or your property tax assessment if you intend to use real estate as collateral.

Money Wise

4. Projected Financial Statements
   TIP: Base you projections on the assumption that you will get the loan. Also, be sure you demonstrate by the numbers that you need funding. If you demonstrate that you don't need a capital investment, the banker won't know why you submitted the loan request.
   a. Balance Sheet: Include a current, startup, or projected balance sheet. If you create a pro forma, or projected, balance sheet, include your use of loan proceeds and the loan amount.
   b. Cash Flow: Month-by-month projections through post investment break-even.
   c. Income Statement: Include a month-by-month statement projected through post-investment break-even.
   d. Key Assumptions: A complete description of any issues that affect the financial projections.

5. Business Financial Statements
   If available, provide the last three years of fiscal statements including a balance sheet, income statement, and the most current interim statements (must be within forty-five to sixty days of date of application). Be sure to sign and date all documents.

6. Business Tax Returns: If available, provide for the last three years.

7. Personal Financial Statements
   Provide a personal financial statement for each person with twenty percent or more ownership. Some banks, such as HSBC, require this information for those with ten percent ownership or more. The lender can provide a form.

8. Personal Tax Returns
   Provide three years of personal tax returns for each person with twenty percent or more ownership in the business.

9. Copy of Lease
   If you are renting space to conduct your business, provide a copy of your unsigned lease agreement (if available) or proposed leasing terms.

   TIP: Don't execute a lease until you have financing secured or the income to cover the huge expense. A lease or rent payment can be between seven and ten percent of your gross income based on industry averages, and industry averages vary! With much more than eight

Money Wise

percent and any business may get itself into a cash crunch. Watch this expense line item. If you feel you must sign a lease to get into that perfect space, then make sure it has a "contingent upon lessee financing" clause. That way, if you don't get the funding you hope for, you can step away from the financial commitment. And watch out for personal guarantees. Most property owners and managers know that a business may not make it, but the owners will go on to live a long and prosperous life. They will likely force you to sign personally for the business expense. We advise against it, but it a tough one to win in your negotiation. Good luck!

Some Alternative Lenders will help you assemble this information; others expect you to do it on your own. If they ask you to do it, find help. The SBA programs, like SCORE and the Women's Business Centers, can help. There are other free technical assistance programs too. Get help. This is a tough process. Some even hire a *CFO to go* service to find loans for them. We don't recommend it—at least not the first time around. You are the business owner and need to know what the banker or lender needs. Plus, you tell your story best, not someone you hire. Later, once you know what the lenders require, hire an expert to help. It will save you time and money while you focus on growing and managing your business.

How are alternative lenders different from a bank?
Unlike a bank, alternative lenders generally are able to stretch a little more in some of the credit evaluation categories.

They look for strengths to offset weaknesses and they can take on more risk. Alternative lenders also provide a higher level of individual attention than banks can afford to do. Most alternative lenders offer training, business consulting, or other assistance to help their borrowers strengthen their management skills, credit capacity, and grow their businesses.

By providing carefully structured loans and customer support, alternative lenders are able to cultivate otherwise unbankable companies into successful and bankable businesses.

Guide 75: Scoring an A+ with the Five Cs of Credit

Positioning for Success

The Five Cs of Credit (and how can I score an A+?)

Securing financing is often one of the first steps to successfully owning and running a business. Even the serial entrepreneur may not realize there are some basic rules to borrowing. So that you don't stroll confidently into a bank for a small business loan only to be turned down, or worse yet, be given no answer at all, here are some tips. Knowing what a lender looks for can help you evaluate which type of financing is right for you and if you are right for financing.

Community development lenders and traditional banks will consider the five Cs of credit each time they make a loan. All borrowers need either a business plan or a marketing plan to present to the lender. The business plan and your financial projections are your opportunity as the borrower to mitigate the risks of the five Cs. Be sure to address each of the five Cs in your business's loan proposal.

Access OPA

Five Cs of Credit

1. Capacity

2. Cash Flow

3. Capital

4. Collateral

5. Character

Capacity

Capacity is your ability to operate your business successfully and, through the course of the business, repay your debts. You can demonstrate your capacity by the thoroughness of your business plan, the quality of your financial projections, your financial and business assumptions, and your personal experience.

How to Score an A+ in Capacity

A+ in capacity is a "been there, done that" business owner who can demonstrate proven success in the same industry.

How to mitigate: If this is your first business or your first business loan, demonstrate to the lender, through your business plan, the experience (hands-on, other work, training, etc.) you bring to the business that will lend to your success—especially in the area of financial management.

Cash Flow

Cash flow shows the lender the probability of successful repayment of the loan. It is the most important of the five Cs to the US Small Business Administration, backers of eighty percent of all small business loans in the United States.

How to Score an A+ in Cash Flow

A+ cash flow will show timing of the disbursements and repayment of the loan. The cash flow from the business will: 1.) pay the entrepreneur, 2.) pay employees, 3.) re-pay the loan, and 4.) should *cash-flow*, or become cash-flow positive, within twelve to fifteen months from the loan request.

How to mitigate: If your business does not demonstrate that it can achieve positive cash flow within one year, then continue projecting your financials until it does. This will usually occur within the second twelve-month period, but in certain equipment heavy industries, it may take longer. This exercise may uncover opportunities for a change in your revenue model, pricing model, or even your target customer.

Capital

Capital is considered the money you personally have invested in the business and is an indication of how much you will lose should the business fail. Capital Demonstrates your cash contribution, and your commitment, to your business.

How to Score an A+ in Capital

An A+ in capital is a business owner who can demonstrate on the balance sheet that they have invested in their business, and that they are able to fund twenty percent or more of the project funding request with cash. In fact, demonstrating that you have cash to contribute can sometimes lower your capital contribution requirement.

Lenders never will invest 100 percent of your project. Rather, they will look at your request for financing and assume that they will contribute up to 80 percent of the project cost in the form of a loan, and the other 20 percent will be investment by the owner(s).

How to mitigate: An A+ in capital requires cash. This can be tricky for a business owner that is seeking financing, but not impossible. The bottom line is that you need to come up with enough of a cash contribution to the project to make the lender feel comfortable.

Sources of capital can include retained earnings from the business, equity investment from friends or family, liquidating investments, or personal savings (from keeping your day job until you can afford to start the business).

Here are some creative ways I have seen clients seek capital and secure the loan:
- Loan your business cash, and subordinate the loan to the bank (let the real lender get paid back first).
- Get a personal loan from friends or family and invest the cash in your business. Make sure to reflect the investment or cash on the balance sheet. Your assets will go up and so will your equity.
- Have friends or family pledge assets to you like cars, boats, land, vacation property, recreational equipment like jet skis. The added collateral might mitigate the capital risk.
- Have a friend or family member provide a guarantee for the loan. Different from a co-signor, a guarantee lends an additional form of repayment in case the cash flow of the business is not sufficient.

Collateral

Collateral or guarantees are additional forms of security the lender looks for in a loan request. Specifically a lender looks for 100 percent to 130 percent of the project's cost in the form of collateral. If the business cannot repay its loan, the bank wants to know there is a second source of repayment. Assets such as equipment, buildings, accounts receivable, and in some cases, inventory, are considered possible sources of repayment if they are sold by the bank for cash. Both business and personal assets can be sources of collateral for a loan.

How to Score an A+ in Collateral

A+ collateral for a loan over thirty-five thousand must include real estate in addition to other forms of collateral to secure the loan.

Ways to mitigate: A guarantee might mitigate the risk of too little collateral. This is when someone else signs a guarantee document promising to repay the loan if you can't.

Character

Character is assessed by your payment history on existing credit relationships—personal and commercial. To a banker, your present credit situation is an indicator of future payment performance. Nonprofit lenders do not look at a *credit score* per se and the credit requirements vary from lender to lender.

How to Score an A+ in Character

A+ in character is reflected in one's credit report by showing no liens, judgments, or bankruptcies and a solid repayment history for the past six months. The credit officer, loan committee, or risk manager will assess your ability to repay debt in a very logical and calculated way. Some considerations from your credit report are demonstration that all monies owed are being paid as agreed and/or have been consistently repaid within thirty days and is your access to revolving credit within a comfortable level considering the new loan debt request.

Ways to mitigate: In some instances, you cannot mitigate poor credit. That said, if a bankruptcy is due to medical reasons, it might not affect the credit review process. Some business owners will bring in a co-signer on the loan or a partner with strong credit history to help mitigate risk.

Your business credit history, your business credit references, and the business credit score can demonstrate business character. The owner's credit score may be considered as well.

A banker will look to your access to other credit as well. If you have credit cards, the available credit on those cards, personal- and business-related, are considered a liability and may count against you as if you have already spent, or used that credit.

They will calculate what your credit limit is on all credit cards or available lines of credit, consider it debt, and add it to their financial ratio calculations.

Also considered is your use of revolving credit. The mechanics of credit scoring is as secret as Google's search engine algorithm. But, the basics are: don't use more than 80% of your available credit—ever—and never close a credit card. However, do reduce your available credit limits to within thirty percent of what you might need.

If you have an excess in credit card limits that you never use or touch, seek advice on whether or not it is a good idea to lower your credit card limits before applying for your business loan.

Getting an A in Credit
Alternative lenders are able to lend in some instances where a traditional bank could not, like poor credit due to medical, divorce, or bankruptcy.

Don't assume that because your credit score is not in the 700's or 800's or because of a former bankruptcy that you cannot access a capital investment for your business.

Credit can be repaired in as little as six months. If this business is your passion and you need an investment of capital to make it happen, then seek advice. Armed with the basic rules of the access to capital game, you can play.

Guide 76: Credit Worthiness Assessment

Access OPA

Based on the five Cs of credit, what are your strengths? What about your weaknesses? This guide will help you assess both strengths and weaknesses to help you prepare your business loan application. You want to be able to mitigate any weaknesses. The better you can address the five Cs of credit with your banker, the higher your success rate will likely become and the lower you interest rate!

5 Cs of Credit Assessment	Strengths	Weaknesses
Capacity Do you have a business plan? Advisory board? Are you a' *been there, done that*' business owner?		
Collateral Do you have collateral lined up in excess of 130% of your project's cost (not the loan amount)?		
Cash Flow Do you have cash flow projections that bring you to break-even? Do you break even within 12-15 months? Are you able to pay yourself, pay your employees, repay the loan, and have excess cash?		
Capital Can you or did you contribute 20 percent of the project's cost?		
Character How is your business credit? Personal credit? Have you repaid debt as agreed? Have you reviewed your revolving credit limits?		

Access OPA

Guide 77: Structure of Debt Financing

There are several different loan programs and loan structuring options when it comes to alternative lenders. What this means to the small business owner, entrepreneur, or *potential* small business owner is that you have research to do before you go out in search of capital.

How do I know how much money I can ask for?

It helps if you know the general rules of lending before you talk to your banker or a potential lender. Here are some standard rules of debt financing to get you started. Just figure that a traditional lender will likely be more conservative on all accounts. Here is a snapshot of the structure of debt financing.

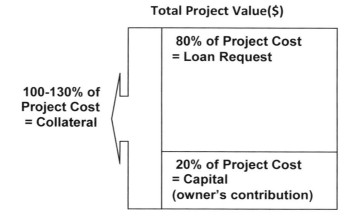

Total Project Value($)

80% of Project Cost = Loan Request

100-130% of Project Cost = Collateral

20% of Project Cost = Capital (owner's contribution)

Project Cost or Project Value
This is the value of your total project—the loan amount needed plus your capital contribution. You never want simply to tell bankers how much you need.

Instead, let them know what the value of the project is, your capital contribution, and pledged collateral first. Then let them know how much you are looking for. If you follow the model, they are already calculating in their head as you share your story, and you are more likely to pique their interest.

Loan Amount
Even alternative lenders prefer to lend only 80 percent of the total cost of your project (a project cost is the total amount of funds you need to accomplish your business goals). They hope that you have at least 20 percent of the total project cost in the form of cash. Your cash. So you are a contributor to your business and have some *skin* in the game. This total is reflected as capital.

Collateral
Also, they look for about 120 - 130 percent of the project cost (not loan amount) in the form of collateral, the assets you plan to pledge to the lender that they will become owners of in case you default on the loan. A traditional bank may have a minimum of 130 percent or higher, while an alternative lender may have some flexibility on collateral. Some alternative lending programs require no collateral at all!

One such example is an SBA Community Express Loan offered through many Community Development Financial Institutions (CDFIs). A Community Express loan is for up to fifty thousand dollars and is unsecured, which means it does not require collateral. Ask your bank or alternative lender if either offers this type of loan and if it might be a good fit for your business.

Capital
The 20 percent that fills the gap between what you ask for and what you need is the cash contribution the bank wants to see that you can make, or have made. Each lender is different; some need this to be actual cash in a business account, while others will look at your owner's equity on the balance sheet to see that over time you have invested back into your business.

The Capital Question

Questions to ask your banker before you apply for a loan:

- What are your loan limits?
- What is the average size small business loan?
- What types of unsecured loan products do you have access to?
- What is your ideal debt structure?
- How much owner's capital do you like to see? Can it be already invested in my business, or do you want to see a capital contribution to this project?
- How much of the project cost can you fund?
- What type of collateral will you accept?
- Do you require real estate as collateral?
- What percent of the project cost do you require in collateral?

How much can an alternative lender actually lend?
Loan limits, interest rates, and terms will vary from fund to fund. However it is typical for a CDFI or alternative lender to be able to loan as little as $500 and up to $250,000. Some lenders can leverage their capital with community banks and lend you even more.

More frequently, an alternative lender provides investment capital under one million dollars and when your business becomes *bankable* by a tradition bank, the alternative lender will graduate you to a non-economic development bank. The traditional bank can then lend you the money to pay off your other loans, usually at a lower rate.

The term of an alternative lender's loan generally varies from institution, but usually lasts from one to seven years, similar to a more traditional lender like a bank.

Et voilà! Whether you are seeking debt or equity financing, or simply need to run the numbers of your business to answer the question, *"When can I stop putting money into my business and start taking it out?"* you are armed with the rules of the financial game.

Guide 78: Introduction to Equity

Access OPA

There are two primary definitions of equity—a definition for business and another for real estate.

1. Equity for businesses or stocks
    Equity is defined as an ownership stake in a company. Shareholder's equity is equal to assets minus liabilities.

2. Equity for real estate
    Equity is defined as the residual ownership claim on a home's value. Equity equals the fair market value of a home, less any mortgage debt or other obligations.

Where to get it—equity

- Personal investment into the business
- Earnings from the business that are kept in the business
- The three Fs: friends, family, and fools
- Investors: angels, sophisticated investors, accredited Investors, and investment clubs
- Venture capital or community development venture capital companies
- Family offices - a wealth management company that caters to an individual family or a small group of families
- Strategic partners, joint ventures, partnerships

Money Wise

TIP: Traditional venture capital companies may be too big to realistically consider as minimum investments average two to $50 million. However, there are patient capital venture capital companies, managing community development venture capital (CDVC) funds. A CDVC might invest between $250,000 and $2 million and can be a fit for an expanding small business.

Access OPA

Guide 79: Show Me an Angel!

Individual private investors are commonly and affectionately known as "angels". Along with family and friends, they provide the vast majority of funding for entrepreneurial companies. They may invest in either debt (typically convertible) or equity or combinations.

How do I find an angel?

There are several angel investment clubs around the country. You will find a list in the back of this section for your use and research.

Further, there are several organizations that serve the angel investment community by offering angel-investment training seminars and tools. One such group is the Kauffman Foundation. The Kauffman Foundation held an Angel Investor 101 class for a full day before a large investment conference years ago. It was neat to see that even the investors needed mentoring and training on how to evaluate an equity investment opportunity.

The Angel Capital Association's website includes a directory of all their angel investment club members, including a link to their website. This is an exhaustive list of active angel-investment groups all over the country.

It will help you as the entrepreneur considering seeking capital from equity investors to know what they look for, how they evaluate investment opportunities, and what happens at the angel-investment luncheons or investment meetings.

You can't play the game if you don't know the rules. Here are some tips from my experience on both sides of the table.

I was a member of the first all women angel-investment club, Seraph Capital, early in my career. I had achieved some success writing business plans for companies that successfully raised millions and was an investment banker (a.k.a. fundraiser), so my experience was relevant. I served Seraph Capital as a volunteer on its investment committee and with a team of about seven other women, we screened each applicant's business plan, based on our screening criteria, for possible selection to present at an investment luncheon.

The investment committee would select only the top three to four out of forty investment candidates to present for a chance at investment capital.

The angel group would have a monthly luncheon meeting where the top selected business teams that were seeking investment from the club investment members would present, one group at a time. The audience, a room full of about forty to fifty angel investors, would ask the business owners questions, hear the responses, and then ask the presenters to leave the room. This gave the angels time to talk with one-another and, in an active, participatory environment, poke holes in the presenter's business plan, business model, strategies, goals, presentation, and anything else that concerned them. Then the next group would present, and the process would begin again.

The investors in an angel investment group, like Seraph Capital, typically will not pool their monies together, but they will make their own investment decisions, separate from one another. This does not mean that more than one person from the group won't invest. On the contrary. Many times several investments come from a single investment group. In fact, many angel investment groups require that the presenter set aside, or allocate a certain amount of equity for that group so they have the ability to invest. No one wants to see a presentation, get excited about the company, and then hear she can't invest because the business leadership team has raised enough money elsewhere.

In an angel investment round, the investment club will ask for between $250,000 and $2,000,000 as a set-aside for their group.

Seraph Capital is still active today, along with Zino Society, Kieritsu Forum, Alliance of Angels, and hundreds more—angel groups are a great place to secure investment capital in the early stages of business.

Guide 80: The Perfect 10-minute Pitch

The Alliance of Angels in Seattle, Washington is home to many Baby Bills—employees of Microsoft in the early days whose stock options turned them into millionaires, many of whom then became angel investors—is one of the oldest angel investment clubs in the United States.

The Alliance of Angels has been vetting upstart businesses for potential investment for years and has the investment pitch down to a streamlined and simplified process. Investment clubs across the United States use this model. It is a great place to start when you are considering putting together an investor presentation to seek angel, or any type, of equity investment.

The following is the best description of what an investor wants to see in a pitch deck, or equity financing presentation.

Angel Presentation Pitch Guidelines

The following is the Alliance of Angels recommendations for each section of the perfect ten minute pitch.

The angel-investment club members are very interested in knowing about the progress and direction of your company. As would any investor, they value transparency and integrity, as well as a succinct, well-thought-out presentation containing the following components:

Introduction - Two elements: First, remember to introduce yourself; and next, in one sentence, tell what your company does. (15 - 20 seconds)

The Problem - Describe the qualitative and quantitative view of the problem. Using a story or scenario is helpful. (30 seconds)

The Solution - Describe your product or service in terms of benefits. Your visual aid should contain screenshots, photos, simple architectural diagram or work flow diagram. Show a value-chain diagram if it is important to show how your solution fits in with other products or services. (1 - 2 minutes)

Traction Slide - Bullet point milestones include: patents filed, signed contracts with partners, revenue booked, number of customers, number of employees, year founded. (15 seconds)

Market Size - Describe the total addressable market. Describe how the market is segmented, ideally in pie graph or some other graphical form. Build these numbers from their constituent parts using drivers that are relevant to your business. (30 seconds)

Start playing chess instead of checkers

Customers - Current and/or potential. There is nothing more powerful than customers to prove your claims about the market. Logos work best. If you have a large number of customers, cite the total number and average revenue a customer is worth to you for emphasis. Be sure to differentiate between paying and non-paying customers. If you have no customers, use this slide to describe who your target customers are and/or who your ideal customer would be. (1 minute)

Business/Revenue Model - State how you price your product/service, what the economics of a sale are in terms of COGS, dealer commissions, distributor percentages if applicable. Explain your one-time vs. recurring revenue sources, estimates, etc. Identify sources of revenue and cost, with an eye to profitability. (30 - 60 seconds)

Marketing Plan/Sales Cycle - How long? Who are the decision makers and influencers of your customers? In what type of sales or sales-support activities are you or your people engaging? (30 - 60 seconds)

Partners - Name names rather than generic categories, qualify the status of agreements or if it is pre-agreement let investors know that X partner has a need, desire, or history of doing what you need him or her to do. (30 seconds)

Competition - Orient investors to your direct and indirect competition. This slide is another opportunity to highlight your differential advantage. A matrix or grid can be compelling. (30 - 60 seconds)

Management Team - Name, title, previous experience. Be brief in your explanation. Do not explain what each person does in your company. Don't forget to include any positions you are seeking to fill. (30 - 60 seconds)

Board of Advisors - Include those business advisors who help you, know you, believe in you, and agree to be spokespeople for your company if called. (15 – 30 seconds)

Financial Projections - Show your "hockey stick" in bar graph form with bars for revenue and income for five years of projections. Clearly bullet point assumptions that drive these projections. (30 seconds)

The Offer (a.k.a Funding Slide) - Describe prior funding, current round offer, pre-money valuation, use of proceeds/milestones, any future rounds of financing anticipated, commentary on exit strategy. For our group, we recommend this as the closing slide. (30 seconds)

The above are guidelines, not absolute rules. You should use your own discretion as to how these guidelines apply to you and your company. Angel investment clubs, like the Alliance of Angels, will typically work with applicant companies on messaging that resonates with their angel investor community.

What does an angel investor expect to see?

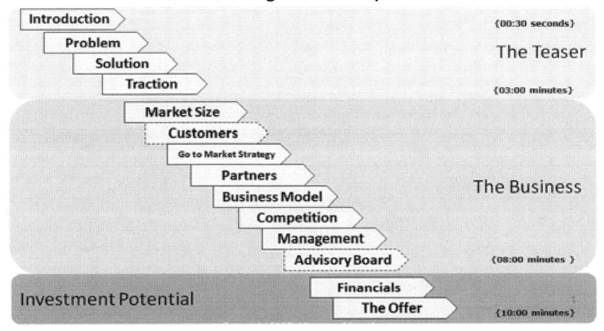

Last: Next Steps

You are armed with solutions, strategies, and tools to help you master two of the Money Rules: Present it! and Access It! When it comes to accessing Other People's Assets—and OPM in particular—knowing the rules of the finance game is key to your success.

Finance and fundraising are an art—not a science. But there are some rules to the game. When you know the rules, you can start playing chess instead of checkers; start being strategic in the game that is business.

Show Me the Money To Do's

- Create my 10 Minute Investor Pitch
- Select my perfect bank--or non-bank
- Pull together my business loan package—so I'm ready when I need it.

Still Ahead

- Create a leadership dashboard
- Learn to implement a relationship sales cycle
- Design my perfect sales process
- Develop a powerful pipeline

Show Me the Money!
Certificate of Completion

The benchmark of business success is the ability to secure outside investment.

If someone else believes in your business enough to risk their capital, then you must have made it. Right? We believe that whether you are bootstrapping your business—or seeking OPM—you can have a successful venture. This section of the *Toolkit* was about understanding the rules of the finance game so that you can play–*if you want to.*

Understanding what a banker wants to see in your business plan and knowing what to include in an investor presentation are necessary tools for entrepreneurs. Now you are armed with the tools. You completed guides 68 through 80 now it's time to reward the commitment.

Completed Guides
Guide 68: Better Borrowing
Guide 69: Get Noticed!
Guide 70: 5 Money Raising Questions
Guide 71: Debt vs. Equity
Guide 72: Finding Funding
Guide 73: Business Loan Checklist
Guide 74: When a Bank Doesn't Feel Right
Guide 75: Scoring an A+ with the Five Cs of Credit
Guide 76: Credit Worthiness Assessment
Guide 77: Structure of Debt Financing
Guide 78: Introduction to Equity
Guide 79: Show Me an Angel!
Guide 80: The Perfect 10 Minute Pitch

Complete your certificate of completion on the following page to memorialize your accomplishments.

Congratulations!

Entrepreneurial Edge

Small Business Toolkit

Certificate of Completion

I certify that I, _____, have successfully completed

Show Me the Money!

Including Core Business Principle™ Debt vs. Equity and
Money Rules: Project It! Present It! Access It! Manage It! and Control It!

SPROUT!

Signature: _____ Date: _____

Chapter 9: **Leading My Business**

Guides

Leadership in real-time.

Takeaways:

Understand the importance of strategic management to a small business.
Implement "FACT-based" financial controls in your new venture.
Design and implement a sales process for your venture.
Understand the importance of controls such as the leadership dashboard in entrepreneurial business management.

Guide 81: Creating Value with a Leadership Dashboard

A leadership dashboard is a key management tool that helps you lead through change, manage day-to-day operations, and grow your business with precision.

Planning for future growth is important. In planning for what is to come, a leadership dashboard can help you stay focused on the important drivers of your business: the customer, your financials, sales and marketing, and the changes that you face during your business life cycle.

Your leadership dashboard includes the top ten value drivers you must understand and control so that you can lead your business through change and toward success. Create yours today.

4 Keys to Creating Value

The four keys to creating value in your business are the following value drivers:

1. Customer Focus
2. Financial Focus
3. Marketing Focus
4. Leadership Focus

We coach dozens of clients whose businesses generate five million dollars in revenue and up. But we coach thousands of clients generating five hundred thousand and less. The key drivers in your financial dashboard are the same, whether you are a very small business or about to reach middle market. Master these leadership dashboard drivers now. You will reap the benefits today and tomorrow.

Create Value by Focusing on Your Customer

Customer Focus

Customers are *key*. We thrive when we have a value-based service or product, know our top customer's characteristics, and plan ahead, based on buying trends.

1. Leadership Dashboard Driver: 80-20 Rule. The top 20 percent of your current customer base <u>drive</u> revenue. To have a forward focus, identify the top 20 percent of your customer base. Learn all you can about this key segment of clients. Refer back to the business design model to help to get clarity on their characteristics. Identifying more customers like them is your forward focus and a key driver in your leadership dashboard. If you are just starting your business, plan for your ideal customer using the guides in this *Toolkit*.

2. Leadership Dashboard Driver: Customer Characteristics. Your customer's buying behavior and spending trends play a part in the seasonality of your business. Knowing your customer's characteristics help you plan for staffing, inventory, and cash management needs. Understanding these drivers will allow you to ramp up staffing or ramp down operations, based on actual data. If you are new to business, seek the advice of other businesses in your business neighborhood through a chamber of commerce or a merchant group to learn the key sales characteristics of the area to help you create value in your business.

3. Leadership Dashboard Driver: Customer Benefits. Focusing on customer benefits will allow you to develop a strategic direct marketing plan to help you reach your ideal customer in more cost-effective and unique ways. Knowing the benefits of your product or service from your customer's perspective helps you embrace and implement strategic direct marketing and relationship selling.

Create Value with a Financial Focus

Financial Focus

Keep score of your business using FACT based financial controls, profit mastery, managing growth, and borrowing properly.

4. Leadership Dashboard Driver: Profit Mastery. Cash is *king*. Stay on top of your cash situation. Take time to prepare cash flow projections for the next twelve to fifteen months and revise weekly if needed. Create a cash budget graph to map out trends. Visit the US Small Business Administration if you need assistance creating a cash flow projection for the first time. QuickBooks will not do this for you.

5. Leadership Dashboard Driver FACT-Based Financial Controls. Create a schedule and set a routine: frequent, accurate, complete, and timely (FACT) financials will allow you to track your key income drivers, cash sinks, and keep you in the driver's seat. Financial controls will be different for each business, but key components include financial tracking and management, financial statement preparation and projections, taxes and tax strategy, budget modeling, expense controls, bank reconciliation, and receivable monitoring.

6. Leadership Dashboard Driver: Plan Properly for Growth and Transition. Talk to your banker! Don't rely on key employees or contractors to meet with your banker for you. Relationships are important. Banking is no different. Meet with your banker at least six months before you need anything. Let them help you prepare for the best possible outcome—before you need any source of financing. Borrow property. Know the five Cs of lending, the appropriate structure of debt financing, and ins and outs of equity financing.

Create Value by Developing Me, Inc.

Marketing Focus

Social media marketing and developing *Me, Inc.* as a brand are key value drivers in your business. And don't forget about your website as a strategic value-creation tool!

7. Leadership Dashboard Driver: Brand You! It's a new brand world. Monitor your online brand presence. You are your brand! Do you have a professional bio? A social media marketing plan? What will someone find when he or she *Google's* your name or your business name? Monitor your online brand presence.

8. Leadership Dashboard Driver: Social Media Marketing. Develop a social media marketing plan. Every business needs a Facebook page, and every business should secure their twitter handle—if nothing else for your use into the future. These are free tools. Over 400 million people are online and 20 million join fan pages each day. Don't let the new social networks scare you! Take a class or go it alone. But, have a plan.

9. Leadership Dashboard Driver: Acquire, Engage, Convert. Take it to the web. Your website can be the hub of customer acquisition and retention. No business should be without a website. Even if it directs people to your Facebook Fan or business page. Use your website for lead qualification, lead generation, prospect engagement and education, and awareness generation. Simple, low-cost options abound!

Create Value by Leading and Managing Change

Leadership Focus

You own your business; now control it. Go with the flow, but also read the tide charts! Make change your friend and not the enemy.

10. Leadership Dashboard Driver: Embrace Change.
Change is inevitable. Extraordinary leaders embrace change.
Pay attention to the life cycle of your business. Are you in startup mode? Might your business be running on empty and need a change? Are your look and feel in line with your new focus? Have you updated your business plan or marketing plan since you started the business? Don't let change happen to you. Control what is easily controlled.

Creating Value with Your Leadership Dashboard

When you have control over your top ten leadership dashboard drivers you will feel in control of your business, and you will be in control of your business. Take charge. Own your processes and manage your controls—your management controls, marketing controls, financial controls and customer controls. The leadership dashboard includes each of the four value drivers for your business. Create a personal leadership tool that you control using the top-ten list as your guide.

Core Business Principle

Implement a Leadership Dashboard

Guide 82: Top 10 Leadership Dashboard Drivers

Leadership Success Drivers 1 through 10

1. 80-20 Rule
2. Customer Characteristics
3. Customer Benefits
4. Profit Mastery
5. FACT-Based Financial Controls
6. Plan Properly
7. Brand You!
8. Social Media Action
9. Acquire, Engage, Convert
10. Embrace Change

Guide 83: Month-end Management

Monthly Financial Control Best Practices

Don't lose control! Following these few—but critical—best practices so you stay in control of your financial future. As the CEO, Chief Visionary, and MIP (most important person) in your business, the buck stops with you. Take full responsibility for all financial controls. Here's how.

1. Determine KPIs (key performance indicators) for the business and monitor frequently and on a schedule

2. Set a month-end meeting with your company controller (bookkeeper, business operations manager, or accountant) to review the following reports or statements:

   - Bank Reconciliation – Ask to see reconciled statement and to be presented with any issues or concerns.
   - Accounts Payable Report – Review accounts payable and ask about his or her issues or concerns
   - Accounts Receivable Report – Ask for report and review for any late payments (over thirty days)
   - Profit-and-Loss Statement – Detailed report (not the summary report). Have the controller highlight and present any deltas (significant differences) month over month. Have the prior month and current month P&L next to each other for review and easy comparison.

Didn't realize it was that simple? It is. Here are some details so you are comfortable controlling and managing by the book.

**Core Business
Principle**

Guide 84: FACT-Based Financial Controls

Are you managing your accountant, or is your accountant or bookkeeper managing you? In so many instances, a company founder is at the mercy of the controller when it is the owner who should be in control.

But how? What if you are not an accountant or financial-oriented person? Most entrepreneurs started a business because of a passion for the thing they are best at—which is not usually managing, projecting, or controlling finances. That's okay!

There are some simple financial controls that any business owner can set up to put them back in the driver's seat—and take control of their businesses financial future.

Losing control of the financial aspects of your business is, sadly, easy to do.

**It's your business—
maintain control**

Most entrepreneurs never really take financial control of their business—until there is a problem. A loan might be declined. A line of credit might be reduced or taken away altogether. Cash might be missing from petty cash or worse—your business checking account. Checks might go unaccounted for. Bank reconciliations might never be done—hiding bigger problems like money pilfering and fraudulent accounts payable.

The good news is that gaining financial control of your business—no matter how long it's been—is simple!

FACT-based Financial Controls

FACT-based Financial Controls—one of your Leadership Dashboard Driver are: Frequent, Accurate, Complete, and Timely. These FACT-based financials will allow you to track your key income drivers, unplanned and formerly unexplained expenses, and keep you in the driver's seat.

Top Three Money Management To Do's

The following are some simple solutions to the three most prominent financial control needs in small businesses:

1. Bank Statement Reconciliation
2. Managing Bills
3. Monitoring a Budget

As a financial consultant to and banker of several startups, I have witnessed first-hand the positive impact for small business owners from implementing financial controls as simple as the top three listed above. Use the *Financial Control* guides to help you create your own.

Spend time on the part of the business you love!

Once you implement these processes, you will feel more relaxed, be able to spend time on the part of the business you love, and feel confident that you are controlling your financial future—and your controller is not controlling you!

TIP: You could use a CPA to set up your financial systems and processes and to perform a month-end close to ensure that your staff remains on track. The CPA would then be familiar with your company for year-end taxes and for uncovering hidden small business or innovation tax incentives or credits you may not have known about. However, you do not need a CPA for month-end management reporting.

Money Wise

**Core Business
Principle**

Money Wise

Guide 85: Bank Reconciliation

Bank Statements. They come so often. What should you be doing with them and what does it matter anyway? A simple monthly bank statement reconciliation—also called reconciliation—can hold your financial team and your bank accountable, and protect you from fraud—which is common in small businesses.

TIP: Usually the statement from the bank is king—not your records.

Time Commitment
This monthly process should take no more than one hour for an experienced bookkeeper or CPA and up to four hours each month if there are difficult-to-find reconciliations, fixes to be made, or if your records don't match the bank statement.

Bank Statement Reconciliation Leadership Control:
1. Establish bank reconciliation process and reporting schedule
2. Bank reconciliation to be completed by the tenth of each month
3. Review with leadership each month
4. Leadership will ask the bookkeeper to describe any discrepancies and/or show journal entries made to correct errors

Money Wise

TIP: Do review journal entries! In most small business record-keeping software, like QuickBooks®, it is easy for anyone to make adjustments to statements and records—anytime. This makes it rather simple to commit fraud—very common among bookkeepers.

Guide 86: Managing Accounts Payable

**Core Business
Principle**

The two most common issues related to bill paying with startup businesses are that they:

1. Pay all bills as they come in, resulting in the lack of control of cash.
2. Let the bookkeeper pay bills and sign checks. This lack of control and oversight increases the risk of fraud, and increases the time required by the CEO to uncover and fix problems when they occur.

You want to be in control of money leaving your business. A best practice for small businesses is to set up a *critical bills* process to help control the flow of cash paid to creditors.

Time Commitment

This weekly or monthly process can take from one to four hours a month for your bookkeeper or business operations manager.

AP Leadership Control

1. Create an accounts payable (AP) schedule and strategy.
2. Task Bookkeeper with creating a critical vs. non-critical pay list.
   a. Critical Bills: Those that, if not paid on time, would result in a detrimental change to credit rating, things being cancelled or shut off, or more fees—like not taking advantage of discounts. These are scheduled to be paid on time.
   b. Non-Critical Bills: Those that can be paid as late as the CEO is comfortable with—like thirty or forty-five days (or more).

3. Set up a financial control system where the bookkeeper:
   a. Enters bills into the accounting software (weekly)
   b. Creates the check payable on the correct date, based on the critical bill-pay list,
   c. Prints the check(s) and places them in the correct folder attached with a paperclip to the bill
   d. Presents status report to leadership weekly
4. Leadership signs checks and has them mailed twice a month or as appropriate.

Accounts Payable Control Example:
I see this all the time. Don't let this happen to you!

- Business owner get's loan to start business based on cash-flow projections.
- Business owner signs lease—without advice or counsel—and opens retail establishment.
- Business owner has free-flowing capital from the investment so pays every bill as it comes in. Early.

Fast-forward six months. Construction begins on street in front of storefront. Marketing efforts returned little to no ROI. Vendors raise prices due to market conditions. You can fill in the blanks here—something always happens so that sales are not what the owner projected.

- Business owner continues to pay bills as they come in—without paying attention to budget, sales, or accounts receivable.
- Sales are down. Bills are up. Business owner is trying new inventory. Investment capital is dwindling faster than projected.
- Within two years the business closes, taking an an additional three years to pay down loan. Ugh.

Without financial controls and monitoring your budget, the worst things can happen. The number one reason businesses fail within the first three years is undercapitalization. Not because they didn't secure enough capital based on their projections—but business happens. Costs slowly go up. Sales may slow. Without cash, you cannot survive. Payables are money you have that you choose to give away. Watch your cash.

TIP: Implement budget monitoring and financial controls from the start to create a sustainable business.

Money Wise

Guide 87: Monitoring a Business Budget

Core Business Principle

When you create a business budget—an action plan as to what you expect your income and expenses to be for each month—you can better notice and control any discrepancies.

Time Commitment
This process can take several hours a month depending on the scope of the budget and the goals of the CEO.

Leadership Control:
1. Create a monthly business budget—use your proforma income projections created in guide *My Bottom Dollar* or for your *Executive Business Plan*

2. Establish a budget review process and reporting schedule

3. Compare your budget to actuals by the tenth of each month

4. Review with leadership each month

5. Leadership will ask bookkeeper or business operations manager (BOM) to describe any deltas—differences—over 5 percent (choose a percent or dollar amount you are comfortable with).

6. Leadership will task the BOM to make changes as appropriate to fix budget issues.

**Keeping you in
control of your cash**

Budget Control Example:
Your company has a travel budget of $10,000 a month for its sales team. Actual expenses for a September were $20,000—double the budget.

Your controller would have uncovered the reason for the high expenses and determined that airline tickets were being purchased by the sales team at the last minute, resulting in higher ticket prices.

With this knowledge, you implement a new travel policy: limit travel expenses to $500 for round trip airfare to the East Coast and $350 for round trip to the West Coast for sales travel, require all tickets to be purchased two weeks ahead of travel time, require CEO-approval for policy deviation, and finally require web-based meetings (like Net Meeting or Skype) for all first and second meetings—reserving travel for deal closing.

You task the controller to craft a policy statement by EOD (end of day) and implement immediately and to monitor the budget line item until expenses are back under control, giving your staff a deadline of one quarter for success. You assign a quality gate of a reduction of travel expenses by 50 percent and allocate a bonus for their success within your timeline.

You then meet with your controller again the following day to review the policy and schedule weekly meetings for his or her report to you on progress toward the goal.

This is a real-world example from a venture-backed company. By implementing travel budget guidelines, the company was able to reduce travel expenses by 8 percent and employees were no longer taking advantage of what seemed like a never ending pool of travel funds!

Don't forget to continue monitoring of the budget to actual. This best practice will uncover even the smallest delta and help keep you in control of your cash.

Guide 88: Managing Progress

Leading your business requires managing progress and monitoring assigned projects and tasks toward a quality gate—a success measure that you determine. Ask yourself, "What does success look like at project completion?" That's your quality gate.

The following are basic components of a project management spreadsheet that you can assign to your team. They will then track their progress and present the spreadsheet along with reports to you as frequently as you need an update. Note that for each assigned project there are the following columns:

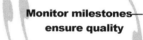

Monitor milestones— ensure quality

- Task Name
- Task Description—this can be as detailed as you require
- Assignment Date—the date project was assigned by leadership
- Due Date—important for tracking timeliness
- Change Date—used when a new task takes priority over a previously assigned task, requiring a change in the original due date. This would not be counted against the employee.
- Quality Gate—what successful completion of the project looks like

Controller Project Tracking	Task	Assigned Date	Due Date	Change Date	Quality Gate
Payroll	Manage payroll process		Ongoing / Bi-Monthly		Payroll submitted accurately and timely
AP Report	Manage AP process		Ongoing / Monthly		AP Report submitted on time and without errors
AR Report	Manage AR process		Ongoing / Monthly		AR Report submitted on time and without errors
Bank Rec	Perform monthly bank reconciliation		Ongoing / Monthly		Bank reconciliation complete, journal entries made, reviewed and approved by CEO
Budget to Actual Report	Budget Monitoring and Reporting		Ongoing / Monthly		Budget to Actual Report submitted on time and with deltas identified and recommended action presented to CEO
P&L Month by Month Report	Financial Statement preparation		Ongoing / Monthly		P&L Detailed Statement printed for current month and prior month; each line item reviewed for deltas; Report and deltas presented to CEO

**Core Business
Principle**

**The old way
of selling**

Guide 89: Developing a Personal Sales Process

Trade is the art of selling—exchanging what you have that is of worth to someone or some other business for (usually) cash. The art of trade is an old one for sure—and it is an art. Master the art and you will never go hungry. You will have all you need—when you need it!

When you own a business, even buying is selling. Whether you manage a team of sales professionals or you are wearing the hat of purchasing agent, you create a customer's relationship to the company.

In this guide, you will gain four trade mastery concepts:
- An understanding of the traditional sales cycle
- The ability to develop your own personal sales process (PSP)
- Introduction to the concept of a sales pipeline
- Introduction to closing techniques

Traditional Sales Cycle

Step 1: Evaluate Opportunities
Step 2: Identify Prospective Customers—Prospects
Step 3: Determine Value or Service Proposition
Step 4: Develop Proposal
Step 5: Engage Prospect—Present Proposal
Step 6: Close/Make the Sale

The traditional sales cycle is tried-and-true. Yes. But, it does not take into consideration vertical market development, positioning you as the expert, strategic coopetition, or relationship selling.

Let's take a fresh look at the sales cycle. This is the model we use in business—you can create your own!

Relationship Sales Cycle
Step 1: Identify a Vertical Market
Step 2: Become an Industry Expert
Step 3: Develop Partnerships
Step 4: Share Your Expertise
Step 5: Proposal Stage
Step 6: Close the Business
Step 7: Referral Request
Step 8: Genuine Thank You
Step 9: Relationship Building
Step 10: Customer Service

Create Connections

It's not a sales cycle...it's a relationship cycle

Four key differences in a relationship selling cycle:
1. Vertical Market Development: Focus on channel sales activities—create a separate value proposition for the various target markets you identified in the *Designing Your Perfect Business* guides and *Startup Success* guides.

2. Become an Industry Expert: Host an event, write an article, lead a workshop, write a blog—there are so many ways to engage your prospective ideal customer using your COIs (centers of influence) to support your activities or simple social media outlets.

Key concept: Prospecting is partnering.

3. Develop Partnerships: Engage in strategic direct marketing—*strategic coopetition*. In the first meeting seek an answer to the question, "Can we work together?" if "yes!," then, work together to uncover the value that you can uniquely add.

4. Share Your Expertise: Serve your prospect. You want them to be able to answer the question, "What did you do for me lately?"

SPROUT!

**Core Business
Principle**

Take this opportunity to develop your own sales cycle. Each business sales cycle will be different. What does yours look like today? How do you need to change it to better meet your business goals? What is your personal sales process?

My Sales Cycle

**Develop a sales
process & plan**

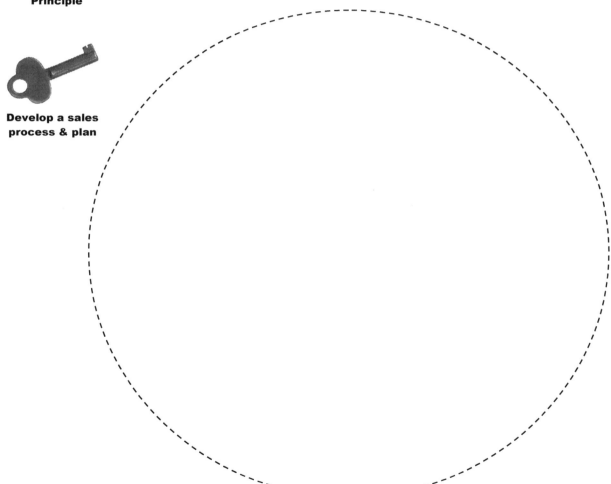

Guide 90: Creating a Powerful Pipeline

Business development is about relationship development. But what do you do if you recently changed industries, or are new to business altogether? What do you do if you don't have existing relationships to build on and need to start from scratch? Simple. Create a powerful pipeline!

So what is a pipeline? No person in business closes—or makes the sale— every time. Just as retail customers may come in and browse instead of buy, you still want their contact with you, your product, and your store to be as positive as possible so that your business is top of mind when they decide to make a purchase.

Core Business Principle

Sales won't feel like sales.

In fact, some people are natural sales people and others think they are terrible at building new relationships. If you remember that sales is all about relationship building, and you believe in your company and product or service—sales will never feel like sales.

Successful selling is an art. But when you know some of the secrets to success—the rules of the game—even a non-sales person can become successful at selling.

Develop a sales process & plan

This model has been taught to business bankers, branch managers, small business owners, and at the Washington State Small Business Conference to teach non-sales people how to sell. Relationship building leads to revenue generation.

Powerful Pipeline Model
Small Business Sales Essentials

Pipeline: 5 new contacts per week = 11-15 meetings per week = Solid Pipeline

Week 1	Week 2	Week 3	Week 4	Week 5	Week 6
5 New Contacts	3 Follow-Up / Drop Off Meetings	2 Proposal Meetings	1 Close the Business		
	5 New Contacts	3 Follow-Up / Drop Off Meetings	2 Proposal Meetings	1 Close the Business	
		5 New Contacts	3 Follow-Up / Drop Off Meetings	2 Proposal Meetings	1 Close the Business
			5 New Contacts	3 Follow-Up / Drop Off Meetings	2 Proposal Meetings

...and so on!

Create a Powerful Pipeline

Powerful Pipeline Formula

5 **New Contacts** per Week

=

11 to 15 **Appointments** per Week

=

- ✓ A Powerful Pipeline of Sales Leads
- ✓ Closed Business
- ✓ New Relationships
- ✓ New Centers of Influence

Identifying Centers of Influence

There is a formula for successful sales—even when you are starting from scratch!

Relationship building leads to revenue

Making Powerful Connections

As a banker, this was the model I used to generate millions in deposits and become the number one ranked banker in the nation for the number two bank in the country. As a business owner, this is the model that service providers use once they have identified their ideal customers and need to start selling.

Notice in the powerful pipeline model that you are to initiate five new contacts each week and set up eleven to fifteen meetings each week. That can sound daunting. But it's not! The magic to making this happen with ease are your centers of influence – COIs!

A center of influence is a connector—someone you look up to or who knows you well—who you feel might be interested in helping you connect to your ideal customer.

Five of your fifteen meetings a week should be with a COI. COIs are easier and more fun to meet with than a pure sales call—prospect meeting—because you may know the person already. So it's more comfortable. You get to ask them how you can help them in business, and they get to ask you the same. Remember—if you are the one who called the meeting—you are the one who pays the bill at the end of the coffee, tea, or lunch meeting!

Use space on the following page to begin to identify your top twenty centers of influence. Your COIs may change frequently, depending on your new contacts and business sales goals.

SPROUT!

Sales success for the non-sales person

My Centers of Influence

Use this model. Follow this formula. Try it for a quarter. You will be pleasantly surprised at the powerful pipeline that a non-sales-person can create!

Guide 91: Making the Sale

In relationship selling your main job is to pay attention to the communication feedback loop.

- Ask what the prospective customers want
- Listen to what they want
- Deliver your message, working to offer a partnership or joint solution to meet their need.

Develop a sales process & plan

Core Business Principle

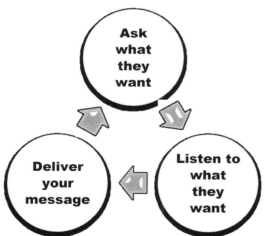

Ask yourself:
- Am I hearing them objecting?
- Am I responding to the rejection?
- Am I asking them to agree with me?
- Am I the one in line for their next order or buying decision?
- Am I a positive part of their buying experience?

Closing Techniques

As small business owners, many times we are the CEO and the lead—or only—sales person. Asking for a prospective customer's business is important and critical to your success. When you love what you do and believe in your products and services, sales really won't feel like sales. It should feel as if you are solving people's problems, meeting their needs, or even making them happy. Imagine your product or service is exactly what they had been searching for—maybe it is!

Practice the art of listening

Once you feel comfortable that you are able to meet the needs of the prospective customer, you can use proven models of bringing that client to a decision point and closing the sale. Here are some of our favorites. If you want to learn more—there are dozens of closing techniques—search online for the term *closing techniques*.

- Alternative Close. Offering a limited set of choices.
- Assumptive Close. Acting as if they are ready to decide.
- Balance-sheet Close. Adding up the pros and the cons.
- Best-time Close. Emphasizing how now is the best time to buy.
- Bonus Close. Offering something more or special to clinch the deal.
- Conditional Close. Linking closure to resolving objections.
- Trial Close. Testing whether they are ready for a close.
- Yes-set Close. Getting them to say 'yes' and they'll keep saying 'yes'.

Determine what closing technique works best for you and practice! Your prospective customer will only be as comfortable as you are when you are asking him or her to buy from you.

Guide 92: 5 Principles for Sustainable Growth

Unlocking the Power of the 80-20 Rule

Discover the secret to creating a sustainable business. Passion inspires entrepreneurs to launch their new ventures. However, when you are in it to win—for the long-term—that passion may fade over time. In order to create a sustainable business—one that can achieve the success you desire—follow these five principles. The secret to creating a sustainable business lays in diligently applying the 80-20 rule in your leadership dashboard.

Core Business Principle

The 80-20 rule simply says that 80 percent of your results come from 20 percent of your efforts. Look around you, and you'll see this rule everywhere in your business and your life. For your business, it means that 80 percent of your sales profits will be produced by 20 percent of your customers and 80 percent of your revenue will be generated by 20 percent of your time, efforts, and activities.

Implement a Leadership Dashboard

The key questions are then:

What is the highest and best use of my time?

How can I spend more time doing the 20 percent that produces results and get more results?

What follows are some simple principles to help you spend more time doing the things you love and the things you know produce the kind of results that flow easily and create a business with sustainable growth, not exhaustion. And you will nurture your passion for your business.

**20% Effort =
80% Results**

80-20 Principle #1 – Valuing Your Time

Cherish the value of your time. As the creator, chief visionary officer, and highest executive of your business, your time is precious. You are a business *owner*, not an employee! Therefore, value your time accordingly, and put a price on it. We suggest a minimum of three times what your hourly rate would be if you worked for someone else—but revisit the guides on pricing to create a strategy that works for your business.

I commit to honoring my time at $_____per hour. Fill in the amount now.

80-20 Principle #2 – Honoring Your Strengths

Know your strengths and honor them. You completed the guide called *Discover Your Strengths* and the *Entrepreneur Assessment* earlier in the *Toolkit*. Even if you haven't yet completed the guides, you likely know what you are good at and what drives you in your business. Are you great at developing relationships, mobilizing partners to take action? Are you the linchpin in your community or a connector? List your top money-making talents now.

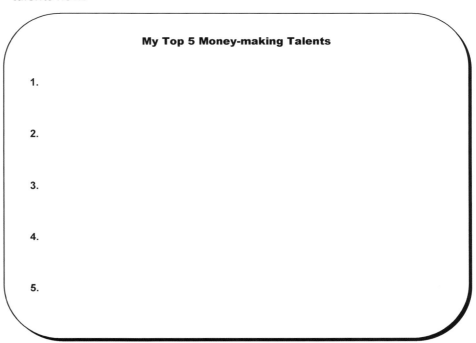

My Top 5 Money-making Talents

1.

2.

3.

4.

5.

Name two talents that you are currently underutilizing and create a plan to apply them to your business:

Apply My Talents Today

1.

2.

80-20 Principle #3 – Keeping Your Eye on the Prize

Talent or time waster? Focus on your talents and rid yourself of the time wasters. Be real about what is a waste of your time and talent. What could be contracted out, hired out, or left undone altogether? Below, list the tasks that represent a waste of your time and talent. Commit now to follow the 80-20 rule and focus on your strengths by ridding yourself of time sinks.

My Top 5 Time-Wasters

1.

2.

3.

4.

5.

Call to Action!

Delegate it, outsource it, or delete it! Use the following space to commit to your top talents now.

Making Change

I commit to stop doing (time-wasting task):

By (date):

80-20 Principle #4 – Setting Powerful Priorities

Make the highest and best use of your time. Commit to tackling the following top three priorities daily. Refer to your money-making talents in Principle #2. Schedule time for these in advance on your weekly calendar.

My Top 3 Priorities (Daily)

1.

2.

3.

80-20 Principle #5—Focus on the Future

Here's how to get strategic! Integrate strategic direct marketing into your marketing strategy. Identify the top 20 percent of your customers—those that produce 80 percent of your profit. Love them and reward them! If you are just starting your business—start strategically. You identified your ideal customer in guides *Who do I Want to Play With*, *Selecting Your Ideal Customer*, and *Target Market*. Implement your powerful pipeline by first reaching out to these top prospects.

Best Practice

> **My Top Customers or Prospective Customers**

Identify the top 20 centers of influence—those referral sources and strategic partners who send you prospective clients. Relationship selling is about relationship building. Celebrate your champions!

> **My Top COIs**

Celebrate your champions!

Maximize Results

Principle #1: Valuing Your Time. This principle becomes the lens through which you will evaluate all your activities. When you focus on your intended results, success is inevitable.

Your responses to Principle 2: Honoring Your Strengths, Principle 4: Setting Powerful Priorities, and Principle 5: Getting Strategic, are clues to help you spend time that maximizes results.

Keep your Eye on the Prize

Principle #3, Ridding Yourself of Time Wasters, identifies time-wasting tasks that represent drains on your energy and passion and take you away from important revenue generating or relationship-building activities. Ironically, these seem to be where we spend most of our time! Break the habit—make your time count.

When in doubt, do the math. Consider how much additional revenue your business would produce in a month if you spent an additional thirty minutes each day on your top 20 percent of revenue-generating activities. What would the impact be on your business?

Source: This guide was modified from an exercise contributed by Pam Jackson, the Northwest's leading certified Growth Coach®.

Last: Next Steps

You are armed with solutions, strategies, and tools to help you master some of the core business principles related to growing and leading your business.

As CEO of a very small business, you wear many hats—from leader to chief sales person. You have the opportunity to design your perfect business—and that means develop the perfect sales cycle too!

In small business leadership, sales needs to be for the non-sales person as well as the pro. Design you're personal selling process—one you feel comfortable with—and practicing listening.

Leading My Business To Do's	Still Ahead
• Implement my own Leadershp Dashboard	• Create a professional bio
• Discover the KPIs for my business	• Learn the secrets to networking with ease
• Implement FACT based financial controls	• Implement social media in 3 steps
• Design my Personal Sales Process	• Set up my free social media accounts
• Identify my Top COIs	
• Follow the 80/20 Rule	

Leading My Business Certificate of Completion

You took the leap to launch your business—now it's time to lead your business.

Leadership means so many things in small business—from managing financial controls to making the sale. With a sales process and plan in place, financial controls under *your* control, and your company's value drivers defined—you are on your way toward leading your business instead of being your business.

Several Keys to Success were integrated into this chapter on leadership: *Designing Your Perfect Business*, *Develop a Sales Process and Plan*, *Design and Use a Leadership Dashboard*.

Completed Guides
Guide 81: Creating Value with a Leadership Dashboard
Guide 82: Top 10 Leadership Dashboard Drivers
Guide 83: Month-End Management
Guide 84: FACT-Based Financial Controls
Guide 85: Bank Reconciliation
Guide 86: Managing Accounts Payable (AP)
Guide 87: Monitoring a Business Budget
Guide 88: Managing Progress
Guide 89: Developing a Personal Sales Process
Guide 90: Creating a Powerful Pipeline
Guide 91: Making the Sale
Guide 92: 5 Principles for Sustainable Growth

Complete your certificate of completion on the following page to memorialize your accomplishments.

Congratulations!

Entrepreneurial Edge

Small Business Toolkit

Certificate of Completion

I certify that I, _____, have successfully completed

Leading My Business

Including FACT Based Financial Controls, Creating Value with a Leadership Dashboard, Developing a Powerful Pipeline, Making the Sale and Keys to Success:Designing Your Perfect Business, Develop a Sales Process and Plan, Design and Use a Leadership Dashboard

Signature: _____

Date: _____

SPROUT!

Chapter 10: **Share Your World**

Guides

Takeaways:

Create a professional bio and "one-breath introduction".
Describe the value and possible pitfalls of barter agreements.
Learn the steps to secure your social media intellectual property.
Evaluate social media return on investment (ROI).

Guide 93: Brand You!

A Professional Biography is a tool to help share your brand with the world. You determined strengths—and possibly uncovered some weaknesses—in in your entrepreneurial capacity in the guide *Discovering Your Strengths*. If you skipped that guide, revisit it now to help streamline writing your professional biography.

SPROUT!

Your professional biography, or bio, is different from a résumé or a list of your accomplishments or experiences. It is a way for you to share your world with those you want to influence. It describes—in as little space as a paragraph but no more than a page—how your background and experience have prepared you to start this business. It shares how you are *the* person to make this company happen.

Use the space below to list those highlights you would want to include in your bio.

Highlights for My Bio

List your strengths as they relate to business ownership.

Sample Professional Bios

Sample Bio 1
Sandy Bjorgen, MA, CPC, President, IMPROV-able Results®
Sandy teaches business people to think and speak under pressure with more cool than they ever imagined and helps them stand out from the crowd as unique, creative, and captivating. She conducts applied improvisation training and communication coaching for organizations, teams, and individuals. Her goal is to provide supportive sessions that are interactive and experiential—allowing participants to accelerate their learning and its application through example and direct experience.

Sample Bio 2
Susan Collins, Principle, Empowerment Enterprises
Susan helps companies (small to Fortune 500) attract customers, reduce attrition, build relationships, and add to the bottom-line. Certified by Dale Carnegie® in leadership, communications, interpersonal skills, and professional sales, Susan has worked for several years in the training and coaching industry. Her relaxed, informal, and positive approach makes it easy for clients to work with her. She is a force for success, helping clients overcome challenges, push boundaries, and embrace change.

Sample Bio 3
Tracey Warren, President, Ready Set Grow Marketing
Tracey has transformed her love of the Internet and passion for marketing into a venture that teaches business owners the value of social media marketing through workshops and one-on-one coaching. As a social media manager, her ability to connect on a personal level with her clients allows her to market for them in their own voices on multiple platforms. Tracey's credentials include a degree in journalism and work as a corporate trainer.

Sample Bio 4
Pamela Jackson, MA, Certified Coach, The Growth Coach
Pam builds upon a seventeen year career in corporate marketing to help small business owners earn more while working less. She and executive coach Dave Hope, co-owners of The Growth Coach® franchise in north King County, offer over forty years combined experience in executive, financial, and strategic planning and marketing leadership. The Growth Coach® is a national leader in small business coaching; its proprietary process helps entrepreneurs create better results in their business and personal lives.

My Professional Bio

Use the following space to write the text you will use in your social media marketing platforms to share your expertise.

My Professional Bio

Name: Date:

SPROUT!

Guide 94: 3 Steps to Networking with Ease

Effective networking is much more than socializing, schmoozing, and selling. The most important things to understand about networking in a group setting are:

1. Networking is a marketing activity, not a sales activity.
2. As a marketing activity, good networking skills focus on building relationships.

Coopetition and Relationship Selling
In the world of coopetition and relationship selling, networking is all about creating a relationship and finding a way to meet the needs of another.

By providing someone with a contact, business development lead, a business, or personal resource, the person will likely want to help you in return. Having a business-grounding statement can often help orient your listener to who you are and what you do.

The following are three simple steps to networking with ease—in any situation.

Step 1: Make a Powerful Impact
The one-breath introduction is a tool used and advocated by the US Small Business Administration. It is a simple elevator pitch which eases the fear of talking about your business and yourself. It should be relatively simple to create a personal introduction that both shares your strengths and will interest those around you.

1

Step

If you can introduce yourself, your business, and what brings you to the event in one breath – you've nailed it. Here's how. First, introduce yourself and the name of your business. Second, share what you do, with whom, and where—your grounding statement. Third, explain why you're there, the type of people you are interested in meeting, and how someone in this group might be able to help you. Simple!

Step 2: Control Your Card

You can use your business card to your advantage, particularly in a meeting when others are speaking. How? The other's elevator-pitch time is not a time for you to chat with your neighbor or to zone out. Instead, it is the perfect time to jot on the back of your business card something that you can offer those speaking that will assist them, solve a stated problem, or introduce them to resources they might want.

Everyone wants my card, right?

By writing something useful on the back of your card for the other person, you accomplish two things.

First, you have a reason to give someone your card. Networking and meeting someone new is much easier if you have a reason to talk. You have something to offer—your business card has meaning. What comes around goes around. When you offer help to someone, that good deed is likely to come back to you.

Second, your contact has a reason to keep your card. Face it, most business cards that we get, we ignore. Your business card is the one they will keep.

Step 3: Make a Connection

Remember the importance of listening to the person who is talking to you. Eye contact is critical, no matter how tempting it is to glance around the room. The most important person in the room is the person with whom you are talking. In the Get Motivated! training summit, I was impressed with so many of the speakers. But two highlighted the importance of listening, Dan Rather and General Colin Powell. In his talk about jumpstarting your dreams, your business, and your career, Dan Rather encouraged the audience of fourteen thousand to "develop yourself as a good listener". He went on to say: "In life, make yourself a good listener—it will pay in positive dividends."

2
Step

3
Step

SPROUT!

Guide 95: Expanding Your Network

One of the best ways to determine whether you are ready to become an entrepreneur is to meet other entrepreneurs, learn what they do, look at their lifestyles, and talk about entrepreneurship. This can help you determine whether you are suited for business ownership.

Identifying an entrepreneur is easier than you might think. You may have a family member or a neighbor who owns a business. You may choose to interview a business owner you have always admired or someone you just want to get to know. You may work with a service provider (an accountant, banker, insurance provider, lawyer, or accountant) who may be an entrepreneur to interview.

Once you complete your first entrepreneur interview, you will want to do another one! It may surprise you how open and willing business owners are to share information. No matter your position, interviewing an entrepreneur will surely be an eye-opening experience.

Increase your confidence by interviewing business owners to learn what they feel is most important to their success.

3 Steps to a Successful Entrepreneur Interview

Based on your entrepreneur assessment, you may want to enhance your management, operational, marketing, sales, or financial skills. The entrepreneur interview may help you expand your business experiences and strengths.

Step 1: Identify Best-in-Class Business Owners

You can use the Internet or conversations with others to help identify business leaders who you feel might be good candidates to interview. This process is strategic. When considering how you may want to interview, do not think about whom you have direct access to today. Think about the future.

As you build your business, you are going to want mentors, personal and business advisors, and one or more advisory boards. Your interview candidates may be the pool of industry leaders you pull from as you build your dream management and advisory team.

Consider identifying entrepreneurs in like industries, who are leaders in their field, and who may be in another state.

Step 2: Do Your Research

The more you know about your potential interviewee, the more comfortable you both will be during the interview. Explore the person's:

- Business website
- Business Facebook pages
- Personal website
- Facebook page
- LinkedIn page
- Do a general Google or Bing search on their name and business name(s)

Look for content, like:

- Business and leadership team
- Current press releases
- Charitable contributions and organizations they support
- Board of directors or advisors

Pay attention to the employers of the company's board of directors or their affiliations. For example, if a board member is from a venture capital company, it is likely this is a venture-backed firm. You could take the research a step further to visit the venture capital company's website to see when or how much was invested in your interviewee's business. This might tell you what state of business it is in and arm you with additional relevant questions.

1
Step

2
Step

3
Step

SPROUT!

Uncover unique and interesting connections that first, might link you to the person in some way through mutual acquaintances and second, so that you can ask questions that will be interesting, engaging, and relevant.

Step 3: Create Compelling Questions
You've done your research. Add to the sample interview questions above as a start. You know a lot about this person's business and interests. Put that information to good use. Create compelling questions that are relevant to the entrepreneur.

How to Interview an Entrepreneur
On my business radio show of BizLine Radio on KKNW for over four seasons, I interviewed dozens of entrepreneurs. The point of this show was to highlight the successes and challenges of business owners, give them an opportunity to share their world, and let the US Small Business Administration share its weekly business tips with my audience.

This experience taught me to research, uncover, and discover the interests, qualities, and passions of my guests before we went on air.

Here are some things you might say when engaging an entrepreneur for your first interview.

What should you say about yourself?
First, let the other person know that you are starting a business and were given advice to reach out to leaders in his or her field. Then, ask for a time for a phone interview. Let the entrepreneur know it will only take about ten to fifteen minutes and ask for his or her availability. Don't be alarmed if the person wants to talk now. That's okay! You are more than ready!

Thank you!
A thank you letter sent to the entrepreneur you interviewed could have a very powerful impact. The person might be an advisor to your business in the future! Don't forget to thank the entrepreneur you interview for his or her time.

Entrepreneur Interview Sample Questions

SPROUT!

Sample Interview Questions

1. What made you want to start your own company?

2. How did you get into this business?

3. Before you started, did you write a business plan? Since starting your business, have you written a business plan or marketing plan? How has it helped you?

4. What personality traits or characteristics have served you well?

5. What have been the most rewarding part and the most challenging part of managing your own business?

6. If you have one piece of advice for a budding entrepreneur, what would it be?

Don't forget to send a thank you note!

SPROUT!

Guide 96: Joining In

Joining the Perfect Business Group

Before you can network, you need to identify the organizations, groups, or associations that might be a good fit and best meet your needs. Some networking functions are free; others have a fee.

Take some time to identify which networking groups you could participate in that could give you access to possible resources for your business, like potential business advisors. If you want some direction on which types of groups will best contribute to the success of your business, visit the guides *B2B or B2C* and *Strategic Coopetition*.

Identify the business networking groups in your area that can connect you to your perfect customer. Some examples might be: industry trade organizations, international trade groups, and chambers of commerce.

My List of Professional Associations: B2B

Professional Development

Also, identify the business groups that can provide you access and personal connections that will help you build your entrepreneurial capacity. Some examples include: MIT Forum, TIE (The Indus Entrepreneurs), NWEN (Northwest Entrepreneur Network), Ladies Who Launch, Young President's Club, Women Business Owners (WBO).

Come up with a list of at least five organizations in each category. Make it a point to visit each group to see if it might be a good for you and help you meet your professional development and business development goals.

My List of Professional Associations: Professional Development

SPROUT!

Access OPA

SPROUT!

Guide 97: Barter Anyone?

Today there are so many ways to engage others to support your vision and business goals. There are websites that help you bid on in-sourced or out-sourced contract services for marketing, brand building, editing, and even business development.

There are colleges in nearly every first and second-tier city and students in your vicinity who are looking for internships and work-study projects—ways to implement their newly learned skills.

In addition, there is a world of bartered products and services.

What if you identify a service that would help your business grow but you don't have the budget? Can you offer your services or products in exchange for theirs? Should you?

What if a prospective client can't pay you your posted hourly rate, but he or she is a strategic fit for your business. That person might lead you to other business—or become a great referral source for additional business into the future. What then? Can you accept the project at a discounted rate with the remainder made up in this person's products or services? Should you?

There are rules—tax and otherwise—to bartering for all or part of a product or service. As long as you know the rules and follow some best practices, you may be able to save some money, expand your business, and fast track your growth using a barter agreement.

We are not attorneys nor accountants and are not giving any tax or legal advice. Be sure to check with your legal counsel and accountant before engaging in a barter agreement of your own.

The Barter Agreement

There are times when an exchange of goods or services is just what you need to get the ball rolling on a particular initiative. As host of the BizLine Radio show on KKNW, a barter agreement was a helpful tool to bring in labor, like a guest recruiter, and production manager. More than identifying and screening potential on-air interview candidates, my barter partner acted more as an assistant producer of the show, making the entire program possible.

Bartering Is legal. Bartering Is Taxable.

Bartering is typically fully taxable to both parties involved when used in business transactions. If one service or product is valued higher than the other being exchanged, you still must report your contribution at the value you exchanged. You would still deduct the exchange at the value of the service or product. For instance, if your services valued one hundred dollars and the other company's services valued fifty dollars, you would still have to claim the $100 as income. However, you could only deduct fifty dollars of the exchange.

TIP: Set a maximum value of the service or products bartered for and try to trade 'like for like'. If the value of each service or product exchanged is equal, they may cancel each other out. If the two transactions match up, then there is truly a "wash", and no income taxes are payable. You may, however, have to pay sales tax on the market value of the goods or services you receive. Be sure to ask a local accountant or tax lawyer for details.

Money Wise

Barter Agreement

The Barter Agreement dated _____ is entered into between_____ (Client) and Attitude Adjustment Music, LLC dba/BizLine Radio hereafter referred to as BizLine Radio in relation to exchange Professional Business Services with visibility on digital properties operated by BizLine Radio. Digital properties may include the BizLine Radio Website, the BizLine Radio show, but are not guaranteed. Further, all obligations of the Barter Agreement shall terminate the sooner of the dilution of BizLine Radio or any of its property(s) or by either party at any time.

Client agrees to providing barter services to the BizLine Radio 2007 season by contributing the following Professional Business Services (please list services to be provided):

- ☐ Marketing
- ☐ Editing
- ☐ Writing
- ☐ Producing / Assistant Producing
- ☐ Advertising
- ☐ Promoting
- ☐ Other_____

In Exchange for above barter services, Bizline Radio agrees to provide best efforts without guarantee the following:
_____ .

Client grants BizLine Radio the unlimited licensing rights to use, free of charge, all content developed for BizLine Radio in perpetuity, for media, public relations, promotions, publishing, web, e-mail, DVD, Radio, advertising or any other such uses. This includes for any sales purposes.

This Agreement shall terminate automatically upon completion by _____ of the Services required by this Agreement.

It is understood by the parties that _____ is fully independent of BizLine Radio, and not an employee, partner or owner of Bizline Radio. Bizline Radio will not provide fringe benefits, including health insurance benefits, paid vacation, paid or filed taxes or any other employee benefit, for the benefit of _____ .

Client owns the copyright on his or her content or images, and can use his or her copyrighted content. There is no restriction on his or her usage of his or her own copyrighted content.

The BizLine Radio logo or name cannot be used without express written consent of BizLine Radio.

Client: _____

Signature: _____
(By this signature, I affirm I am authorized to sign on behalf of this company.)

Printed name: _____

Title: _____

Address: _____

City/State/Zip: _____

Phone: _____

e-mail: _____

Web site: _____

BizLine Radio

By _____

Printed Name: Tiffany McVeety

SMALL BUSINESS TOOLKIT 365

Guide 98: Simplifying Social Media

Social media is all the rage. No, it's more than all the rage. Your colleagues, the retail establishment next door, and suppliers across town, are on board. So why not you? Why not now? It's not too late! In fact, according to notable social media guru, Jamie Turner of the site Mashable, about 50 percent of the business community is still in the launch stage of social media. That is good news for you! If you thought you were behind the curve, and that every one of your competitors is ahead of you, that is not the case. Only half of them are ahead of you—so let's get moving!

SPROUT!

Social media is a part of your overall marketing plan but can seem daunting because it requires our input and energy to make it work.

Two business owners came into GROW Washington, a nonprofit entrepreneurial development center, for a social media marketing assistance the other day. The two women, one a real estate professional and the other a retail-store owner in a destination town, had attended countless of social media marketing classes, and were ready to execute.

Instead of jumping on the computer, I knew better. We needed a plan, and I needed to share with them some simple steps to help them create their own social media marketing plan and execution strategy before we jumped to a computer.

Here are the three steps to your social media marketing execution plan. Execute this plan, and you will gain followers, build a community, and avoid a false start.

The strategies and recommendations that follow, are a melding of what I have learned and what I have seen work with my clients and colleagues. The point is to get started!

Here is a simple solution to getting set up on the most popular social media platforms. In this section you will be introduced to all sorts of information that you may have learned in social media classes. Here is the simple solution to actually executing what you may have already learned.

Stop waiting. Start now!

Follow these simple steps to implement your social media marketing plan.

3 Steps to Develop Your Social Media Strategy
Planning for your social media marketing efforts will take three steps:

1. Planning
2. Execution
3. Optimization

Goal Setting
First is goal setting. You need goals for your social media marketing efforts so you can optimize and assess your return on investment.

Securing Intellectual Property
Second, is securing your intellectual property. We will show you how to sign up on the top social media sites.

Results, Return, Impact
Finally, you will learn how to maximize your time by scheduling your posts and tweets for future dates using free scheduling tools.

Guide 99: Social Media Marketing Roadmap

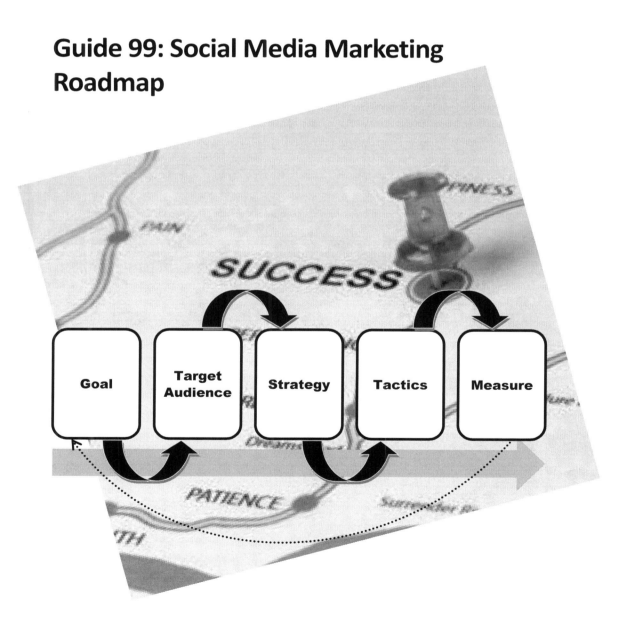

Guide 100: Social Media Planning

Every marketing activity should support a business goal. Design a strategy with goals in mind. Before launching into social media marketing have a plan in place. Be clear about your goals. You should be able to answer the following questions before you get started:

- Who is your target audience?

- What are your social media marketing goals?

- What do you want to happen when you set up your Facebook page? Twitter? Your blog? Other marketing tactic?

- What outcomes are you hoping for when you become active in social media?

- What is the estimated time for implementation? Ongoing time?

- Who is going to manage this new marketing tactic, as content intensive as it can be? Do you need to get help?

- What will this cost?

- How will you gauge success? What is your expected marketing return? Is it based on new customers? Added revenue? Lower cost of new customer acquisition?

With some basic goals understood and on paper, you can begin. In the following guides, you will find screen shots from some of the top social media sites so you can execute your plan simply and with ease.

Guide 101: Top Social Media Marketing Tactics

Why reinvent the wheel? Over 200 readers took the poll and made their choices. The digital media research company *Top Rank* surveys and compiles the top digital marketing tactics and strategies every year. The most recent report, 2011 shares that while there are many signs of marketing budgets making a recovery, the vast majority of marketers are still focused on planning the most efficient and effective online marketing mix they can—here are the top tactics.

Search engine optimization (38%, 87 Votes)

Social network participation (Facebook, LinkedIn) (34%, 78 Votes)

Blogging (30%, 69 Votes)

Email marketing (15%, 35 Votes)

Content marketing (15%, 35 Votes)

Pay per click (15%, 34 Votes)

Video marketing (13%, 29 Votes)

Microblogging (Twitter) (12%, 28 Votes)

Social media advertising (8%, 19 Votes)

Corporate web site (7%, 16 Votes)

The top responses in this year's survey reflect a more holistic perspective that includes search, social media, advertising, content, and email. While social media marketing continues to get a lot of media attention and companies are investing more ($1.2 Billion 2011, Forrester), search marketing (PPC and SEO) gets the majority of digital marketing budgets ($20.7 billion 2011, Forrester).

Top 5 Social Media Tactics In a Nutshell

1. Search Engine Optimization – SEO
What is it?

Search engine optimization (SEO) is the process of improving the visibility of a website or a web page in search engines via the *natural* or *un-paid* ("organic" or "algorithmic"), search results.

What's the fuss?

Top search engine results equals top rank and top of mind for your customers and prospective customers.

There are over 200 SEO factors that Google uses to rank pages in the Google search results (SERPs). What are the search engine optimization rules? Speculation—it's very secret—identifies the following top tips:

- Keyword in URL
- Keyword in Domain name
- Keyword in Title tag
- Keyword in H1, H2 and H3
- Freshness of Pages
- Freshness - Amount of Content Change

Find a hands-on social media consultant to help guide you in the above tactics, or research the phrases on your own to learn more. Either way—don't miss out! Sixty-two percent of all businesses using social media marketing outsource some or all of their marketing tactics.

2. Social Network Participation
What is it?

Connecting to friends, associations, clients, products, services, and everything-in-between using using social network websites. Social network marketing generally tends to focus on two main objectives: 1.) generating some action and 2.) creating brand awareness. We include step-by-step guides to help get you connected using the top social networking sites later in this Chapter.

What's the fuss?

The belief that social networks are limited to teenagers is looking increasingly misguided. Thirty-two percent of Internet users between the ages of 50 and 64 are now using a social networking site such as Facebook, LinkedIn or Twitter on a daily basis—up from just 20 percent at this same time last year. Social networking participation among the highly coveted group—Baby Boomers—has grown 20 percent in the past year according to the Pew Research Center.

Forrester Research finds that more than four in five US adults online use social media at least once a month, with half engaging with friends, family, colleagues and strangers via social network sites such as Facebook, LinkedIn, Twitter, Digg and Reddit. Among those who embrace social media tools, adults age 35 to 54 boosted their participation by more than 50 percent, with more than half of adults age 35 to 44 now in social networks.

3. Blogging

What is it?

Here are popular definitions:

- A frequent, chronological publication of personal thoughts and Web links.
- A blog is basically a journal that is available on the web. The activity of updating a blog is "blogging" and someone who keeps a blog is a "blogger."
- A blog is a website in which items are posted on a regular basis and displayed in reverse chronological order.

What's the fuss?

Business blogs are sweeping the business community. According to About.com:

- Blog software is easy to use. Simply write your thoughts, link to resources, and publish to your blog, all at the push of a few buttons. Blog software companies such as: Movable Type, Blogger.com and Typepad all offer easy blogging tools to get started.
- Blogging is a low-cost alternative to having a web presence. For small business owners without the time to learn web html or the money to hire a designer/developer, blogging offers an inexpensive method to get your company's name out on the Internet.
- Updating the weblog is a much quicker process than contacting a web designer with changes or doing the coding and uploading yourself.
- Business blogs provide your small business with a chance to share your expertise and knowledge with a larger audience. A powerful benefit for consultants and knowledge workers.

4. **Email Marketing**

What is it?

Email marketing is directly marketing a commercial message to a group of people using electronic mail email. According to Forrester Research, US firms spent US $1.51 billion on email marketing in 2011 and will grow to $2.468 billion by 2016.

What's the fuss?

Email marketing is popular with companies for several reasons:

- An exact return on investment can be tracked ("track to basket") and has proven to be high when done properly. Email marketing is often reported as second only to search marketing as the most effective online marketing tactic.
- Advertisers can reach substantial numbers of email subscribers who have opted in (i.e., consented) to receive email communications on subjects of interest to them.
- Almost half of American Internet users check or send email on a typical day.

5. **Content Marketing**

What is it?

Content marketing includes all marketing formats that involve the creation or sharing of content to engage potential prospects or current consumers. Quality content brings prospects to a brand's site so brands can develop a relationship with the prospective customers and nurture them towards a purchase.

What's the fuss?

The goal of content marketing is usually to inspire trust, and grow your reputation and influence your market. Marketers are leveraging new media content products more than ever tough with nearly three fourths leveraging their content through social media networks, blogs, and e-newsletters. White papers and case studies are mainstays in a content marketing portfolio.

- Nine out of ten organizations market with content marketing.
- Marketers, on average, spend over a quarter of their marketing budget on content marketing with small businesses spending 66 percent.

Guide 102: Securing Your Social Media Space

Step 2 of three steps to develop your social media strategy: Social Media Execution

Facebook, Twitter, LinkedIn, Google Places...and more! Secure your business name and set up accounts on relevant social media marketing sites. Here are our top recommendations, but if there are others in your area, by all means set up accounts! In most instances, they are free.

Don't pay anything yet. Stick with the free options if they are available to you. When you have used the sites, and are comfortable with all your options, then consider upgrading one or two to a fee for service option. However, I am all for free. Keep it simple to start. Stick with the free options.

1. Facebook – www.facebook.com
2. Twitter – www.twitter.com
3. LinkedIn – www.linkedin.com
4. Google Places – www.google.com/places
5. Your favorite?

There are new social media sites popping up all the time. Participate in your local business accelerator or business incubator programs—or look at your local community college class schedules to keep abreast of all the changes. Or just start. Once you have accounts on the social media properties above, you will have more connection than you can manage!

Guide 103: Setting Up Your Facebook Fan Page

Facebook

Bright Idea

Facebook

Everybody loves, and uses, Facebook these days to communicate with customers, build community, support like-minded businesses and colleagues, promote events, and stay connected, in a personal way, with your new fans—friends, clients, potential clients, and interesting people who add value to what our mission is by simply being connected.

Use Google! Going to Facebook.com and searching for some sort of "how to" set up a business page is daunting, and actually, I found impossible. The site is updating and changing so fast, that the best way to learn how is, literally, to research how to on your favorite search engine.

TIP: Names for these pages and sites change often!

Here are the steps, one by one, as of January 2012. My business incubator clients always want me to walk them through the process, so here it goes.

It will take only a few minutes on each site to set you up. And that's where we'll stop for now. Executing takes some work on your part. I will guide you through the process, though. If you feel ready to execute now, then do it!

To locate the latest and greatest Facebook business page set-up option, I used Google and simply typed "setting up a fan page on Facebook". Choose the option that is an actual Facebook page and not a person writing about Facebook. You will get to your destination faster.

Below is exactly what I typed into the search engine:

Et voilà! But so many options! You are a business. Choose the "Local Business or Place" option and click on the picture.

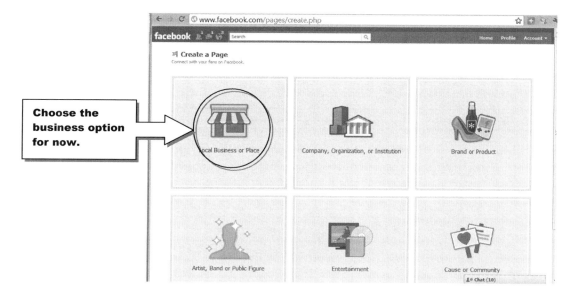

On the Facebook.com website, when you find the business fan page set-up option of the day—this site changes frequently so the images below may not be the same—simply fill in the information for your business (name, location, phone) and agree to the service.

You are asked to choose a category for your business. If you own a retail store, choose retail. Otherwise, there are about a hundred options.

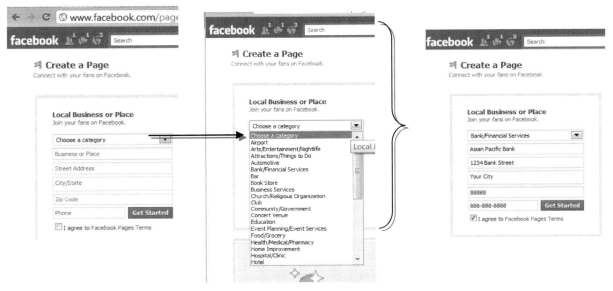

When you hit the enter key, you are set. You have your page!

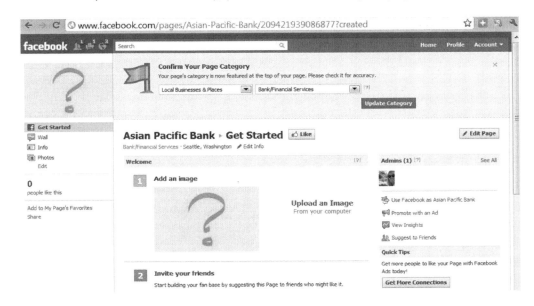

I chose a bank, and not a retail store, because I am helping start one presently. Every name and business you select becomes live! Your business name will appear, you will be the administrator, and you will have a business page on Facebook.com. Simple!

TIP: You need a personal Facebook page to start. So if you have not set one up yet, start there!

Use this space to brainstorm your Facebook page names and other social media intellectual property you may want to secure (in case your business name is taken).

Bright Idea

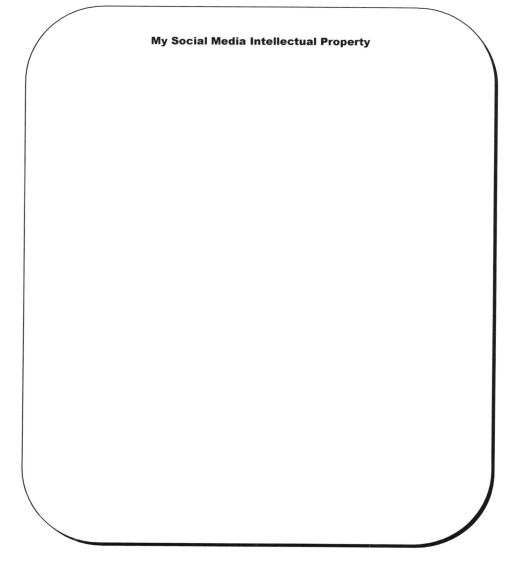

My Social Media Intellectual Property

Guide 104: Getting Started with Twitter

Twitter

Twitter account set up is just as simple, especially when you start with a Facebook account first. Twitter will simply ask if you want to use your Facebook account information to set up your Twitter account, and you want to say (or really click) yes.

Here we go! Visit Twitter.com and click on the sign-up button on the right hand side of the screen.

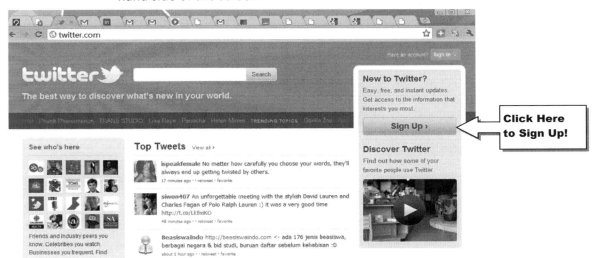

This is the Twitter sign up page. Fill in the blanks and the site will tell you within moments if your chosen username is available. If at first your name is not available, try something similar that matches your Facebook page name. Alternatively, use your personal name for everything. You are your own brand after all!

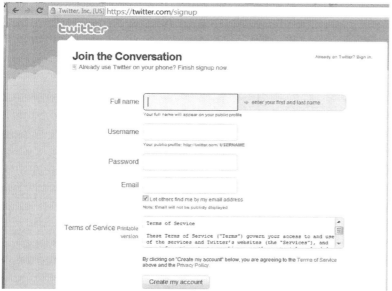

Simply fill in the blanks and click Create My Account

Once you have chosen a Twitter name that is accepted (it may take a few tries!), this is the next page. When your Twitter name, or handle, has been confirmed, enter a unique email account for each Twitter name you choose. You may have more than one Twitter name, but I don't recommend that yet.

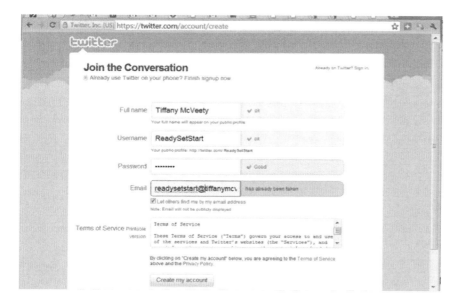

The site will make you enter what you see on the page to confirm that you are not a computer randomly setting up Twitter handles! No big deal. Enter what you see, and hit the" Create My Account" button.

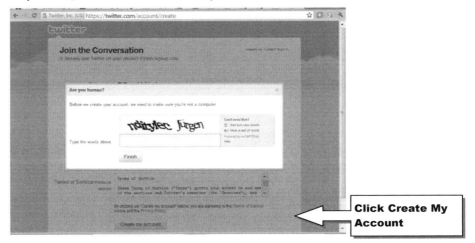

Et voilà! again, so simple! You now have a new Twitter account! This one might be for my next book!

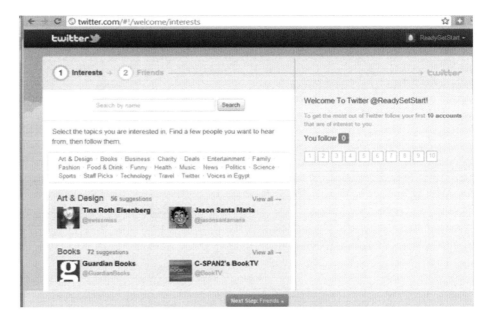

Guide 105: Making Connections with LinkedIn

LinkedIn.com

LinkedIn is a business connector website. It helps you establish your professional profile. LinkedIn gives you the keys to controlling your online identity. Have you Goggled yourself lately? You never know what may come up.

LinkedIn

LinkedIn profiles rise to the top of search results, letting you control the first impression people get when searching for you online. Every business owner should have a LinkedIn profile–they are free!

Guide 106: Plan Now, Schedule for Later

Hootsuite

Setting Up Your Social Media Dashboard

Choose Your Favorite Social Media Content Management Tool

You no longer need to rely on posting content consistently. There are websites that will do this for you! It can still be your brilliant idea, thought, quote, or content ...but you are busy business owners. Let a free content management system post the content you want, when you want it to go out. There are several options like TweetDeck and HootSuite. HootSuite allows users to monitor all of their social profiles, including popular networks Facebook, Twitter, and LinkedIn. There are others—just search for social media dashboard in your favorite search engine. For me, HootSuite was the first, and that is what my mentors chose to use.

Pick a social media content management account and set it up. Later you can add an administrator other than yourself so that an employee, intern, or student can update your current events, classes, or blog.

Bright Idea

TIP: You will need to remember your user names and passwords for each social media account you own. A pain—but critical! Don't worry, if you recall your username (email address) but forget your password, the site will email you a link to your email account to let you reset your password. Write it down somewhere!

Let's look at setting up a HootSuite account.

Choose the free option if there is one. If not—look more closely!

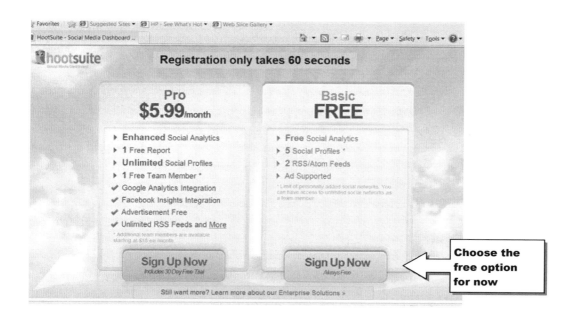

Simply fill in the blanks, and click *Create Account*.
Et voilà! Again, within sixty seconds you have a social media dashboard!

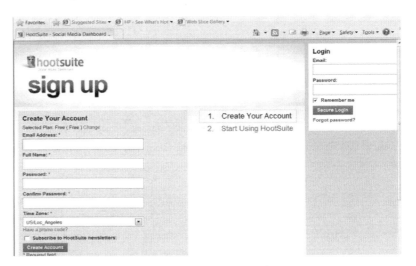

Now you can add up to five social media sites to post and or push content to like Facebook, Facebook Business/Fan Page, Twitter account, and LinkedIn account! This will be the next step!

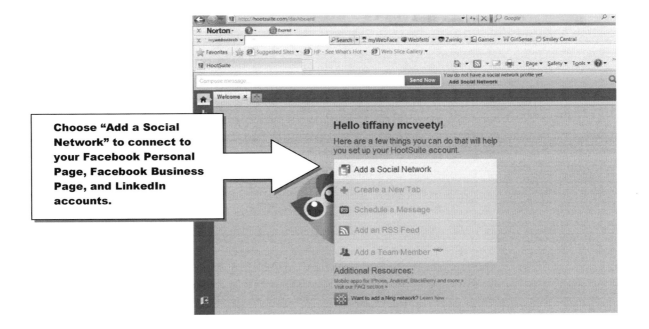

Choose "Add a Social Network" to connect to your Facebook Personal Page, Facebook Business Page, and LinkedIn accounts.

Guide 107: Going Places with Google Places

Google Places

Google is emerging as a forerunner in creating social media tools for business owners that get you noticed—fast! Ever notice that map that shows up when you perform a search using Google and wonder how your business can be listed?

Almost all – 97 percent of consumers – search for local online.

Here's how—and it's free!

The steps are simple!
1. Visit google.com/places
2. Choose the "Get Started" option
3. Choose "Sign Up for a New Account." This is important. You have the opportunity to have your new Google Place associated with whatever email account you want.

Bright Idea

TIP: If you use an email account for your business that is different from your personal email account, then use that business email address. You can have a separate Google Place for each of your businesses whether you are a service provider or have a brick and mortar location.

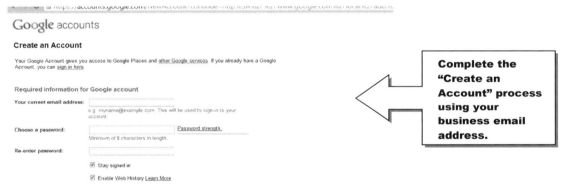

You will then get an email confirmation in your email box that you used to set up the account. When you receive the email, just click on the link to verify your email address and set up your business information. The link will place you back at the Get Started page. This is what your setup page will look like.

Choose "List your Business," and then follow the steps to enter your business information as you would like it to appear on the web. The page should then look something like this, with your listing on the right:

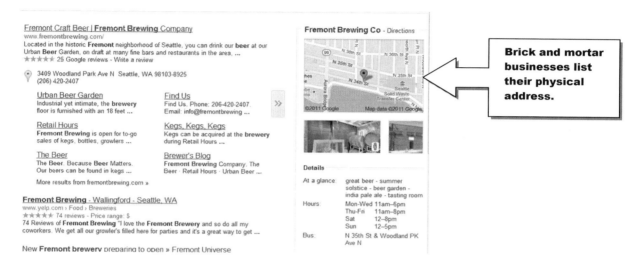

When you've submitted your details, you will need to validate your listing. This means that Google will contact you by post, phone call, or text message, to verify that your business exists. Follow the instructions on the screen to do this. When you've finished validating your listing, then Google will tell you when to expect it to go live on the web. When your listing is live, you can always modify the details or view statistics by going to www.google.com/places/.

Special Features: You can add times of operation, pictures, and even coupons—free! There is an analytics tool built in so you can track your customers and get feedback on your Google Place listing.

Bright Idea

Guide 108: Unleashing Your Social Media Savvy

Choose Your Top 20 Sites to Follow

Identify your top twenty companies, people, associations, and otherwise like-minded potential stakeholders that you want to follow (a Twitter term) or be associated with that you feel can add value to your customer, your business, your brand, or your customer. I know I said "your customer" twice. It really is all about reaching your customer, developing a relationship with your customer, letting your customer get to know your brand, and eventually selling to your customer once you have his or her attention and trust.

Unsure of your stakeholders? The following questions may help:
- What industry are you in?
- What associations are there for your industry?
- What magazines reach your customers?
- What networking groups or business associations serve your industry or your greatest customer base (the top 20 percent of your best customers)?

Bright Idea

TIP: Go back to the *Designing Your Perfect Business* chapter of the *Toolkit* and review your strategic direct marketing ideas.

Search (Google is my favorite, but use yours!) the top one hundred Twitter followers that follow others (you want followers!). Select the top five to ten that match or resonate with your interest base from above, and follow them. Don't be surprised when they follow you back!

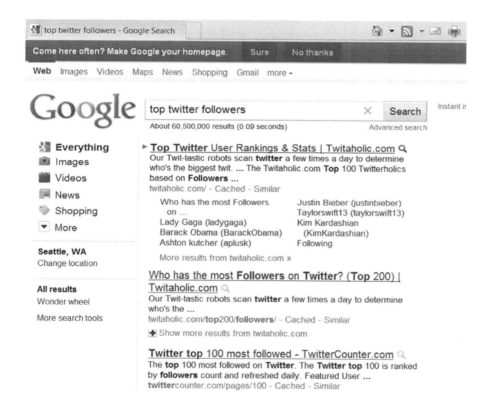

Yes, there are multiple sites that track Twitter accounts, both followers and those who also follow back. The top followed tend to be celebrities and music and movie stars. Move on to the business related moguls, magazine publishers, and social media mavens.

Tip: You have a limited number of twitter accounts to follow—so be selective (today that number is one hundred). Remember, your customers and friends will want you to follow them so leave some room for that!

Bright Idea

Guide 109: Plan Ahead to Share Often

In order to remain relevant, you must post something to your social media sites at least once a week–but twice is better. Oh my! I realize this sounds like a lot of posts when you are trying to run a business. Let the computer do it for you!

There are fifty-two weeks in a year. If you decide to post twice a week, that's only one hundred and four very short posts! So let's break this job down.

Remain Relevant.

What days of the week are you interested in your fans, customers, and friends hearing from you? How about a neat quote that you like on Fridays? Or a tip of the week on a Tuesday? How about using a magazine as an example. Create different departments and seasonal highlights for your posts. This can be a good strategy for a retail store. You may have a dozen posts on "Top Design Tips" for spring, summer, fall, and winter. Or a dozen posts on "Using Color".

You get the idea! Look at your favorite relevant magazines for ideas. This way you can satisfy your 104 social media posts simply and with ease! Plan them now.

You can always post up-to-the-minute relevant information during the weekday, any time, but we need some consistency at the onset. This is one way to strategically plan now for future execution.

Congratulations, you have now entered into the management stage of your social media marketing campaign!

Execute! Plan, Schedule, Share

Your goals might be to create brand awareness, and to engage your customers or prospective customers and call them to action. Action might be to buy something, to respond to a survey, to like a Facebook page, or some other measurable evidence that they are connecting with your company and your brand.

You don't need to be tied to the computer when you are using a social media content dashboard! You already set up your HootSuite or TweetDeck account. Now it's time to use it!

Take Action!
- Compose your weekly or bi-weekly tweets/posts.
- Schedule your weekly–bi-weekly Tweets (for the quarter or year–it's up to you!)
- Follow your top twenty sites to follow–you are only ready to follow once you have scheduled your Tweets!
- Post your upcoming events and announcements

Don't leave your social media to the pre-scheduled posts. Stay relevant and current. Share your successes and your clients' successes. Make special offers and invitations available to your friends, fans, and followers.

Guide 110: Optimizing Your Social Media ROI

Relationship and community building is a key outcome for social media marketing efforts. Check in with your Twitter followers and Facebook friends and fans. Are they posting back to your sites? Do they like your posts? Are people you have never met *friending and following* you?

Are you getting calls from publications for interviews or speaking engagements?

When you put on an event, are the signups faster or greater than before your social media efforts? If so, these are indicators that you are building a community and brand awareness.

And how about sales. Have they increased? Are you tracking sales compared to your marketing efforts?

Do you know the value of your perfect customer so you can benchmark your marketing efforts against new customer acquisition? If not, here's how.

ROI and New Customer Acquisition

In the Chapter Designing Your Perfect Business, you identified the buying behavior of your perfect customer. Now use that buying behavior to calculate the total value of the customer over the lifetime or Lifetime Value (LTV). Here is a basic Marketing ROI formula:

$$ROI = Expected\ LTV\ /\ Marketing\ Investment$$

Example: If your perfect customer spends an average of twenty-five dollars with you a visit, and they shop with you four times a year, that customer's annual value is one hundred dollars. Let's say, you expect that he or she will be a loyal customer for three years. The total lifetime value of that customer is three hundred dollars. But what about profitability? If your gross profit per customer is 60%, then for each customer, the Net LTV is one hundred and twenty dollars.

$$\text{Gross Profit: } 300 \times .6 = 180$$
$$\text{Net LTV: } 300 - 180 = 120$$

Let's say you have a budget of one-thousand dollars for your social media marketing campaign. What would you expect your marketing return on investment to be?

$$\text{Marketing ROI: } 1000 / 300 = 3.33$$

When you calculate the average profit you make from a customer in twelve months you have a benchmark for your ROI. Then you can determine the expected incremental income from the marketing campaign to gauge its success.

$$\text{ROI Break-even} = \text{Marketing Investment} / \text{Net LTV}$$

If each new customer nets your business one-hundred and twenty dollars, then a one thousand dollar marketing investment needs to generate nine new customers to break even. Marketing ROI Break-even: 9 new customers

$$\text{ROI Break-even: } 1000 / 120 = 8.3$$

Understanding the revenue generated per dollar spent for each marketing activity can be sufficient enough to help make important decisions to improve the entire marketing mix.

Improving your marketing ROI leads to improved marketing effectiveness, increased revenue, profit, and market share for the same amount of marketing spend. Social media marketing is still marketing. Think back to your best marketing campaigns and think about how you can use today's technology to achieve the results you want.

Social Media Summary

At the rate the technology changes, there are likely new and amazing social media tools out there even now, that I have not covered. Attend workshops and classes to keep up on the latest, or just ask a tech savvy friend. Change your strategy, tactics, and marketing efforts as needed to get the results you want.

- Plan with the end goal in mind! Know the intended outcome of your social media marketing efforts, and benchmark your goals against your marketing expense.
- Plan ahead, and schedule in advance. A social media content dashboard can save you time, and help you share your world frequently and consistently.
- Follow others who follow you back. Your placement on the search engines will be higher when you do.
- Strengthen your online community by sharing current events and relevant content with your *fans, friends,* and *followers.*
- Become the expert using a content marketing tactic! Share your world.

Last: Next Steps

Change is inevitable. Keep up by getting involved and staying current in your industry. Change your strategy, tactics, and marketing efforts to get the results you want. You are the expert in your business—share your world with these tools, tips, and strategies. Get to work!

Share Your World To Do's

- Create your professional bio
- Join your top three business development networking groups
- Get connected with a LinkedIn account
- Launch your Facebook Business Page
- Plan and schedule your first quarter Tweets.
- Get social with your Social Media Marketing Plan!

Still Ahead

- Visit the website the Entrepreneurial Edge Academy for tips, free downloands, and more!
- Create Your Social Media Platform
- Get followed on Twitter
- Genterate fans on Facebook

Share Your World!
Certificate of Completion

Whether you are a social enterprise or not, social media is important to your business. Get connected. Share your expertise. Get social. Get started!

Completed Guides
    Guide 93: Brand You!
    Guide 94: 3 Steps to Networking with Ease
    Guide 95: Expanding Your Network
    Guide 96: Joining In
    Guide 97: Barter Anyone?
    Guide 98: Simplifying Social Media
    Guide 98: Simplifying Social Media
    Guide 99: Social Media Marketing Roadmap
    Guide 100: Social Media Planning
    Guide 101: Top Social Media Marketing Tactics
    Guide 102: Securing Your Social Media Space
    Guide 103: Setting Up Your Facebook Fan Page
    Guide 104: Getting Started with Twitter
    Guide 105: Making Connections with LinkedIn
    Guide 106: Plan Now, Schedule for Later
    Guide 107: Going Places with Google Places
    Guide 108: Unleashing Your Social Media Savvy
    Guide 109: Plan Ahead to Share Often
    Guide 110: Optimizing Your Social Media ROI

Complete your certificate of completion on the following page to memorialize your accomplishments.

Congratulations!

Entrepreneurial Edge

Small Business Toolkit

Certificate of Completion

I certify that I, _____, have successfully completed

Share Your World

Including: Brand You!, Networking With Ease, Entrepreneur Interview Skills, and Social Media Unleashed!

Signature: _____   Date: _____

SPROUT!

Entrepreneur Resources

Business Design Resources

A good reference librarian can get you further faster than your own Internet research. Visit you college or local business reference librarian and let them know what you are researching.

Market Research Resources
The World's Largest Collection of Market Research
www.marketresearch.com

American Marketing Association's Market Research Website
www.marketingpower.com

Federal Government Data
A great deal of demographic data is either free or inexpensive because it is collected and published by the federal government. The following publications are from the Commerce Department and Census Bureau.

Statistical Abstract of the United States (annual)
Published by the US Department of Commerce, this publication provides one-stop shopping for a demographic portrait of life in the United States. Tables include information on just about everything: employment projections, production figures, family income.
www.census.gov/prod/www/abs/statab.html

United States Census
The most current census is available in print format in many libraries. For the first time, the census is also available in CD-ROM. The Census Bureau also monitors the population through its regular surveys, including the monthly Current Population Survey (CPS). www.census.gov

County and City Data Book
Contains data for 50 states, more than 3,000 counties or county areas, 243 SMSA's, and 840 cities of 25,000 inhabitants or more.
www.census.gov/statab/www/ccdb.html

State and Metropolitan Area Data Book (annual)
The *SMA Data Book* provides demographics for each state and metropolitan area, as well as counties and central cities.
www.census.gov/statab/www/smadb.html

US Small Business Administration
This is an official site for the US Small Business Administration (SBA) and provides a wealth of information on starting and running your own small business. The topics covered range from the early planning stages, to starting up, running, and exit strategies, as well as links to many other resources for startups.
www.sbaonline.sba.gov

Money Rules Resources

Free Business Templates
US Small Business Administration SCORE Business Templates
For the best, and most simple, 12 Month Cash Flow template available free.
www.score.org/template_gallery.html

Some of the templates available that I recommend are the following:
- Startup Expenses
- Cash-flow Statement (12 Month)
- Profit-and-loss Projection (12 Month)
- Profit-and-loss Projection (3 Years)
- Opening Day Balance Sheet
- Balance Sheet (Projected)
- Break-even Analysis
- Sales Forecast (12 Month)

Angel Investment Clubs and Associations
An exhaustive list of angel investment clubs and associations can be found as a free download at www.EntrepreneurialEdgeSeries.com.

Angel Capital Education Foundation
Angel Capital Education Foundation (ACEF) is a charitable organization devoted to education and research in the field of angel investing.
www.angelcapitaleducation.org

International Angel Resources:
European Business Angel Network is a listing of angel networks in Europe.
www.eban.org

Resources for Women Entrepreneurs

Find a special list of resources for women entrepreneurs as a free download at www.EntrepreneurialEdgeSeries.com.

Nationwide SBA Women's Business Centers
Providing free business assistance, mentoring, access to resources, access to capital, and access to markets to women entrepreneurs, don't miss out on this great free business resource. A list of all Women's Business Centers by state and including contact information can be found as a free download at www.EntrepreneurialEdgeSeries.com.

Non-bank Business Loan Resources
Community development financial institutions (or CDFIs) provide a great service to small businesses. But many potential borrowers don't know they exist. CDFIs Alphabetical by State and City can be found as a free download at www.EntrepreneurialEdgeSeries.com.

Inventor's Resources

US Copyright Office
This is the official site of the United States Copyright Office, where you can find general copyright information, search copyright records, registration forms and fees, publications, law and policy, and more.
www.copyright.gov

US Patent and Trademark Office (USPTO)
This is the official site of the United States Patent and Trademark Office, where you can find a wealth of information about the patents and trademarks, from general to legal, and more. The site also allows you to search the patents and trademark databases. The site includes an inventor support section, which, in addition to more detailed information and guidance on patents and trademarks, includes the Inventor's Online forum chat transcripts as well as links to patent and trademark-related information in libraries across the country. www.uspto.gov

Inventors Assistance Center (IAC)
A division of the USTPO, the IAC can assist you with filling out forms, provide you with general information concerning rules, procedures, and fees, and send you patenting information via mail or facsimile.
www.uspto.gov/inventors/iac/index.jsp

Inventor Resources - US Patent and Trademark Office

The US Patent and Trademark Office (USPTO) publishes inventor resources on the agency website. The Inventor Resources site is dedicated to serving the special needs and interests of the inventor and entrepreneur. www.uspto.gov/inventors/index.jsp

SBIR Gateway

The most comprehensive and easy to use SBIR information site, this website lets the inventor or entrepreneur search all SBIR and STTR grant opportunities and solicitations from all federal offices in one location. ww.zyn.com/sbir

World Intellectual Property Organization (WIPO)

World Intellectual Property Organization (WIPO) is roughly the international/global equivalent of the US Copyright and Patents and Trademarks Offices. The site allows you to search the copyright, patents, and trademark databases for international applications and issued documents. www.wipo.int

Google Patents

Google provided US patent database search. In addition to having the familiar flavor, Google Patents is somewhat easier to use than the USPTO search engine and displays patent documents and images using the standard web helper applications (Adobe Acrobat and JPEG). www.google.com/patents

List of Guides

Start here if you aren't sure where else to start! In the following List of Guides, find the guide number, followed by the guide title, page number, and brief description. The Guides are in chronological order based on the Core Business Principles.

Guide 11: Determining Your EQ, 41
Every year, hundreds of thousands of people like you make the transition from employee to entrepreneur. How do you know if the entrepreneurial life is for you?

Guide 12: Realizing Your Values, 45
When your values and goals are aligned, you jump on a fast track to success. Uncover your values.

Guide 13: Aligning Your Entrepreneurial Intention, 51
Align your personal values with your entrepreneurial intention.

Guide 14: Discovering Your Strengths, 53
Every entrepreneur needs some expertise in the main functional business areas—but you don't need to be an expert. Discover your strengths and create a strategy for success.

Guide 15: Entrepreneurial Goal Setting, 61
Business planning is personal planning. Learn the four factors in entrepreneurial goal setting and how to set SMART goals in this holistic goal setting exercise.

Guide 16: Defining Your Vision, 70
Business planning is an art, not a science. A strategic vision is a roadmap of a company's future. Create your own business vision statement.

Guide 17: The Art of Business Formation, 74
There is a strategic art to the start. Yes, there is a perfect process. Create a business structure that will last your business's lifetime.

Guide 18: Steps to the Start, 81
There is a right way to start a business. We feel the right way is the option that lets you meet your goals in the most simple and cost-effective way. Learn how.

Guide 19: Identifying Advisors, 86
What type of team do you need to support your goals?

Guide 20: Engaging Advisors, 90
Broad stakeholder involvement and support is required to build a fast growth or capital-intensive company. Learn how to mobilize OPA (other people's assets) to support your venture.

Guide 21: Business Design Roadmap, 103
The business process diagram is your business planning roadmap. How can you decide what to do if you don't know where you want to be after you've done it?

Guide 48: My Perfect Pitch, 205
Write a compelling business description—in four sentences or less! Executive Business Plan Step 1 of ten.

Guide 49: Perfect Players, 207
Tell the world—or your potential investor—why you are the one to pull this business off. Executive Business Plan Step 2.

Guide 50: Right Place, Right Time, 209
Get an investor interested. Executive Business Plan Step 3.

Guide 51: Piece of the Pie, 211
What piece of the pie will you plan to reach? Executive Business Plan Step 4.

Guide 52: Honorable Prosperity, 212
Earning an income from your own efforts used to be called honorable prosperity. What does your business sell? Executive Business Plan Step 5.

Guide 53: Profitable Interactions, 214
You make money on the buying—not the selling. Executive Business Plan Step 6.

Guide 54: The Price Is Right, 216
Describe your pricing strategy—this time in a few sentences. Executive Business Plan Step 7.

Guide 55: The Lay of the Land, 217
Having a competition section in a business plan is not self-defeating—it lends credibility. Executive Business Plan Step 8.

Guide 56: Creating Connections, 218
A marketing plan includes a marketing strategy—it is not *the* marketing strategy. Executive Business Plan Step 9.

Guide 57: Presenting Projections, 222
There is a specific format an investor is used to seeing when looking at a business plan. Learn it. Use it. Executive Business Plan Step 10.

Guide 58: Executive Business Plan Template, 225
Here's the Executive Business Plan template. Answer the questions to create a simple, single page business plan—*that works.*

Guide 59: Executive Business Plan Sample, 226
So you know where you're going. The Executive Business Plan example.

List of Guides – Alphabetical Order

To help you navigate. Here are the guides in alphabetical order followed by their page number.

Index

Core Business Principles Index

Entrepreneurial Edge Core Business Principles

Core Business Principles are best practices taught by certified business incubators, advocated by Microentrepreneur Development Organizations, and delivered to you throughout the Entrepreneurial Edge Series.

The *Entrepreneurial Edge Small Business Toolkit* introduces you to eighteen of the 20 Core Business Principles. In the following Index, look for the Core Business Principle you are interested in spending time on. Page numbers follow the titles of the respective guides.

Core Categories	Core Business Principles
Startup Success	1. Values 2. Vision 3. Business Formation Strategies 4. Business Model 5. Advisory Board
Designing Your Perfect Business	6. Revenue Model 7. Pricing Model 8. Customer Identification 9. Competitive Advantage 10. Market Opportunity 11. Target Market
Idea to Market	12. Features vs. Benefits (Value Proposition) 13. Strategic Direct Marketing 14. Components of a Marketing Plan 15. Intellectual Property Protection 16. Sales Process Design
Show Me the Money	17. Debt vs. Equity 18. Pro forma Financial Statements
Managing Your Venture	19. Chart of Accounts 20. RMA Ratios

About the Author

Tiffany McVeety, MBA, Author, Economic Gardener

Mrs. McVeety has a unique ability to mobilize resources—time, talent, and capital to support entrepreneurship. She has directed, developed, and launched several award-winning and internationally recognized business incubation programs. She served as a Director of an award-winning US Small Business Administration Women's Business Center and launched an award-winning Latino-focused micro-loan fund and an award-winning entrepreneurial development center serving indigenous populations. Leaders from forty countries have visited her business centers as demonstration of best practices in both access to capital and advanced technical assistance programs.

Speaking at QuickStart Shoreline,
Women's Business Summit,
City Hall, Shoreline, WA.

Today she designs and builds sustainable programs to vitalize, optimize, and unleash entrepreneurship, innovation, and leadership through advanced workforce skills training and outreach programs for colleges, countries, companies, and communities. She is founding director of GROW Washington, the premiere product-focused business incubator in that state. She was awarded an export grant by the Department of Commerce that took her to Greece during the financial crisis to support their efforts to empower entrepreneurs. The efforts are ongoing. Tiffany welcomes other international engagements to support small business.

Sponsor/Speaker at the
Women in Small Biz Conference.

Tiffany has delivered over 200 custom presentations to groups from five to five-hundred—global and local—for organizations like the United States Small Business Administration, the United States Navy Transitional Assistance Program, the National Business Incubation Association, and small cities seeking to vitalize their business communities. She continues to provide custom, advanced, workforce-development solutions to the global community with a focus on entrepreneurship, leadership, capital investment strategies, and innovation.

In Shanghai, China
Promoting EB5
Investment in small biz.

As author of the Entrepreneurial Edge series of guidebooks Tiffany distills complex business hurdles into simple solutions and strategies the very small business owner—or multi-national—can take to the bank. Her experience in business and as an international business banker gives her clients and readers an edge—we call it the *entrepreneurial edge*.

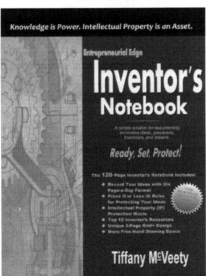

Entrepreneurial Edge Academy
Entrepreneurial Edge Pro

Professional Entrepreneur Training Certification

Certified Online Startup Training

Welcome to Entrepreneurial Edge Pro

Are you overqualified and underworked looking to create your destiny through self-employment?

Are you a business coach, business incubator professional or workforce development professional looking for some proven tools to lead clients to success?

Are you seeking a simple solution, based on best practices, to asses, train, and mentor entrepreneurs from idea to funding?

Entrepreneurial Edge Pro is a fully online entrepreneurship training course that guides you through the key guides from the Small Business Toolkit. Upon completion you are armed to start your business or train others to start their own.

Professional entrepreneurial training offered online, on-demand with built-in flexibility and support. Entrepreneur assessment tools and entrepreneurial training for entrepreneurs and the workforce development professionals, business coaches, and technical assistance providers who train them.

Get *Your* Edge at **Entrepreneurial Edge Academy.com**

A Certified Self Employment Training Solution Provider.

Visit www.CareerBridge.wa.gov and search for "Entrepreneurial Edge" for a list of Self Employment Training eligible courses.